Counseling the Procrastinator in Academic Settings

Counseling the Procrastinator in Academic Settings

Edited by Henri C. Schouwenburg, Clarry H. Lay,
Timothy A. Pychyl, and Joseph R. Ferrari

American Psychological Association, Washington, DC

Published by
American Psychological Association
750 First Street, NE
Washington, DC 20002
www.apa.org

To order
APA Order Department
P.O. Box 92984
Washington, DC 20090-2984
Tel: (800) 374-2721; Direct: (202) 336-5510
Fax: (202) 336-5502; TDD/TTY: (202) 336-6123
Online: www.apa.org/books/
E-mail: order@apa.org

In the U.K., Europe, Africa, and the Middle East, copies may be ordered from
American Psychological Association
3 Henrietta Street
Covent Garden, London
WC2E 8LU England

Typeset in Goudy by Stephen McDougal, Mechanicsville, MD

Printer: United Book Press, Inc., Baltimore, MD
Cover Designer: Go! Creative, Kensington, MD
Technical/Production Editor: Rosemary Moulton

The opinions and statements published are the responsibility of the authors, and such opinions and statements do not necessarily represent the policies of the American Psychological Association.

Library of Congress Cataloging-in-Publication Data

Counseling the procrastinator in academic settings / edited by Henri C. Schouwenburg . . . [et al.].
    p. cm.
Includes bibliographical references and indexes.
ISBN 1-59147-107-9 (hardcover : alk. paper)
1. College students—Time management. 2. Counseling in higher education.
3. Procrastination. I. Schouwenburg, Henri C. II. Title.
LB2395.4.C68 2004
378.1'94—dc22   2004000025

British Library Cataloguing-in-Publication Data
A CIP record is available from the British Library.

Printed in the United States of America
First Edition

CONTENTS

CONTRIBUTORS

Sabina Beijne, MSc, Psychological Counseling Service, Leiden University, Leiden, the Netherlands

Kelly Binder, MA, Department of Psychology, Carleton University, Ottawa, Ontario, Canada

Richard A. Davis, PhD, Department of Psychology, York University, Toronto, Ontario, Canada

Eric Depreeuw, PhD, Center for Study and Student Counseling, Catholic University of Brussels, Belgium

Wendelien van Eerde, PhD, Department of Technology Management, Eindhoven University of Technology, Eindhoven, the Netherlands

Tanja van Essen, MSc, Academic Assistance and Counseling Center, University of Groningen, Groningen, the Netherlands

Joseph R. Ferrari, PhD, Department of Psychology, DePaul University, Chicago, IL

Gordon L. Flett, PhD, Department of Psychology, York University, Toronto, Ontario, Canada

Sary van den Heuvel, MA, IVLOS Institute of Education, Utrecht University, Utrecht, the Netherlands

Paul L. Hewitt, PhD, Department of Psychology, University of British Columbia, Vancouver, British Columbia, Canada

Walter van Horebeek, MSc, Psychotherapeutic Student Center, University of Louvain, Louvain, Belgium

Dieta Kruise, MSc, Psychological Counseling Service, Leiden University, Leiden, the Netherlands

Clarry H. Lay, PhD, Department of Psychology, York University, Toronto, Ontario, Canada

Harvey P. Mandel, PhD, Department of Psychology and Institute on Achievement and Motivation, York University, Toronto, Ontario, Canada

Sofie Michielsen, MSc, Psychotherapeutic Student Center, University of Louvain, Louvain, Belgium

Anne Neyskens, MSc, Psychotherapeutic Student Center, University of Louvain, Louvain, Belgium

Jean O'Callaghan, MSc, School of Psychology and Therapeutic Studies, University of Surrey Roehampton, London, England

Marjan Ossebaard, MSc, IVLOS Institute of Education, Utrecht University, Utrecht, the Netherlands

Timothy A. Pychyl, PhD, Department of Psychology, Carleton University, Ottawa, Ontario, Canada

Henri C. Schouwenburg, PhD, Academic Assistance and Counseling Center, University of Groningen, Groningen, the Netherlands

Simon B. Sherry, MA, Department of Psychology, University of Saskatchewan, Saskatoon, Saskatchewan, Canada

Robert M. Topman, MSc, Psychological Counseling Service, Leiden University, Leiden, the Netherlands

Bruce W. Tuckman, PhD, Psychological Foundations of Education Program and Academic Learning Lab, Ohio State University, Columbus

Lilly J. Schubert Walker, PhD, Division of Student Affairs and Services, Memorial University of Newfoundland, St. John's, Newfoundland, Canada

PREFACE

This book is about counseling students who procrastinate. It consists of a collection of experiences, procedures, and research provided by psychologists who specialize in counseling students who seek help for their dilatory tendencies.

Although procrastination, or putting off until tomorrow what one should do today, is a phenomenon well-known for thousands of years, it is only recently that systematic research has been conducted with respect to its manifestations, causes, and cures. One probable reason for studying procrastination is that procrastinators continually fail to adhere temporally to schedules they and others have set, which in industrial societies is an important precondition for the efficient use of technology, time, and other resources. In addition, the negative moral connotation of procrastination creates much distress in people who procrastinate. This may be a reason for the recent heightened interest in studying procrastination.

Of course, this interest in procrastination treatment reflects a strong cultural bias. In academic settings in North America and Europe, to be academically successful, students need to be able to control tendencies to procrastinate in doing their academic work. In other cultures, however, the implied emphasis on the timely completion of a started task may not have such a high value. Yet as long as the educational and professional contexts in this part of the world are as they are, students and other workers will have to comply to some extent with the expectation of timeliness.

Although procrastination in the Western world has long been a problem well worth studying, the first scientific studies date only from the mid 1980s (e.g., Lay, 1986), and the first book summarizing research results in the area dates to 1995 (Ferrari, Johnson, & McCown), followed five years later by a special issue of the *Journal of Social Behavior and Personality* (Ferrari & Pychyl, 2000b).

In some ways, the present volume can be regarded as a sequel to these pioneering publications, as it is an early attempt to apply the findings of procrastination research. This book, in essence, describes a collection of intervention methods presently being developed by counselors at universities in both North America and Europe. These interventions, although differing from one to another in their details, all have in common the goal of helping procrastinating students to develop self-regulation skills and an accompanying sense of personal power or self-efficacy.

This volume is intended as a handbook for counselors, student advisers, and psychologists seeking to prevent or treat procrastination in students. It is organized into three parts. Part I is theoretical, and it begins with two relatively short theoretical background chapters. Schouwenburg's introductory chapter 1 highlights and summarizes a number of important issues that have emerged from procrastination research, and chapter 2 by Ferrari continues to provide an overall context for the book with an overview and broad summary of research results with respect to procrastination in academic settings. Chapter 3, by van Eerde, examines the relation of procrastination as a trait to the Big Five model of personality structure. Taken together, these three chapters provide a comprehensive overview of the theoretical and empirical state of the art with respect to procrastination in students and others.

The next 10 chapters form Part II—the body—of this book. Part II presents, in a somewhat arbitrary sequence, a number of counseling and intervention models developed for procrastinating students. It opens with chapter 4, an account of Lay's group approach in counseling procrastinating students. The guiding principle of this chapter and the intervention is that learning to act in a timely manner on one's intentions is the key to success in life, or at least to preventing unhappiness. Next, in chapter 5, van Essen and her colleagues outline a group training method that is directed at learning time management techniques and changing unproductive thoughts in relation to academic work with the help of rational–emotive behavioral therapy. Chapter 6 is a detailed description of Walker's group counseling approach directed at helping students overcome the patterns of powerlessness that may lead to procrastination. Chapter 7 contains two different purely behavioral approaches to counseling groups of procrastinating students. The first, by Tuckman, makes use of a comprehensive Web-based program to increase students' motivation to study, and the second, by Schouwenburg, involves so-called task management groups. Both approaches make use of various techniques drawn from self-help protocols for the treatment of addicts.

In chapter 8, van Horebeek and his colleagues present a cognitive–behavioral group treatment for procrastinating students along the lines of applied behavioral analysis. Chapter 9, by Mandel, gives an extensive demonstration of the author's approach of constructive confrontation in a counseling session with a certain type of procrastinating underachiever. Chapter 10, by Topman and his colleagues, demonstrates in detail how the Internet can be mobilized in counseling procrastinating students. In chapter 11, Pychyl and Binder discuss the use of the Personal Projects Analysis questionnaire as a research tool to examine the effectiveness of counseling students who procrastinate in their academic work. Another more or less unconventional approach, described by O'Callaghan in chapter 12, uses a narrative method in dealing with procrastination in students. Part II concludes with a description by Flett and his colleagues of the perfectionistic procrastinator (chap. 13) that provides a rich description of this subgroup of procrastinating students and ends with implications for counseling.

Finally, Part III is an epilogue consisting of one somewhat critical final chapter (chap. 14, by Schouwenburg) on the status and future of intervention models for counseling the procrastinator in academic settings. In this chapter, the author identifies different underlying interpretations of the nature of the procrastination problem in the intervention programs described in this book. He then concludes by presenting an outline of an "ideal" intervention program to be developed in the future. Thus, whereas Part I provides a good theoretical background on the problem and Part II stresses practical models of intervention, Part III can be interpreted as a research program for the future with a view to developing effective intervention methods. Not all readers, however, are expected to have a comprehensive background in academic psychology. We have written the theoretical and research summaries with a general reader in mind. But more practice-oriented readers may want to turn immediately to chapters 4 and 14 to get an overview of the big-picture issues in counseling procrastinators and then focus on the chapters in Part II they find most relevant and helpful for their specific roles.

Finally, ours is a continuing journey of research and intervention. We welcome your comments on our collective work, and we invite you to share your own approaches with us.

I

THEORETICAL BACKGROUND

1

PROCRASTINATION IN ACADEMIC SETTINGS: GENERAL INTRODUCTION

HENRI C. SCHOUWENBURG

In comparison with research on other psychological problems, research on the nature of procrastination began relatively late, in the 1980s. It has been carried out mainly on students, sometimes taking the academic setting for granted as a representative for other settings in which achievement may be at stake and sometimes with an explicit interest in procrastinatory behavior in the academic setting. The latter point of view was especially adopted by researchers with some connection to student counseling. Their aim was to develop scientifically based intervention methods for helping students to overcome procrastinating in their academic tasks. In doing so, they encountered a number of problems of a more general nature that became issues still dominating procrastination research.

This introductory chapter discusses these issues and introduces general guidelines for therapeutic intervention derived from procrastination research. It thus sets the stage for the presentation of intervention methods in the chapters to follow. This chapter begins with a definition of procrastination that draws a clear distinction between dilatory behavior and procrastination as a trait. I then move to a causal explanation of procrastination as derived from the research literature, with a specific focus on self-control and self-regulatory failure. With these important issues as a conceptual background, I then discuss the prevalence of procrastination in the academic context, its specificity or lack thereof, and issues of manifestation as related to personality in particular. The chapter ends with a brief outline of promising approaches for intervention. Throughout the discussion, I intend to link this summary of theory and research to the chapters that constitute this book and in doing so set out a conceptual framework for procrastination intervention.

PROCRASTINATION AS A BEHAVIOR

Merriam-Webster's dictionary (Gove, 1976) dates the term "to procrastinate" to as far back as 1588, with *pro* meaning forward and *cras* meaning tomorrow, which together provide the meaning: to put off intentionally and habitually something that should be done. The Cambridge dictionary (Procter, 1995) defines the term as the act of continuing to delay something that must be done, often because it is unpleasant or boring. A third dictionary, Collins Cobuild (Sinclair, 1987), asserts that if one procrastinates, one is very slow to do something, because one keeps leaving it until later. From these definitions it becomes clear that there are at least two ways to interpret procrastination: (a) as a behavior and (b) as a generalized habit or trait.

Early researchers on procrastination focused entirely on a behavioral interpretation, regarding procrastination as a task-specific avoidance behavior. Accordingly, the treatment they offered consisted of behavioral interventions such as improved time management and the application of study habit techniques (see Milgram, Sroloff, & Rosenbaum, 1988). Today, this behavioral interpretation forms the basis for pragmatic intervention methods aimed at creating a kind of maintenance schedule for keeping one's procrastinatory tendencies within socially acceptable limits. Chapter 7 in this volume presents two successful examples of such an approach.

Deficiencies in time and task management are indeed essential in this interpretation. They manifest themselves in temporal gaps between intentions and their corresponding goal-directed behaviors. Behavior-oriented measurement scales, such as my own Academic Procrastination State Inventory (APSI; Schouwenburg, 1995), investigate whether students had begun studying when they had intended, had studied the subject matter they had planned to, interrupted or gave up studying, and the like. Only behavior from the past week is investigated through this measure, and a summed score on this scale provides a summary of current levels of dilatory behavior.

Not all postponement, however, should be considered dilatory behavior. Deferment can be purposely planned, and it can be wise to postpone doing something. For example, in Europe, for many students at university, it would be wise to postpone preparing for an examination until the exact subject has been announced. If postponement is unplanned, however, this is dilatory behavior. When dilatory behavior becomes habitual, or chronic, delaying can be interpreted as a typical response or as a habit or trait; in that case, it is considered trait procrastination.

To avoid conceptual confusion, one can refer to each manifestation of procrastination with a different term. Following Lay (1986), I refer to procrastination as a behavior using the term *dilatory behavior* and reserve the term *procrastination* for the trait. Trait procrastination is to dilatory behavior as trait anxiety is to state anxiety (Schouwenburg & Lay, 1995). This is an important and useful distinction and one that the reader should keep in mind.

PROCRASTINATION AS A TRAIT

Currently, most researchers and counselors regard procrastination as a personality trait—that is, as a tendency to exhibit a typical response in a variety of situations. In accordance with this view, Lay (1986) defined *trait procrastination* as the tendency to postpone that which is necessary to reach some goal.

Traits are inferred tendencies to produce consistent patterns of individual behavioral responses that are repeatedly aroused by a wide range of stimulus situations (e.g., Allport, 1937). Accordingly, measurement scales for traits, such as Lay's Procrastination Scale (see Ferrari, Johnson, & McCown, 1995), inquire into behavior that is displayed often, usually, or generally, in a variety of situations. In terms of Eysenck's perspective, such scale items constitute habitual responses (e.g., Eysenck, 1970). A trait is inferred from the observed intercorrelations of a number of different habitual responses. For example, Lay's Procrastination Scale consists of 20 habitual responses that are strongly intercorrelated, producing one single trait: procrastination. Other instruments for measuring procrastination may be found in Ferrari, Johnson, and McCown (1995).

On the basis of their intercorrelations, traits can be grouped into higher order concepts in the analysis of personality (e.g., Costa & McCrae, 1992; Eysenck, 1970; John, 1990). One of the most impressive achievements in personality psychology during the last 15 years is the consensus that most traits can be grouped into a very limited number of higher order concepts or factors, of which the so-called Big Five model is one of the most prominent (e.g., John, 1990). By convention, these five factors are numbered as follows: (1) Surgency, or Extraversion–Introversion; (2) Agreeableness; (3) Conscientiousness; (4) Emotional Stability; and (5) Intellect or Openness to Experience.

Procrastination as a trait appears to be strongly associated with low levels of Conscientiousness (3) and to a lesser extent with low Emotional Stability or Neuroticism (4). There are also relatively small effects of Introversion (1) and low Agreeableness (2; J. L. Johnson & Bloom, 1995;

Schouwenburg & Lay, 1995; Watson, 2001). These results have been corroborated by a meta-analysis of the research literature provided in chapter 3 of this volume. In sum, then, Factor 3 (Conscientiousness) plays a dominant role in explaining the variance in procrastination trait scores. Some additional variance is explained by other Big Five factors, notably by Neuroticism, but to a much lesser degree (e.g., Watson, 2001). Consequently, the overall personality profile of procrastinators, in terms of the Big Five factors, may provide some general guidelines for therapeutic interventions.

As their position on Factor 3 (Conscientiousness) ranks people in terms of behavior (e.g., active vs. lazy), basic intervention methods for procrastinators should be directed at behavior. Additional therapeutic principles might be derived from secondary factors involved. For example, Factor 4 (Emotional Stability) ranks people in terms of sensitivity. Interventions for people low on this factor should therefore be directed at affect. A ranking on Factor 1 (Extraversion–Introversion) reflects how people view themselves in terms of temperament: exuberant versus inhibited, self-directed versus other-directed, primary versus secondary reacting, and the like. Therefore, interventions with respect to this factor should be directed at self-evaluation, self-worth, self-efficacy, and so forth. The intersection of three Big Five factors (3, 4, and 1, respectively) will cover most of the variance in trait procrastination.

The other two factors, however, also contribute, although to a lesser degree (Schouwenburg & Lay, 1995). Of these factors, Factor 5 (Intellect) ranks people in terms of reflective thinking. Interventions should therefore be directed at cognition. Finally, Factor 2 (Agreeableness) ranks people in terms of basic social attitude: kind versus hostile. Corresponding interventions should therefore be directed at attitude change.

TRAITS AS SOURCES OF BEHAVIOR

Strictly speaking, traits are nothing more than summary variables, describing and summarizing the common variance in the responses to the items that constitute personality questionnaires. For example, in Lay's Procrastination Scale these items all refer to behavior: missing events, being prompt at something, delaying before starting to do something, not doing things as planned, and the like. Trait procrastination, as measured by this scale, is a summary of the predisposition to engage in dilatory behavior, that is, to manifest intention–behavior gaps (Schouwenburg & Lay, 1995).

Behavior never occurs alone, however; it is accompanied by thoughts and feelings. This insight is central to rational–emotive behavioral therapy (REBT; e.g., Ellis & Knaus, 2002). The notion of challenging this three-part complex of behavior, cognition, and affect by focusing on maladaptive thinking is fundamental to various treatment approaches, such as the REBT-based intervention described in chapter 5 and the cognitive–behavioral group treatment described in chapter 8 in this volume. Also, the counseling intervention discussed in chapter 6 and the narrative approach to counseling procrastinators discussed in chapter 12 follow this line of thinking.

In contrast to simple descriptive summaries, traits have also been understood as source variables (Cattell, 1965): single, unitary influences or sources that produce specific behavior. As a consequence, measures like the one derived from Lay's Procrastination Scale could be regarded as representing the source of dilatory behavior, rather than just a summary. Such an interpretation would require a perfect correlation between the trait and the behavior of which it is the source. Procrastination as a trait, however, correlates only .60 with dilatory behavior as measured by the APSI (Schouwenburg, 1995). Corrected for measurement error, this correlation may be somewhat higher, but it would not reach unity. This correlation suggests that other traits and other factors may function as additional sources of dilatory behavior.

In this context, one must realize that there is no sharp distinction at the behavioral level between dilatory behavior and avoidance. Both terms refer to instances of not doing something; only psychological interpretation makes one behavior dilatory and the other avoidance. For example, the observation that a student failed to turn in his or her homework should not automatically lead to the conclusion that this is a sign of procrastination. The student may be afraid of the teacher involved, making this neglect an instance of avoidance behavior. Questioning followed by interpretation should clarify exactly what is involved.

Other well-researched candidates for additional source variables for dilatory behavior or task avoidance are anxiety (Solomon & Rothblum, 1984), depression or dejection (Lay, 1995), and indecisiveness (Effert & Ferrari, 1989). It is well-known that anxiety produces avoidance behavior. As a consequence, it may be expected that procrastinators who are also anxious will show even stronger rates of postponement. However, anxious people are subjects par excellence for counselors. It is therefore not unusual to find a strong component of anxiety in populations of procrastinators seen by counselors.

Another interesting candidate as a source of procrastinatory behavior could be the well-researched trait of optimism (Lay & Burns, 1991). In nonprocrastinators, this trait seems to spur students to more hours of study (the upside of optimism), whereas in procrastinators this trait seems to lead to fewer hours of study (the downside of optimism) and to the expressions of unrealistic optimism so familiar to student counselors (see, e.g., chap. 9, this volume).

Although recent research has also addressed a wide variety of other traits that may be additional candidates for sources of dilatory behavior (a review of this research is provided in chap. 2, this volume), in sum, there is a good claim for trait procrastination to be a main source of dilatory behavior.

Still, one could suspect this to be just another manifestation of ancient faculty psychology. The position of trait procrastination in as robust a frame of reference as the Big Five model, with related trait variables (Schouwenburg, 2002), may point to a way out of this dilemma. Plotting correlations of traits with two Big Five factors, (low) Conscientiousness and Neuroticism, obtained in various studies shows a very distinct clustering of related traits: trait procrastination, weak impulse control, lack of persistence, lack of work discipline, lack of time management skill, and inability to work methodically. In this constellation, there seems to be little justification for viewing procrastination as a separate trait. It is possibly more fruitful to label this cluster as (lack of) self-control.

TRAIT PROCRASTINATION AS LACK OF SELF-CONTROL IN SELF-REGULATION

One can do but one thing at a time, so there is always competition among possible activities. It is a rational assumption that the activity or project that will win out will depend on the project that is judged most important. Self-control theory (e.g., Logue, 1988) postulates (a) that people continuously evaluate the importance of competing personal projects, (b) that people engage in activities corresponding to the project they evaluate as most important, (c) that subjective importance is a function of both "objective" importance and delay, and (d) that the "objective" importance of a behavioral alternative is largely a function of the perceived reward associated with it. This theory implies that at every moment the subjective importance of an event that is relatively far away is discounted from its objective importance, as shown in Figure 1.1.

This theory is especially relevant for students. When studying, they are typically engaged in activities that are directed toward relatively faraway deadlines. Obtaining the reward involved will take a long time. At any moment, there will be other personal projects in their agenda, such as desire and plans for social contact or the need and intention to water their plants, that are judged "objectively" as much less important but present themselves as rewarding in a much shorter term. As a consequence of discounting, these lesser projects frequently take precedence over the objectively judged much more important task of studying. In other words, their intention to study will be put off in favor of the less important but nondiscounted tasks or activities. This general and well-documented psychological mechanism may account for the intriguing high base rate of dilatory behavior in the population.

In self-control theory, the term *self-control* is used for the behavior of persisting in the pursuit of a long-term goal in spite of the influence of competing short-term temptations; the opposite behavior is called *impulsiveness* (Logue, 1988) but may also be identified with procrastination (Schouwenburg,

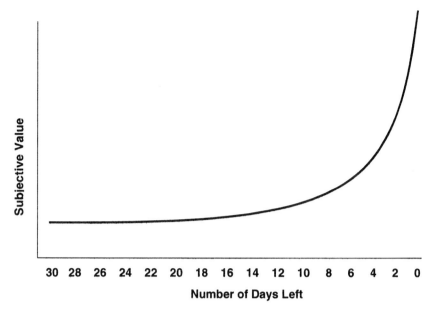

Figure 1.1. Subjective value of a reward (on an arbitrary scale) as a function of the number of days left to receive it.

1994). Keeping oneself to the task of working on a long-term (study) goal in an environment characterized by the influence of temptations of various kinds requires not only "willpower" (e.g., Ferrari & Pychyl, 2004; Muraven, Tice, & Baumeister, 1998) but also regulation of a number of other study-related psychological processes. These related processes include the students' ability to concentrate, to protect their study intentions from other temptations, and to persist at the task, as well as their overall satisfaction with their understanding of the subject matter.

In other words, students have to self-regulate (Baumeister, Heatherton, & Tice, 1994). The prefix *self* in *self-regulation* refers to the more or less automatic way in which these types of control operate, whereas the term *regulation* refers to a mechanism of negative feedback (Carver & Scheier, 1998). In the basic paradigm of regulation, an ongoing behavior is monitored and compared with a norm or goal. The detection of discrepancies triggers compensatory behaviors, the effect of which is fed back to the monitor. It can be argued that procrastinators are weak in all components of this control mechanism. For instance, there is ample research evidence that they are weak, or deficient, in setting norms or goals (e.g., Eerde, 1998; Lay & Schouwenburg, 1993).

Monitoring involves self-reflection, and this is generally not a strong point with procrastinators. They find it difficult to focus their attention on their study behavior, their concentration is often impaired, they underestimate the time needed for completing study tasks, and they are unrealistically optimistic about the effectiveness of their studying behavior (DeWitte & Lens, 2000; McCown, Petzel, & Rupert, 1987; Pychyl, Morin, & Salmon, 2000).

Valid comparisons of monitor values and norms can be made by the individual only if the "comparator" functions well. There is some evidence (e.g., Silver & Sabini, 1981) that in procrastinators this is not so. In procrastinators, the comparator function seems to be biased in such a way that they seem to discount the value of future events much more strongly than other people do, which makes them unprepared victims of short-term temptations (Pychyl, Lee, Thibodeau, & Blunt, 2000).

An assessment of self-control theory provides a number of ideas for successful intervention methods (see also Figure 1.1). For example, as a first component of intervention, an increase in the reward value of a long-term goal may be considered. Although this may not be feasible materially in academic settings, an immaterial way of increasing the reward value of passing an exam or handing in a writing assignment may consist of putting the student's reputation among peers at stake. This is exactly what happens in group interventions that continue long enough for participants to witness the attainment of long-term goals, such as task management groups, as described in chapter 7 in this volume.

A second component of intervention consists of blocking access to short-term temptations, thereby decreasing their reward value. Such effects are produced by common study skills techniques for preventing distraction, such as studying in a library, with a clean desktop, with the door closed, and so on. All cognitive–behavioral interventions presented in the present volume include this component.

Finally, a third component of intervention may involve an explicit increase in the height of the motivational curve in Figure 1.1, done by splitting up the task of the long-term goal into many short-term subgoal tasks—for example, weekly study tasks, as advocated by study planning techniques. Again, task management groups, as discussed in chapter 7, offer a good illustration of this principle. A related procedure is to decrease the height of the motivational curves of short-term temptations by deliberately considering the importance and urgency of any disturbance of the studying process. This is the essence of the time-management techniques that are used in most of the cognitive–behavioral interventions proposed in this volume.

The exertion of corrective action to address discrepancies detected between ongoing behavior and a norm requires considerable effort by individuals. The aim of this corrective action is to make higher processes override lower processes (Baumeister et al., 1994). A certain amount of willpower is necessary to complete such corrective action successfully. This is a vital weak point in the character of procrastinators. To assist students in this optimizing process and to help them develop willpower, an extensive program of intervention comparable to the psychotherapy process may be necessary.

PREVALENCE AND BASE RATE OF PROCRASTINATION
IN A STUDENT POPULATION

How widespread is procrastination among students? Figures in the literature vary from 20% to 70%, but these figures are usually poorly documented, if at all. It may therefore be helpful to look at the distribution of scores on Lay's Procrastination Scale collected from 2,088 university students in the first half of the last decade (Figure 1.2). The first thing that is apparent in the figure is that the scores are approximately normally distributed ($M = 58.82$, $SD = 10.30$, range = 20–100), which means that almost everybody procrastinates to some extent and that a considerable amount of procrastination is average and thus normal. Now, what amount of procrastination should be considered problematic? There are a few arbitrary conventions, such as the upper three stanines (67 and over), the upper 10% (71 and over), or the upper 5% of the distribution (77 and over), whereas for research purposes a simple median split dichotomization is the rule. Another arbitrary rule is to consider persons more than a standard deviation above the mean of the distribution as problematic or severe procrastinators. In our data, this rule would result in 190 participants, which is roughly 10% of students. So the question, How widespread is procrastination among students? can be answered in an exact way by pointing to the above score distribution and its characteristics, but it cannot very well be answered without reference to some comparison group. Unfortunately, reliable information regarding groups other than students is still largely lacking.

It is therefore useful to reflect on the above score distribution itself. Its mean, for example, reflects a relatively high base rate of habitual procrastination in the (academic) population. Why is this so? To understand this, it is important to realize that procrastinating is not the same as doing nothing. It is simply doing things other than the activity that was intended. People in everyday life, and students in particular, pursue a multiplicity of goals and intentions that call for corresponding activities. These activities may vary in their importance or priority at some point in time. They have been termed *personal projects*, and chapter 11 in this volume is dedicated to a study of counseling based on this view.

In contrast, the normal distribution of procrastination scores implies that there is a considerable number of students who have a below-base-rate procrastination score. These students obviously succeed in counteracting the effects of discounting. They display self-control, a characteristic that has been extensively researched (e.g., Ainslie, 1992; Mischel, 1981).

Students showing base rates in procrastination well above the norm may be viewed as excessive in their behavior, and this behavior may be problematic in their lives. In various areas of their lives, notably in their studies, they experience a repeated discrepancy between what they intend to do and what they do in reality. They can therefore be viewed as chronic procrastina-

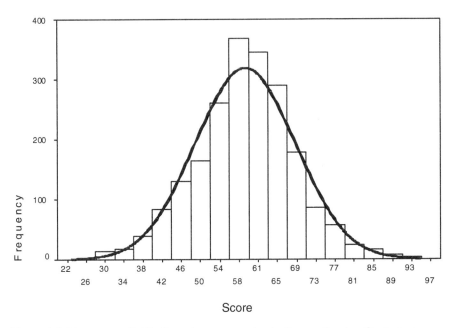

Figure 1.2. Frequency distribution of scores on Lay's Procrastination Scale in a large student sample (*N* = 2,088).

tors (Ferrari, Johnson, & McCown, 1995; Ferrari & Pychyl, 2000b) or, to use my earlier term, trait procrastinators. These students follow the discounting rule but possess in addition a trait called procrastination. The focus of the present volume is on the counseling of these students.

PROCRASTINATION IN DIFFERENT SITUATIONS

As indicated before, research on procrastination has been conducted mainly among students. Most dilatory behavior in this situation concerns the completion of academic assignments, such as preparing for examinations, doing homework, and writing term papers. Some researchers refer to such dilatory behavior as *academic procrastination.*

Trait procrastination in students is a source of their dilatory study behavior, resulting in intention–behavior gaps with respect to study tasks. This disposition may also be viewed as a source trait in their engagement in other activities, activities that are often less important but more rewarding in the short term. Trait procrastination probably impairs the self-regulation of both academic performance and other task or personal project behaviors (see Ferrari & Emmons, 1995; Ferrari & Pychyl, 2004; Senécal, Koestner, & Vallerand, 1995; Tice & Baumeister, 1997).

In other specific situations, dilatory behavior is concerned with the completion of nonacademic life routines, such as getting up, paying bills, washing dishes, returning telephone calls, and the like (Milgram, Mey-Tal, & Levison, 1998). On the basis of recent research, in which they observed a correlation of .65 between academic and life routine procrastination in students, Milgram and his colleagues suggested that procrastination is a generalized behavioral disposition, consistent across very different kinds of tasks.

My own research data suggest a similar point of view. For example, in data collected among university students in various phases of their academic career, median splits of both scores on Lay's Procrastination Scale and academic dilatory behavior measured by the APSI resulted in three subsets; see the diagram in Figure 1.3. In this diagram, Subset 1 contains students high on trait procrastination who reported little academic dilatory behavior (24%), Subset 2 contains students high on trait procrastination who reported strong academic dilatory behavior (48%), and Subset 3 contains students who reported strong academic dilatory behavior but who were low on trait procrastination (28%). Measuring academic dilatory behavior with a different instrument, the Procrastination Checklist Study Tasks (see Ferrari, Johnson, & McCown, 1995), resulted in a slightly different mix: 22%, 50%, and 28%, respectively.

Looking at the data, one can see there is little doubt that academic dilatory behavior can best be understood as the expression of trait procrastination in an academic situation. The trait is expressed explicitly in the students of Subset 2. They are the focus of this volume. However, students in Subset 1 may report little dilatory behavior in an academic setting because they have adapted to a nondilatory style of studying as a result of high intrinsic motivation or effective training, or simply because they study under a strict regimen of relatively short study tasks. Their high level of trait procrastination, however, reveals that there must be other areas in which their procrastinatory tendencies do show. These students may also benefit from interventions as proposed in the present volume; they are, however, not explicitly addressed.

Finally, students in Subset 3 may report strong dilatory behavior in relative absence of the trait as a result of loss of motivation, evaluation anxiety, influence by the peer culture at school, or a strong preference for other activities. These students do not show the trait, so many of the interventions proposed in the present volume obviously do not apply to them. The exception to this may be the purely behavioral interventions proposed in chapter 7 and in other chapters in this volume, which do not rely on the trait concept.

PROCRASTINATORS: THE SEARCH FOR TYPES

Clinical observations (e.g., Burka & Yuen, 1983) suggest that there are at least three fundamental types of procrastinators: anxious procrastinators, happy-go-lucky procrastinators, and rebellious procrastinators. Many student counselors share the conviction that anxiety is involved in student procrasti-

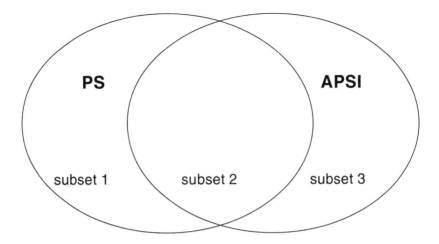

Figure 1.3. Venn diagram of subsets of procrastinating students, based on median-split scores on Lay's Procrastination Scale (PS) and the Academic Procrastination State Inventory (APSI).

nation. Empirical research among student populations, however, shows that on average anxiety and procrastination are unrelated (Schouwenburg, 1995). This result may point to a selection effect, because counselors are apt to see students as being in need of help, implying some extent of anxiety, but it does not exclude the possibility that there may exist homogeneous subsets of procrastinating students with mutually different characteristics.

In procrastination research, only two studies have addressed the issue of separate types of procrastinating students explicitly. Lay (1987), using a technique of modal profile analysis, managed to identify two different types of procrastinators in a sample of 94 "normal" students. He subsequently identified them as disorganized and rebellious (11%) and as disorganized, lacking energy, and lacking achievement motivation (10%). In a subsequent study among 337 students and nonstudents, these findings were largely confirmed. One of Lay's main conclusions was that both anxiety and achievement seemed to be relevant for discriminating different types of procrastinators.

The second study (McCown, Johnson, & Petzel, 1989) examined a sample of 227 extreme procrastinators who were also underachieving. Using principal components analysis, they identified three types of procrastinators: (a) a "tough minded," extraverted, low anxiety, low time management type; (b) a neurotic extraverted type; and (c) a neurotic, depressed, and introverted type.

In spite of possible methodological shortcomings (Costa, Herbst, McCrae, Samuels, & Ozer, 2002), these few studies seem to confirm earlier clinical observations to some extent. Combining these results with the established Big Five factors, I propose the following hypothetical taxonomy: All procrastinators share extremely low scores on Conscientiousness, which predisposes them to disorganization, lack of time management, weak impulse control, and lack of work discipline. As a result, their academic achievement tends to be lower than could be expected on the basis of ability scores. In addition, some of these procrastinators are also high in Neuroticism (or low in Emotional Stability), making them anxious, fearful of failing, and perfectionistic, and they probably work hard to compensate for their lack of organization. Their worries make them seek help at counseling services. Chapter 13 in this volume is concerned with this type of procrastinating student.

Some procrastinators, however, do not combine low Conscientiousness with high Neuroticism. This makes them free of anxiety and therefore not prone to consulting counseling services. Their academic underachievement, however, will not be compensated by neurotic dutifulness, so they will be identifiable in general student populations by high scores on trait procrastination, low scores on Neuroticism, and low achievement. Chapter 9 deals extensively with counseling this type of procrastinator.

My own archived data provide some support for this distinction. These data include 118 cases in which Lay's Procrastination Scale scores and Study Problems Questionnaire scores (Schouwenburg, 1995) are available. One of these study problems, lack of work discipline, is highly saturated with (low) Conscientiousness, whereas another study problem, fear of failure, is highly saturated with Neuroticism or low Emotional Stability. Figure 1.4 shows the scores on these two study problems of 190 students with a Lay's Procrastination Scale score higher than 1 standard deviation above average. These study problem scores were standardized with respect to student populations. Figure 1.4 shows that almost all the procrastinators lacked work discipline. In addition, they were more or less continuously distributed on fear of failure. Although not an indication of "types" in a strict sense (Costa et al., 2002), this distribution underlines the clinical usefulness of discriminating between emotionally stable and unstable trait procrastinators.

This taxonomy could be extended meaningfully by individual positions on Extraversion–Introversion. For example, neurotic procrastinators who are also extraverted, and thus easily distracted by social interactions, may show feelings of guilt as the most prominent clinical symptom, whereas neurotic procrastinators who are introverted may rather be prone to feelings of depression. However, emotionally stable (i.e., not neurotic) procrastinators who are also extraverts may constitute the familiar type of unrealistically optimistic, happy-go-lucky procrastinator, whereas the introverted emotionally stable procrastinator may be typified as rather a dreamer.

CONCLUSION

In this volume, dilatory behavior is regarded primarily as a product of trait procrastination. Behavioral control techniques may be called for to coun-

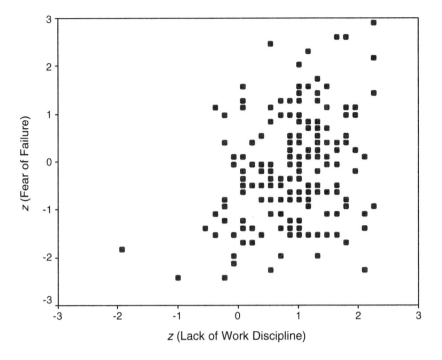

Figure 1.4. Bivariate scores on two scales of the Study Problems Questionnaire of 190 severe procrastinators (scoring more than 1 standard deviation above the mean on Lay's Procrastination Scale).

teract this primary effect. Besides behavior, however, there are other effects of the trait, including cognitions such as false estimates of the time needed to complete a study task, misconceptions about the influence of discounting on study motivation, and low self-efficacy. These side effects may themselves contribute to continued procrastinating. Interventions may be directed at promoting cognitive control to break the reinforcing effects of cognitions on dilatory behavior. Finally, procrastination may frequently be accompanied by negative feelings or affect, such as depression or feelings of dejection. Tackling these negative feelings by promoting emotional control may be another way of trying to weaken the effects of trait procrastination on academic behavior.

Depending on the particular point of view of the authors, the chapters on interventions in this book all reflect a distinct mix of these principles (see Table 1.1). In addition, the intervention methods presented differ considerably in approach (e.g., Web-based interventions in chaps. 7 and 10, personal project analysis in chap. 11, and narrative approach in chap. 12), selection of clients (notably in chaps. 8, 9, and 13), use of supportive materials (such as personality questionnaires in chaps. 5 and 6), and evidence collected regarding the effects of the intervention (e.g., effects on project systems, chap. 11, vs. changes in specific behaviors, chap. 5).

TABLE 1.1
Features of Interventions Presented in This Volume

Chapter/authors	Behavioral control	Cognitions	Feelings

4: Lay	Goal setting
	Planning &
	  Scheduling
	Right place
	More time
		School work = job
		  success =
		  completion of
		  intentions
			Feeling better after
			  change

5: van Essen et al.	Time management
	Goal setting
	Planning
		Changing
		  unproductive
		  thoughts (REBT)
		Self-efficacy	

6: Walker	Goal setting Planning Monitoring	Productive thinking Focus on successes	Personal power Facing fears

7: Tuckman &
  Schouwenburg
	Goal setting
	Planning &
	  scheduling
	Using models
	Monitoring
		Taking
		  responsibility	

8: van Horebeek et
  al.
	Goal setting
	Planning &
	  scheduling
	Monitoring
		Time is up!
		Cognitive
		  restructuring	

9: Mandel	Monitoring	Exposing
		  ambivalence
		Confronting
		  excuses	

10: Topman et al.	Goal setting
	Planning &
	  scheduling
	Monitoring
		Confronting
		  excuses
		Self-efficacy
			Overcoming
			  shame

11: Pychyl & Binder	Goal setting
	Time management
	Monitoring
		Changing
		  unproductive
		  thoughts
			Reducing guilt &
			  anxiety

12: O'Callaghan		Flexible &
		  supportive
		  narratives	

13: Flett et al		Control of negative
		  automatic
		  thoughts
			Stress inoculation

Note. REBT = rational–emotive behavioral therapy.

Thus, the practical counseling methods described in this volume seem to vary considerably. Yet they are all aimed at promoting new intervention that can lead to change. Which of these methods will prove most fruitful, and for whom, the future will show.

2

TRAIT PROCRASTINATION IN ACADEMIC SETTINGS: AN OVERVIEW OF STUDENTS WHO ENGAGE IN TASK DELAYS

JOSEPH R. FERRARI

Imagine the following common scenario: It is the middle of the class term, and the instructor reminds the students that a term paper, a major part of their grade, will need to be handed in by the last day of class. The instructor asks for a show of hands if anyone needs any help so far. No one raises a hand. The instructor asks for a show of hands if anyone has had problems getting resources, references, or other materials for their paper. No one raises a hand. The students begin to squirm and look down at their papers and materials, instead of maintaining eye contact with the instructor, who begins to get a sense that not much progress has occurred so far. Finally, the instructor asks, "Have you selected your topics?" Asked to announce, again, the exact date the project is due, the instructor provides the date, pauses, and then asks, "Has anyone begun to work on the paper?"

It is no surprise to most instructors that students report *procrastination*, defined here as the purposive delay in the start or completion of tasks. *Procrastinatory behavior*, as illustrated in the preceding scenario, means the

19

expression of a personality trait in an academic setting (see chap. 1 of this volume for further details). The perspective of when the procrastinatory behavior "begins" may depend on who is observing the inertia. For the instructor, procrastination may begin just after he or she assigns the project; for the student, procrastination may not begin until he or she has decided that it is time to actually begin the project, perhaps a week after the project was assigned.

It is important for readers to understand, however, that calling all persons who procrastinate "chronic" or trait procrastinators would be incorrect (see Ferrari, Johnson, & McCown, 1995). That is, just because a student delays the start or completion of term papers does not mean that this student also delays in other aspects of campus life (e.g., eating dinner, accepting free concert tickets, calling friends, or e-mailing others) or personal life (e.g., going out with friends, purchasing a new CD, working a part-time job, or listening to music).

On the other hand, considerable research has begun to explore a pattern in which frequent delays in tasks is a way of life across settings and situations for an individual, and this dispositional tendency is postulated as caused by *trait procrastination* (for details see chap. 1; Ferrari, Johnson, & McCown, 1995; Ferrari & Pychyl, 2000b). Trait procrastination is a summary of the predisposition to engage in frequent procrastination (see chap. 1; Schouwenburg, 1995). Chapter 3 (this volume) shows how trait procrastination is anchored within a state-of-the-art model of personality, the Big Five model. No detailed discussion of the underlying personality structure associated with trait procrastination is covered in this chapter (see instead chap. 3). In the present chapter, procrastinatory behavior in an academic setting is conceived of as the trait expression of procrastination as well as situation-generated behavior. I will use the label ATP for *academic trait procrastination* or *academic trait procrastinator*, depending on the sentence context. This label refers to the Trait × Situation interaction related to academics.

Educational administrators and research psychologists have examined systematically the antecedents and consequences of ATP among students for several decades. In this chapter, I present a review of the characteristics of trait procrastinators in academic settings, the situations that elicit these academic task delays, the motives and purposes for academic task delays, and the consequences of academic task delays for academic performance and student well-being. The goal of this chapter is to create a context in which to assess and implement preventive and intervention strategies for those who engage in ATP.

Research psychologists have assessed ATP using a few reliable and valid measures. These scales include the Student Academic Procrastination Scale developed and used in Israel by Milgram and colleagues (Milgram, Batori, & Mowrer, 1993; Milgram, Mey-Tal, & Levison, 1998), the Academic Procrastination State Inventory and the Procrastination Checklist Study Tasks used in the Netherlands by Schouwenburg and associates (Lay & Schouwenburg, 1993; Schouwenburg, 1993, 1995), and the Tuckman Procrastination Scale (Tuckman, 1991) used in the United States by others (Burns, Dittmann, Nguyen, & Mitchelson, 2000; Jackson, Weiss, & Lundquist, 2000). However, the most widely used instrument is the reliable and valid Procrastination Assessment Scale–Students, or PASS, developed by Solomon and Rothblum (1984; Rothblum, Solomon, & Murakami, 1986).

The PASS assesses the prevalence of, and reasons for, academic procrastination across six academic areas (writing a term paper, studying for an exam, keeping up with weekly reading assignments, performing administrative tasks, attending meetings, and performing academic tasks in general). Respondents indicate both their tendency to procrastinate (frequency) and their perception of whether the delays cause them difficulties (problem). Most of the results in this chapter about ATP have been based on data collected with the PASS. Future research comparing and contrasting measures seem warranted.

CHARACTERISTICS AND DEVELOPMENTAL ORIGINS OF TRAIT PROCRASTINATORS IN ACADEMIC SETTINGS

Research studies that include demographic information indicate that persons who report ATP tend to be young, traditional-age, male students who do not self-identify with any particular racial category (Clark & Hill, 1994; Prohaska, Morrill, Atiles, & Perez, 2000). Trait procrastination on academic tasks also extends to graduate students, who report higher rates than undergraduate students (see chap. 6, this volume; Jiao & Onwuegbuzie, 1998; Onwuegbuzie, 2000; Onwuegbuzie & Collins, 2001; Onwuegbuzie & Jiao, 2000), and even to faculty, who may not obtain tenure and promotion because of few or no publications in professional journals (see Boice, 1992, 1993, 1995).

In terms of psychological variables, Table 2.1 shows positive and negative correlates between ATP and a number of attributes and characteristics self-reported by undergraduates. The sample sizes on which the coefficients are based are included in the table, and nearly all these significant coefficients were based on U.S. samples. (See the appendix to chap. 3, this volume, for a list of sources of these data.) As noted in Table 2.1, ATP is significantly positively related to a number of variables, especially fear of failure, self-handicapping, depression, guilt affect, and state anxiety. Alternatively, ATP is significantly negatively related to optimism and self-confidence when making decisions. Although omitted from this table (but still of interest), studies reported that ATP was not significantly related to general intelligence, private self-consciousness, interpersonal control, self-monitoring, or Myers–Briggs typologies (for details, see Ferrari, Johnson, & McCown, 1995; Ferrari & Pychyl, 2000b). Clearly, ATPs are individuals with a complex nomological network.

TABLE 2.1
Psychological Correlates of Academic Procrastination

Psychological variables	Academic trait procrastination correlates	n
Positive correlates		
Fear of failure	.63	211
Self-handicapping	.53	185
	.51	169
	.48	99
Depression (Australian sample)	.44	210
	.27	297
Guilt affect	.42	225
State anxiety (Australian sample)	.40	297
Evening proneness	.38	107
Rebelliousness (Australian sample)	.32	297
Indecision (Australian sample)	.32	297
Social anxiety	.32	234
Irrational cognitions	.30	210
Public self-consciousness	.29	185
	.24	185
Socially prescribed perfectionism	.24	135
Parental criticism	.24	210
Parental performance expectations	.21	210
Trait anxiety	.13	220
Negative correlates		
Self-efficacy	−.54	182
Optimism	−.42	208
Decisional self-confidence	−.40	99
Organization	−.37	210
Work discipline	−.35	220
General motivation	−.32	96
Personal self-confidence	−.30	157
Personal control over life	−.30	157
Personal performance standards	−.30	210
Dominance	−.27	220
Self-esteem (Australian sample)	−.35	297
	−.26	169
	−.23	210
Global life satisfaction	−.25	225
Intrinsic motivation	−.21	110

Note. All coefficients were significant at least at the .05 level. Variables with multiple coefficients reflect multiple studies reporting that relationship. All samples are U.S. undergraduates, unless otherwise indicated.

A few studies have examined the origins of ATP among students by focusing on parental influences, child rearing practices, and family life situations. Ferrari and Olivette (1993) found that indecisive moms, but not dads, influenced their daughters to be procrastinators, whereas Pychyl, Coplan, and Reid (2002) reported that parenting style mediated the effects through self-systems, and gender influenced whether daughters engaged in ATP. Milgram et al. (1998), in contrast, found no significant relationship between parental characteristics and reported ATP among children. However, moms involved with their children's education were less likely to have children who engaged in procrastination. Scher and Ferrari (2000) reported that a student's ability to recall academic tasks completed or not completed from the previous day was related to whether the task was perceived as important to his or her family, but not friends. Together, these studies suggest that the dynamics of a person's family and home life influence his or her engagement in procrastination.

Thus, procrastination may occur in a variety of students with a wide range of characteristics. In short, there may be no "typical" profile of the ATP toward which to address preventive and intervention strategies, because his or her nomological network of psychological variables seems complex. Instead, there may be typical profiles of some classes of procrastinators in academic settings (see, e.g., chap. 9 on underachiever procrastinators and chap. 13 on perfectionist procrastinators). In the next section, research on when people engage in ATP is presented. Varied methodologies have been applied to address this topic that may yield some useful and interesting results for treating high ATP rates.

PREDICTING WHEN STUDENTS MAY ENGAGE IN ACADEMIC TRAIT PROCRASTINATION

Studies indicate that fear of failure and aversiveness of the task may be two general, primary motives for ATP (e.g., Blunt & Pychyl, 1998, 2000; Milgram et al., 1993; Schouwenburg, 1993; Solomon & Rothblum, 1984). Ferrari, Keane, Wolfe, and Beck (1998) further demonstrated that ATP was motivated by task aversiveness for students at a selective-admission college (e.g., an Ivy League liberal arts college) but by fear of task failure and fear of social disapproval for students at a non-selective-admission college (e.g., an open-enrollment college). The motives for ATP, therefore, may depend on the type of institution a student attends.

Among college students ATP also has been predicted by an avoidant, fearful, diffuse sense of personal identity (Ferrari, Wolfe, et al., 1995), and ATP occurred on academic tasks that students perceived as unpleasant, boring, or difficult rather than on pleasant and easy tasks (Milgram et al., 1993). In addition, students who regarded themselves as less capable than other students delayed on academic tasks and expressed an interest in changing their delaying behaviors (Milgram, Marshevsky, & Sadeh, 1995). Therefore, not surprisingly, students engage in ATP when they find course-related tasks distasteful and when they lack self-confidence in their skills to master the material.

Few studies have explored the contexts when ATP may occur. Ferrari, Wolfe, et al. (1995), for instance, found that ATP rates differed among students from different-quality institutions. Students from institutions with very selective admission standards reported higher rates of ATP than students from institutions with moderate or no selection standards. These researchers proposed that students' perceptions of themselves as engaging in ATP may be relatively subjective. For the very talented student, to wait more than a day or two to start a term paper due in 10 weeks might be perceived as ATP, whereas for a poor student who may require remedial instruction skills, ATP occurs only when the term paper is started 1 or 2 days before it is due.

Some researchers (Ferrari & Scher, 2000; Milgram et al., 1998; Pychyl, Lee, et al., 2000; Scher & Ferrari, 2000) used a short-term daily log or diary procedure to explore the context and nature of tasks that people delay or complete. Typically, participants listed each day for approximately 5 to 7 days all the tasks they intended to complete and completed in the last 24 hours. In some cases, the students were paged or beeped randomly during the day to ascertain what tasks they were delaying or completing. The listed tasks were the unit of analysis, as opposed to exclusively personality factors of persons.

As one might expect, researchers examining the daily diary or log procedure found that people delay the completion of aversive, difficult, and unpleasant tasks (Pychyl, Lee, et al., 2000; Scher & Ferrari, 2000). In one study, for instance, students delayed the start or completion of academic tasks but not nonacademic tasks—unless the latter tasks were perceived as boring and tedious (Ferrari & Scher, 2000). Another study found that students paged randomly during the day at the time of the page reported delaying unpleasant, stressful, and difficult tasks; they were engaging in activities significantly more pleasant or fun (Pychyl, Lee, et al., 2000). Another study using daily recordings found that procrastination on tasks generalized even to postponement of nonacademic life routines (Milgram et al., 1998).

In summary, it seems that ATP occurs because of individual-differences factors (e.g., how the person perceives the act of task delays, a student's ego identity) and the context or nature of the target task. Diaries or logs and event-recording procedures suggest that students report procrastinating on academic tasks that they find boring and unpleasant. Knowing how to measure this concept, who is likely to demonstrate this behavior pattern, and in what settings this behavior pattern is most likely to occur may be useful information for practitioners. Still, that information does not tell us why some people are motivated to engage in high ATP rates.

PROCRASTINATION IN ACADEMICS: THE USE OF EXCUSES

Besides understanding the characteristics and family impact of trait procrastination by students, it is important for educators and policy administrators to understand the motives for student ATP. Ferrari et al. (1998) examined the use of fraudulent and legitimate excuses by students at different levels of institutional selectivity as the subjective reasons why they engaged in ATP. The purpose of the study was to ascertain whether students from varied types of institutions used fraudulent excuses for delaying or procrastinating on academic tasks. Surprisingly, these college students, regardless of the institution's admission selectivity level, willingly admitted that more than 70% of the time, when they gave an instructor an excuse for nonperformance of an assignment, exam, or task, they generated a fraudulent reason (i.e., a "lie"; Ferrari et al., 1998). Sample lies included "I left it home/in my dorm room," "A relative/friend just passed away," and "I had computer/printer problems" (Ferrari et al., 1998, pp. 199–215).

Furthermore, regardless of the level of admission selectivity, most instructors (over 90%) did not require substantiation of the excuse. Fraudulent excuses were most commonly used in large lecture classes taught by young "lenient" women instructors (Ferrari et al., 1998). At the nonselective college only, ATP students reported using both legitimate and fraudulent excuses more often than non-ATP students throughout college and during the semester surveyed. Therefore, the motives for students who engage in ATP may vary depending on the academic rigor of the institution. Administrators and educational personnel need to consider both individual and situational differences when implementing interventions for ATP. Instructors also may want to be more cautious about giving extensions to students at their institution who are ATP.

Related to the use of fraudulent excuses for ATP, Ferrari and Beck (1998) explored the emotional consequences for fabricating a false excuse (i.e., telling a lie). They reported that college students, irrespective of the admission selectivity of the institution, claimed to experience a positive feeling when falsifying to an instructor in order to delay an assigned task. However, these same students experienced negative feelings during, after, and when recalling that lie.

Taken together, it seems students do not "feel bad" when they engage in ATP behaviors or when they lie to permit procrastination for a class. However, when students think about the use of that lie for ATP, they do experience negative feelings. These negative effects seem not to prevent students from lying in the future (Ferrari et al., 1998). Additional research on the role of affect as a motive for and consequence of engaging in ATP seems to be warranted and should be considered when designing interventions targeted to reduce this form of delay behaviors.

One other investigation explored the role of motivation for ATP in college students. Brownlow and Reasinger (2000) asked students to complete the PASS and a self-report measure of intrinsic and extrinsic motivators toward getting academic tasks completed. Results indicated that high-ATP students made more external attributions for their successes, whereas only low-ATP students saw intrinsic and extrinsic factors as important motivators to complete a task. In addition, for women, but not men, low extrinsic motivation (and perfectionism) contributed to high ATP rates. Thus, gender differences in motivation for frequent ATP seem a factor to consider.

In this chapter, task aspects, personal fears, and setting characteristics were described as important contributors to why students engaged in ATP. In fact, it seems that students are motivated to use fraudulent excuses as a way to get out of starting or completing academic tasks, and instructors and administrators need to be cautious about simply accepting student excuses. Although students seem to experience negative emotions after lying to get out of an academic task, they continue to lie.

EDUCATIONAL IMPLICATIONS OF ACADEMIC TRAIT PROCRASTINATION

Much of the research on ATP has relied on self-report measures. However, it is important to examine the academic consequences of ATP in terms of objective behavioral indexes. Table 2.2 contains the correlates reported in the literature between ATP and a wide range of behavioral indexes of academic performance by undergraduates and other students in the United States and other countries. (See the appendix to chap. 3, this volume, for a list of many sources of these data.) It appears that ATP is significantly positively related to the time used to turn in assignments, time used to hand in term paper outlines, hours spent studying or working on projects, and academic dishonesty (i.e., cheating and plagiarism). This table also indicates that ATP has serious negative outcomes for class, course, and cumulative grade measures. Overall, ATP is negatively related to poor English and math course grades, completion of homework, and amount of time spent studying. In fact, many of these behavioral outcomes reported in the literature occur for students from different countries and suggest that ATP hinders student performance. These behavioral outcomes are useful verifications for instructors and researchers, who always knew that ATP did not reflect constructive student performance; now, they can show students what the research shows.

CONCLUSION

This brief overview provides a context in which to understand ATP among students. It extends chapter 1 by reporting the who, when, why, and what of trait procrastination across international academic settings with undergraduate and graduate students. Furthermore, this overview sets the stage for chapter 3, which examines the personality structure of trait procrastination in academic settings.

Clearly, more research is needed to determine additional antecedent factors that predict who will engage in ATP, the role of social systems (e.g.,

TABLE 2.2
Behavioral Outcome Correlates of Academic Trait Procrastination

Behavioral outcomes	Academic trait procrastination correlates	n
Positive correlates		
Time to return class assignments	.58	190
	.40	201
(Doctoral student sample)	.22	151
Time to hand in paper outlines		
(Australian sample)	.36	297
Hours spent working on projects	.31	178
	.27	220
Cheating	.30	285
Plagiarism	.30	285
Time to hand in final paper (Australian		
sample)	.23	297
Late start to work on a project	.24	220
Negative correlates		
English performance grades (Australian		
sample)	−.62	380
Mathematics performance grades		
(Australian sample)	−.61	380
Completion of homework assignments	−.54	183
(Australian sample)	−.30	380
Time spent studying	−.29	220
(Medical student sample)	−.27	135
Term paper outline grade (Australian		
sample)	−.26	297
Final term paper grade (Australian		
sample)	−.24	297
Final course grade (Australian sample)	−.30	297
	−.22	161
Cumulative grade point average	−.12	271

Note. All coefficients were significant at the least at the .05 level. Variables with multiple coefficients reflect multiple studies reporting that relationship. All samples are U.S. undergraduates, unless otherwise indicated.

family and friends) and other situations that promote ATP, and the development of theoretical models that explain why ATP exists and continues. The challenge for educators, counselors, and researchers is to address academic procrastination in ways that enhance the well-being of present and future generations of students.

3

PROCRASTINATION IN ACADEMIC SETTINGS AND THE BIG FIVE MODEL OF PERSONALITY: A META-ANALYSIS

WENDELIEN VAN EERDE

Everyone may procrastinate on some occasions, but typically *procrastination* has been defined as a trait or behavioral disposition to postpone or delay performing a task or making decisions (e.g., Milgram et al., 1998). The trait definition appears to indicate that the individual generally delays, independent of the appropriateness to a particular situation, and this characteristic would automatically make procrastination a dysfunctional tendency. Conversely, it would also be dysfunctional to always stick to a plan without looking at the context. A closer look at when people typically procrastinate and when they typically do not sheds a different light on the phenomenon (see chap. 2, this volume), and some research has paid attention to this issue, for example by identifying tasks typically procrastinated on (e.g., Blunt & Pychyl, 2000; Ferrari & Scher, 2000; Lay, 1992; Milgram et al., 1995). However, the majority of studies have been conducted with the idea that individual differences are most important in determining procrastination, without much further investigation of the processes that are triggered in a certain type of person by certain situational aspects (see also Mischel & Shoda, 1998).

The broader context of the situational aspects described in this chapter is the academic setting, or procrastinating in relation to studying. Most studies on procrastination have been conducted in this setting. Although procrastination may be seen as an outcome of several processes, determined by personality, motives, task, and context as antecedents, procrastination usually has been studied as an independent trait variable, and the relations with other traits, motives, affect, and performance have been assessed concurrently or at a later point in time (see van Eerde, 2003, for a review). Most studies have compared procrastinators with nonprocrastinators using a median split on the self-report scale, and most studies have been conducted using a cross-sectional correlational design.

The results from the previous studies are used in this chapter, which addresses the extent to which self-reported procrastination in an academic setting is related to the Big Five model of personality (Costa & McCrae, 1992). Do people who report a tendency to procrastinate have a specific profile according to this model?

Several studies have addressed this question for two or more factors at the facet level of the Big Five model (J. L. Johnson & Bloom, 1995; Milgram & Tenne, 2000; Schouwenburg & Lay, 1995; Watson, 2001). This meta-analysis builds on these studies by systematically comparing and combining the studies on the relation between procrastination and the Big Five model of personality. That is, the results of studies that explicitly addressed this question were combined and compared, and where available, results from other studies were added.

METHOD

Study Selection

A search for empirical studies on procrastination was conducted using the PsycINFO database of the American Psychological Association, limiting the search by using "procrastination" in the key phrase or descriptor fields and limiting publication type by empirical studies to find the studies in which procrastination was actually measured. Also, this computer search was supplemented by a so-called ancestry approach: Articles were traced through reference lists and when possible obtained. Retrieved studies were included in the meta-analysis if they met the following three criteria:

1. A self-report scale of procrastination was used, independent of whether it was aimed to measure the traitlike or statelike nature of procrastination (for an overview of several scales, see Ferrari, Johnson, & McCown, 1995). Practically, this limited the studies to those conducted after 1982, after which scales were used to measure procrastination.

2. An effect size could be found in the article that indicated the direct relation between procrastination and a Big Five facet or factor. When a relation was called "nonsignificant" in the article, a conservative estimation (i.e., an effect size of 0) was included.
3. The sample in which the effect size was obtained consisted of students, whether elementary school children, high school children, undergraduate students, or graduate students.

Independent subgroups reported within an article were included separately. If several effect sizes applying to the same effect category were available in one sample, then these were averaged (via a Fisher's z transformation) before inclusion.

Variables

The effect sizes were correlations or other indicators of effects (F, t, χ^2) transformed to correlations (see Mullen, 1989). The effect sizes were grouped according to the Big Five model of personality and contained the correlations between procrastination and the following:

- Neuroticism factor and the facets Anxiety, Hostility, Depression, Self-Consciousness, Impulsivity, and Vulnerability
- Extraversion factor and the facets Warmth, Gregariousness, Assertiveness, Activity, Excitement Seeking, and Positive Emotions
- Openness to Experience factor and the facets Fantasy, Aesthetics, Feelings, Actions, Ideas, and Values
- Agreeableness factor and the facets Trust, Straightforwardness, Altruism, Compliance, Modesty, and Tender-Mindedness
- Conscientiousness factor and the facets Order, Dutifulness, Self-Discipline, Achievement Striving, Competence, and Deliberation

Integration of Effect Sizes

The Rosenthal (1991) meta-analytic procedures were used to compare and combine the effect sizes (for a comparison with two other meta-analytic approaches, see B. T. Johnson, Mullen, & Salas, 1995). The correlations were transformed to Fisher's z and multiplied by their degrees of freedom ($n - 3$). These weighted Fisher's zs were summed across studies within each effect category and divided by the total degrees of freedom in the category to obtain the average weighted Fisher's z of each effect category. This Fisher's z was transformed back into r to obtain the weighted mean correlation for the effect category, and 95% confidence intervals were computed for the weighted means. Subsequently, the χ^2 for homogeneity of results was computed within each effect category (Rosenthal, 1991) to establish whether the findings could be interpreted as belonging to the same population of effect sizes.

RESULTS

After examination of the articles, the results found in 41 articles (see Appendix 3.1) were included, from which I retrieved the effect sizes of 45 independent samples with a total of 9,141 participants. Sample sizes in the studies ranged from 58 to 618, with an average of 203 per study (median n = 173). The percentage of women in the samples (not reported in eight studies) ranged between 0% and 100%, with an average of 63%, indicating that women were overrepresented in the studies.

The range of ages in the samples was between 7 and 58 years. In 32 samples, the age of the samples was reported as a mean or median. Averaging these statistics over the samples resulted in a mean of 21, which indicates that the participants were relatively young. The types of participant were recorded: 18 samples consisted of college psychology students, 21 samples were college students with majors other than psychology, and 6 of the samples comprised schoolchildren. Most samples were North American (71%).

Not all studies reported a coefficient alpha for the scale used to measure procrastination; 23 did. Generally, if the alpha was reported, it indicated that the scale was internally consistent, with a minimum of .66 to a maximum of .92. Most studies used Lay's Procrastination Scale (k = 19; Lay, 1986; see also Ferrari, Johnson, & McCown, 1995) or the Procrastination Assessment Scale for Students (k = 11; Solomon & Rothblum, 1984, see also Ferrari, Johnson, & McCown, 1995) to measure procrastination.

Table 3.1 contains the number of studies (k) examining procrastination and a factor or facet of the Big Five model, total sample size per category, the average results of each category weighted by the degrees of freedom of the total sample size in that category, the 95% confidence interval around the average, the homogeneity of the findings (χ^2), and the minimum and maximum effect size in each category. The effect sizes can be considered to be significantly different from 0 when the confidence interval does not include a 0.

Looking at the facets of Neuroticism in Table 3.1, it can be seen that most research related to the Big Five model has been conducted on anxiety and depression. Although relatively few studies have been conducted on impulsiveness, it has the largest relationship within this factor (r = .35).

The Extraversion factor was overall slightly negatively related to procrastination. The large variation in effect sizes on Extraversion has been noted before (Steel, Brothen, & Wambach, 2001). On inspection of the seven individual effect sizes on the factor Extraversion, the r of .63 reported by McCown, Petzel, and Rupert (1987) appeared to be a clear outlier, because five of the correlations were negative, and only one was positive and much smaller.

Openness to Experience was only marginally positively related to procrastination. The only facet of Openness to Experience that appeared to be more relevant to procrastination was Fantasy; its effect size ($r = .25$) was equally high as the effect size for, for example, Neuroticism, which—in contrast to the Fantasy facet—has received much attention in research, indicated by the higher number of related studies in this meta-analysis.

In regard to the results for Agreeableness, the negative sign appears to indicate that generally, those who report the tendency to procrastinate are slightly less likely to report they possess Trust, Straightforwardness, Altruism, and Compliance as traits. The largest average effect size of all categories was found for the Conscientiousness factor ($r = -.65$). The effect size of the factor was much larger (in a negative direction) than the individual facets, but all appear to be relevant in relation to procrastination. The four facets Feelings, Values, Modesty, and Tender-Mindedness were not related to procrastination, as can be concluded from the confidence intervals, which included the zero.

HETEROGENEITY

Many of the effect sizes within the facet categories were heterogeneous. However, to test whether there are systematic differences between the studies, there should be some explanation as to why some studies would have a higher or lower relationship to procrastination. For the factor Neuroticism, I tested whether the use of a certain scale to measure procrastination could explain the variance in effect sizes, based on Milgram and Naaman's (1996) assertion that the PASS (Solomon & Rothblum, 1984) confounds procrastination with concern about procrastination. This scale consists of four parts (prevalence of, concern with, reasons for, and wish to change procrastination). Some researchers use all four parts, and some use fewer. I tested the assertion that the relation between Neuroticism and procrastination would be higher when the PASS was used by comparing the weighted effect sizes from the studies that used the PASS to those that assessed procrastination with other scales. The assertion was confirmed for the Neuroticism factor score. The weighted effect sizes for the PASS were $r = .41$ ($k = 2$) versus the other tests, $r = .24$ ($k = 8$), $Z = 4.26$, $p < .001$, and the facets Anxiety, $r = .26$ ($k = 8$) versus $r = .19$ ($k = 18$), $Z = 3.31$, $p < .001$; Depression $r = .34$ ($k = 5$) versus $r = .26$ ($k = 10$), $Z = 3.53$, $p < .001$; and Vulnerability $r = .38$ ($k = 1$) versus $r = .15$ ($k = 2$), $Z = 2.79$, $p < .01$. There were no significant differences between the effect sizes of the scales for the facets Angry Hostility (both $rs = .17$, $k = 2$ and $k = 1$), Self-Consciousness (both $rs = .19$, $k = 5$ and $k = 3$), and Impulsiveness ($r = .32$, $k = 1$ vs. $r = .37$, $k = 3$, $Z = 1.12$).

TABLE 3.1
Average Effect Sizes

Factor or facet	Number of studies (k)	Sample total (n)	Average weighted r	95% confidence interval	$\chi^2(k-1)$	Min	Max
1. Neuroticism	11	2,748	.26	.23 to .29	36.97***	.05	.42
Anxiety	26	5,529	.22	.19 to .25	65.25****	–.10	.40
Angry hostility	3	905	.17	.10 to .24	.66	.12	.19
Depression	15	3,330	.29	.26 to .31	26.98*	.08	.44
Self-consciousness	8	1,928	.19	.15 to .24	27.74***	.03	.37
Impulsiveness	4	1,047	.35	.30 to .41	2.04	.30	.40
Vulnerability	3	905	.30	.26 to .39	6.79*	.17	.38
2. Extraversion	8	2,142	–.08	–.12 to –.04	160.96***	–.34	.63
Warmth	2	703	–.16	–.23 to –.09	1.18	–.20	–.12
Gregariousness	2	703	–.11	–.20 to –.02	.18	–.12	–.09
Assertiveness	3	1,043	–.14	–.20 to –.04	14.18***	–.28	.00
Activity	2	703	–.20	–.27 to –.13	27.88***	–.22	–.18
Excitement seeking	4	900	.11	.04 to .18	6.13	.06	.28
Positive emotions	2	703	–.15	–.22 to –.08	.18	–.16	–.13
3. Openness	6	1,811	.07	.02 to .12	13.38*	–.07	.31
Fantasy	2	703	.25	.19 to .32	1.28	.21	.29
Aesthetics	2	703	.04	–.03 to .11	5.69*	–.05	.13
Feelings	2	703	.00	–.07 to .07	.28	–.02	.02
Actions	2	703	–.06	–.13 to .01	.03	–.06	–.05
Ideas	2	703	–.08	–.15 to –.01	1.13	–.12	–.04
Values	2	703	.00	–.07 to .07	.63	–.03	.03
4. Agreeableness	5	1,811	–.10	–.15 to –.05	11.58*	–.22	.13
Trust	2	703	–.14	–.21 to –.07	.65	–.17	–.11
Straightforwardness	2	703	–.11	–.18 to –.04	4.07*	–.19	–.04
Altruism	2	703	–.14	–.21 to –.07	.07	–.15	–.13

Compliance	3	845	-.07	-.14 to .00	1.89	-.12	-.02
Modesty	2	703	.05	-.02 to .12	3.44	-.02	.12
Tender-mindedness	2	703	.02	-.05 to .09	1.43	-.02	.07
5. Conscientiousness	11	2,870	-.65	-.67 to -.62	73.85***	-.79	-.49
Competence	4	1,185	-.47	-.52 to -.42	2.01	-.52	-.42
Order	6	1,403	-.45	-.49 to -.41	20.15**	-.56	-.31
Dutifulness	5	1,261	-.45	-.49 to -.40	16.27**	-.58	-.33
Achievement striving	6	1,558	-.38	-.42 to -.34	119.63***	-.59	.12
Self-discipline	7	2,018	-.45	-.49 to -.42	95.56***	-.75	-.21
Deliberation	4	1,185	-.35	-.41 to -.30	1.96	-.40	-.31

Note. Min = minimum; Max = maximum.
*p < .05. **p < .01. ***p < .001.

DISCUSSION

This meta-analysis provided a systematic overview of the relation between procrastination and the Big Five model of personality among students. The largest average correlation was found between procrastination and the factor Conscientiousness (negative). The largest number of studies addressed the relation with the Neuroticism factor and facets (see Table 3.1), and these studies indicate a moderate relation between procrastination and Neuroticism.

Of the other three Big Five factors, only the Fantasy facet of the factor Openness was more than marginally related to procrastination. It may come as a surprise that Self-Consciousness, which includes Shame and Guilt, was not highly related to procrastination ($r = .19$). This finding goes against the idea that the moral component of procrastination is important and needs further investigation. In addition, studies using the PASS to measure procrastination revealed an overestimation of the relation between procrastination and Neuroticism (including some of its facets) in comparison to studies measuring procrastination with other scales.

When all results are combined, a profile arises of a certain type of student. This student is not conscientious, somewhat neurotic, has a lively fantasy life, and is slightly introverted and unsociable.

LIMITATIONS

Although a general profile has been shaped by these results, this profile is not altogether unproblematic. Alternative interpretations of the results are possible; it would be simplistic to say that each student who procrastinates has this profile.

First, not all characteristics of the Big Five profile have to be found combined in one person, because the relation between the effect size categories has not been assessed. There may be multiple profiles. For example, it may well be that in one group procrastination is paired with Depression and in another group with Anxiety and that other groups have no emotional concerns.

Second, because the effect sizes are correlations, most from cross-sectional studies, it is impossible to check whether they indicate a true relation with, a confounding relation with, or a spurious relation with the Big Five model of personality. In particular, because both procrastination and the Big Five model have been measured using self-reports, it is not possible to determine whether a general self-image may have influenced the procrastination and Big Five model measures. Also, common method bias may have caused the correlations to be inflated. The use of peer ratings and observations and the measurement at different points in time may help to identify the extent to which the effect sizes obtained by self-reports, combined in this meta-analysis, are similar to those obtained when other data sources and points in time are used.

Third, considering that some of the results of this meta-analysis are heterogeneous, indicating the variation in effect sizes in different studies, the search for moderators is important. In some instances, the use of a test or a particular sample may explain a different relation between procrastination and the Big Five model. For example, the use of a certain test can explain some of the variance, as was the case in the Neuroticism factor by comparing the PASS and the other tests. However, sometimes it is not easy to identify why there might be a different relationship. For example, in the case of Extraversion, one study obtained a positive relation of $r = .63$ between Extraversion and procrastination, whereas five other studies indicated a negative relation between the variables. However, as far as the measurement and sample are concerned, these are not particularly different from the other studies. Other factors may play a role that cannot be found in the study results.

IMPLICATIONS FOR COUNSELING

Some implications for counseling arise from this study. First, low Conscientiousness is associated with procrastination. Not being conscientious may lead to several problems in an achievement-oriented society. Conscientiousness is the only factor of the Big Five model related to study results (e.g., Costa & McCrae, 1992; Paunonen & Ashton, 2001; Schouwenburg, 1997). Overcoming the negative effects of low Conscientiousness can probably be taught by techniques that help the student to be more organized and that stimulate self-control. In addition, social control can be helpful by other students, counselors, or professors.

However, over different academic settings the degree of Conscientiousness required may differ, and perhaps a very high degree of Conscientiousness may impede other behaviors. For example, conscientiousness was negatively related to behavioral flexibility (Griffin & Hesketh, 2001), which may not be useful in all performance situations, particularly those that require innovative solutions. Some studies have found a negative relation between Conscientiousness and creative behavior (Feist, 1998; King, McKee-Walker, & Broyles, 1996; Wolfradt & Pretz, 2001).

Second, although there is a relation between procrastination and Neuroticism, the relation is not very strong. Some of the higher relations may be explained by the use of the PASS, which includes the concern with procrastination in the measurement of procrastination, causing the effect sizes with emotional variables to be higher. Still, for some students in counseling, interventions may be necessary that help to overcome the negative emotions associated with procrastination.

Third, some studies have found that procrastination can be induced by situational variables, such as task difficulty and interest (Pychyl, Lee, et al., 2000; Senécal, Lavoie, & Koestner, 1997), or that the negative outcomes of procrastination on performance can be limited by the use of tests (Tuckman, 1998). These studies illustrate that the context of the behavior also must be taken into account. Procrastination is a matter not only of personality, but also of motivation.

Finally, it is important to distinguish the individual and social outcomes of dilatory behavior from the tendency to procrastinate. In other words, not everyone who procrastinates is a low performer and a neurotic person. It would be useful to focus on the question of whether and when procrastination becomes dysfunctional and to deal with the consequences in these situations, rather than assuming that all procrastinators have a dysfunctional personality profile and need counseling to correct this.

APPENDIX 3.1: STUDIES INCLUDED IN THE META-ANALYSIS

Beck, B. L., Koons, S. R., & Milgrim, D. L. (2000). Correlates and consequences of behavioral procrastination: The effects of academic procrastination, self-consciousness, self-esteem, and self-handicapping. *Journal of Social Behavior and Personality, 15,* 3–13.

Beswick, G., Rothblum, E. D., & Mann, L. (1988). Psychological antecedents of student procrastination. *Australian Psychologist, 23,* 207–217.

Fee, R. L., & Tangney, J. P. (2000). Procrastination: A means of avoiding shame or guilt? *Journal of Social Behavior and Personality, 15,* 167–184.

Ferrari, J. R. (1991). Compulsive procrastination: Some self-reported characteristics. *Psychological Reports, 68,* 455–458.

Ferrari, J. R. (1992a). Procrastinators and perfect behavior: An exploratory factor analysis of self-presentation, self-awareness, and self-handicapping components. *Journal of Research in Personality, 26,* 75–84.

Ferrari, J. R. (1992b). Psychometric validation of two procrastination inventories for adults: Arousal and avoidance measures. *Journal of Psychopathology and Behavioral Assessment, 14,* 97–110.

Ferrari, J. R., & Emmons, R. A. (1995). Methods of procrastination and their relation to self-control and self-reinforcement. *Journal of Social Behavior and Personality, 10,* 135–142.

Ferrari, J. R., & Gojkovich, P. (2000). Procrastination and attention: Factor analysis of attention deficit, boredomness, intelligence, self-esteem, and task delay frequencies. *Journal of Social Behavior and Personality, 15,* 185–197.

Haycock, L. A., McCarthy, P., & Skay, C. L. (1998). Procrastination in college students: The role of self-efficacy and anxiety. *Journal of Counseling and Development, 76,* 317–324.

Hess, B., Sherman, M. F., & Goodman, M. (2000). Eveningness predicts academic procrastination: The mediating role of neuroticism. *Journal of Social Behavior and Personality, 15*, 61–74.

Johnson, J. L., & Bloom, A. M. (1995). An analysis of the contribution of the five factors of personality to variance in academic procrastination. *Personality and Individual Differences, 18*, 127–133.

Lay, C. H. (1986). At last, my research article on procrastination. *Journal of Research in Personality, 20*, 474–495.

Lay, C. H. (1992). Trait procrastination and the perception of person-task characteristics. *Journal of Social Behavior and Personality, 7*, 483–494.

Lay, C. H. (1994). Trait procrastination and affective experiences: Describing past study behavior and its relation to agitation and dejection. *Motivation and Emotion, 18*, 269–284.

Lay, C. H. (1997). Explaining lower-order traits through higher-order factors: The case of trait procrastination, conscientiousness and the specificity dilemma. *European Journal of Personality, 11*, 267–278.

Lay, C. H., Edwards, J. M., Parker, J. D. A., & Endler, N. S. (1989). An assessment of appraisal, anxiety, coping, and procrastination during an examination period. *European Journal of Personality, 3*, 195–208.

Lay, C. H., Knish, S., & Zanatta, R. (1992). Self-handicappers and procrastinators: A comparison of their practice behavior prior to an evaluation. *Journal of Research in Personality, 26*, 242–257.

Lay, C. H., Kovacs, A., & Danto, D. (1998). The relation of trait procrastination to the big-five factor conscientiousness: An assessment with primary-junior school children based on self-reports. *Personality and Individual Differences, 25*, 187–193.

Lay, C. H., & Silverman, S. (1996). Trait procrastination, anxiety, and dilatory behavior. *Personality and Individual Differences, 21*, 61–67.

Martin, T. R., Flett, G. L., Hewitt, P. L., Krames, L., & Szanto, G. (1996). Personality correlates of depression and health symptoms: A test of a self-regulation model. *Journal of Research in Personality, 31*, 264–277.

McCown, W., Petzel, T., & Rupert, P. (1987). An experimental study of some hypothesized behaviors and personality variables of college student procrastinators. *Personality and Individual Differences, 8*, 781–786.

Milgram, N. A., Batori, G., & Mowrer, D. (1993). Correlates of academic procrastination. *Journal of School Psychology, 31*, 487–500.

Milgram, N. A., Gehrman, T., & Keinan, G. (1992). Procrastination and emotional upset: A typological model. *Personality and Individual Differences, 13*, 1307–1313.

Milgram, N. A., Marshevsky, S., & Sadeh, C. (1995). Correlates of academic procrastination: Discomfort, task aversiveness, and task capability. *Journal of Psychology, 129*, 145–155.

Milgram, N., & Tenne, R. (2000). Personality correlates of decisional and task avoidant procrastination. *European Journal of Personality, 14*, 141–156.

Milgram, N., & Toubiana, Y. (1999). Academic anxiety, academic procrastination, and parental involvement in students and their parents. *British Journal of Educational Psychology, 69*, 345–361.

Owens, A. M., & Newbegin, I. (1997). Procrastination in high school achievement. *Journal of Social Behavior and Personality, 12*, 869–887.

Rothblum, E. D., Solomon, L. J., & Murakami, J. (1986). Affective, cognitive, and behavioral differences between high and low procrastinators. *Journal of Counseling Psychology, 33*, 387–394.

Saddler, C. D., & Sacks, L. A. (1993). Multidimensional perfectionism and academic procrastination: Relationships with depression in university students. *Psychological Reports, 73*, 863–871.

Sarmány Schuller, I. (1999). Procrastination, need for cognition, and sensation seeking. *Studia Psychologica, 41*, 73–85.

Schouwenburg, H. C. (1995). Academic procrastination: Theoretical notions, measurement, and research. In J. R. Ferrari, J. L. Johnson, & W. G. McCown (Eds.), *Procrastination and task avoidance: Theory, research, and treatment* (pp. 71–96). New York: Plenum.

Schouwenburg, H. C. (1996). *Personality and academic competence.* Unpublished report, University of Groningen, The Netherlands.

Schouwenburg, H. C. (1997). *Results of a questionnaire among participants of skills courses taught by the Academic Assistance Center of the University of Groningen from January 1995 to August 1996.* Unpublished report, University of Groningen, The Netherlands.

Schouwenburg, H. C., & Lay, C. H. (1995). Trait procrastination and the big-five factors of personality. *Personality and Individual Differences, 18*, 481–490.

Senécal, C., Koestner, R., & Vallerand, R. J. (1995). Self-regulation and academic procrastination. *Journal of Social Psychology, 135*, 607–619.

Solomon, L. J., & Rothblum, E. D. (1984). Academic procrastination: Frequency and cognitive–behavioral correlates. *Journal of Counseling Psychology, 31*, 503–509.

Specter, M. H., & Ferrari, J. R. (2000). Time orientations of procrastinators: Focusing on the past, present, or future? *Journal of Social Behavior and Personality, 15*, 197–202.

Stainton, M., Lay, C. H., & Flett, G. L. (2000). Trait procrastinators and behavior/trait specific cognitions. *Journal of Social Behavior and Personality, 15*, 297–312.

Steel, P., Brothen, T., & Wambach, C. (2001). Procrastination and personality, performance, and mood. *Personality and Individual Differences, 30*, 95–106.

Stöber, J., & Joormann, J. (2001). Worry, procrastination, and perfectionism: Differentiating amount of worry, pathological worry, anxiety, and depression. *Cognitive Therapy and Research, 25*, 49–60.

Watson, D. C. (2001). Procrastination and the five-factor model: A facet level analysis. *Personality and Individual Differences, 30*, 149–158.

II

INTERVENTION METHODS

4

SOME BASIC ELEMENTS IN COUNSELING PROCRASTINATORS

CLARRY H. LAY

Nothing beats the timely pursuit of one's intentions. It is *the* measure of success in life.

In thinking about success in life, I propose that the most encompassing yardstick for people is the timely pursuit of their intentions. I mean this on a daily basis, and to include intentions in the interest of all goals and necessary aspects of a person's life. These intentions concern academic tasks, social and leisure activities, exercise and hobbies, attention to one's physical and psychological well-being, everyday tasks like doing the laundry, and anything else that is a part of a person's life experiences and goals. People feel best when they accomplish things, and the most elementary form of accomplishment is the timely pursuit of their intentions. I also contend that the timely pursuit of these intentions supercedes, or should supersede, other indicators of success, such as performance, money, prestige, promotion, recognition by others, and top grades in school. The latter are all good, but they are secondary.

Given this thesis, trait procrastinators are, by definition, unsuccessful. The trait procrastinator's daily, weekly, and lifetime experiences are replete with extended temporal gaps between their intentions and their actions. This is what is meant by dilatory behavior, and it is the defining behavior of trait procrastinators.

Trait procrastinators who seek counseling find this idea of success in life compelling, although threatening. On the one hand, it is reassuring for many to think of success in such a simple and attainable way, independent of other, more prevalent, and sometimes more distant indicators. On the other hand, this idea is highly threatening, because it defines the procrastinator as unsuccessful to date, regardless of any other dimensions, and heightens the implications of any subsequent failure to change. Whatever the procrastinator's response, this general thesis is a starting point and a simple one in counseling those who seek help to change. It is one of a number of simple points that I make in trying to help them bring about this change.

POPULATION COUNSELED

For the past 10 years I have worked through the Counseling and Development Center of my university in counseling groups of students and others who identify themselves as trait procrastinators. The others include staff and faculty, although I see them much less frequently. Graduate students also are occasionally among the group members.

The mean score obtained by group members as a whole on my Trait Procrastination scale (Lay, 1986) is over 16. The version I use is a 20-item true–false scale, so the maximum score is 20. The mean score for the general student population on this scale is around 9. The majority of the students who seek counseling procrastinate in all aspects of their lives (hence, the high mean score on the procrastination scale). There are exceptions, however. Some students in the groups indicate that they procrastinate only on academic tasks or only on certain academic tasks, particularly the writing of essays. On occasion, some students obtain average scores on the procrastination scale, and it has become apparent over time that they are in the procrastination group only because they are generally troubled individuals who have decided to take a large number of different counseling groups offered by the university.

Given the pervasiveness of their dilatory behavior across all aspects of their lives, most students are not attending simply because they want to learn to follow their study plans more consistently or get better grades, but because they have become very dissatisfied with their lives in general. At the same time, because the group sessions are held during the school term, students focus to a large extent on academic tasks during the counseling sessions.

The group sessions are advertised around campus and in the main campus newspaper. For the most part, students decide themselves to register. There are few referrals. For each group there are generally 12 to 20 students who initially register, and perhaps 20% fail to attend the first session. The dropout rate over the following sessions varies from group to group. Given the nature of the group involved, I have to be prepared for people signing up for the group at the last minute; signing up early, but never attending; missing the first session, but attending thereafter; coming to the sessions late; coming to the sessions sporadically (sometimes because they cannot afford the time that day); and otherwise demonstrating a lack of organization and commitment or certainty. Unlike some other programs described in this book, there are no penalties attached to nonattendance. We often develop a core of 6 to 10 students who attend the sessions regularly.

COMMON PROBLEMS

I typically begin the first session by asking students why they are here. I hear the usual reasons about procrastinating on their academic tasks and in other areas of their lives. They talk essentially about their inability to carry through on their plans, and often their specific examples have to do with everyday tasks like paying bills or doing laundry. They will sometimes spontaneously speak about some specific academic task, but mostly, when it concerns academic tasks, their descriptions are very general and fuzzy.

As already mentioned, group members often indicate that they have come to a point where they are simply very dissatisfied with themselves and with their lives. This appears, sometimes, to be prompted by being in university. They may mention that they have been procrastinators all their lives, but that back in high school it did not really seem to matter. At the extreme, I hear stories like that of one young man, who lived across the street from his public school and, at age 8, was put out the front door in his underwear by his very frustrated mother to get him on his way to school, because he habitually put off getting dressed in the morning.

OVERALL GOALS OF THE INTERVENTION

The basic tenets of the program are summarized in Exhibit 4.1. These begin with the underlying premise of the meaning of success in life: *Nothing beats the timely pursuit of your intentions. It is the measure of success in life.* The exhibit also lists orientations toward change and operations toward change, as well as some reminders to trait procrastinators that address their particular perspectives in approaching task actions.

In the sessions, I strive to give the group participants a better understanding of why people procrastinate and why they, themselves, procrastinate and a better understanding of their own personality and their goals and motivations in this context. To this end, I ask participants to complete a personality questionnaire and return it before the second session. This questionnaire contains scales to measure the following traits: procrastination, neurotic disorganization, optimism, energy level, rebelliousness, achievement,

GENERAL THESIS

Nothing beats the timely pursuit of your intentions. It is *the* measure of success in life.

ORIENTATIONS TOWARD CHANGE

1. You must spend more time working on the tasks that are most important.
2. You must spend less time on less important tasks.
3. Once you have formed intentions regarding some task, you have an obligation and responsibility (primarily to yourself) to act on them.
4. The ultimate payoff for change is that you will feel better about yourself.

OPERATIONS TOWARD CHANGE

1. You must spend more time in the right places.
2. Form highly detailed intentions regarding each task that specify day, time, place, and for how long.
3. Write down the details of your intentions and refer to them often on a regular basis.

REMINDERS

1. Your intentions should override how you feel at the moment.
2. Procrastinators tend to overestimate the degree of unpleasantness of a task.
3. Work on your task at any level, and think of the task at the simplest level when necessary.
4. Focus on one task at a time.

perfectionism, time management, breadth of interest, stimulus screening, self-esteem, and anxiety. The rationale for the selection of many of these traits is based on Lay (1987). The group members receive feedback about their trait scores in the second session.

The personality feedback is also intended in a very general way to prompt participants to think more about their own characteristics and to focus on the self. Trait procrastination has much to do with self-concept and self-identity. Procrastinators may be characterized by a *diffuse identity* (Berzonsky & Ferrari, 1996), a term used by Berzonsky (1989) to describe individuals who are uncommitted to a personal involvement in the beliefs, aspirations, and values that one professes to hold. Baumeister (1985) linked the absence of a clear identity to the experience of conflict between wanting to commit to one desirable course of action but not being prepared to give up others. Furthermore, procrastinators experience inconsistencies in their self elements. That is, they lack what McGregor (2003) called *identity consolidation*, with important implications for self-regulation. Thus, the diffuse or inconsistent self elements of the procrastinator may promote dilatory behavior. In this context, along with the personality feedback and discussion, the dynamics of the group and the group interchanges during the counseling sessions are intended to contribute importantly and positively to each individual's sense of self.

A further goal of the intervention program is to bring about a change in how the participants think about their intentions and their actions and to enable them to self-instruct differently in this regard. The importance of self-talk or self-instruction in self-regulation is stressed (Meichenbaum, 1977; Mischel, Cantor, & Feldman, 1996).

Intentions may be the forerunner of behavior (Ajzen, 1985), but the quality of intentions can vary dramatically from person to person, and it is the quality that we focus on in the groups. Researchers interested in motivation and goal pursuit often equate the formation of intentions with commitment (e.g., Gollwitzer & Brandstatter, 1997), an equation that could be uttered only by a nonprocrastinator. In reality, this is very much a limited position when describing the procrastinator. Indeed, a major problem with trait procrastinators is their lack of a sense of *ought*, or obligation, tied to their intentions (Lay, 1995, based on Higgins, 1987). Intentions for procrastinators, in contrast to nonprocrastinators, are often wishes or mere indications of the ideal self. Their intentions are more often ideals or hopes— "Wouldn't it be nice if I started studying for my history test tomorrow," or "I hope to start studying for my history test tomorrow"—and seldom take the form of "I intend to, and thereby have an obligation to, start studying for my history test tomorrow." This is one important manifestation of the procrastinator's lack of conscientiousness, or will, or willpower, and procrastinators need to learn to talk to themselves differently in this regard.

Furthermore, the distinction by Warshaw and Davis (1985) between behavioral intentions and behavioral expectations is relevant here. Behavioral intentions concern specific actions in engaging in some task, whereas behavioral expectations refer to people's estimations that they will act on their intentions. Warshaw and Davis viewed the latter as the better predictor of subsequent behavior. Procrastinators are well aware of their dilatory behavior in the past and exhibit greater discrepancies between their behavioral intentions and their behavioral expectations compared with nonprocrastinators. A greater sense of obligation to their intentions, along with other aspects considered in the counseling sessions, may serve to lessen this discrepancy.

With many intended tasks, most individuals would rather be doing something else, primarily because the intended behavior or task is perceived to be less interesting, or more aversive, or less voluntary, than some other activity. With trait procrastinators, this may be a heightened distinction (Lay, 1992; Milgram, Sroloff, & Rosenbaum, 1988); they may be more likely to act on such a preference. In contrast, nonprocrastinators will more often do what they intended, regardless of the task characteristics and the presence of alternative activities. This is a point that the procrastinator must come to appreciate. That is, the behavior of the nonprocrastinator in this regard must be put forward as a model.

To a large extent, procrastinators believe that they would rather be doing something other that what they ought to be doing. They may engage in some other activity deliberately, or they may simply end up doing so without any specified intention. That they would rather be doing something else is not always an accurate belief on the part of procrastinators, but it is one that they often succumb to, nevertheless. It is a belief that needs to be addressed in counseling sessions and incorporated into the procrastinator's self-talk. To a large extent, this belief involves not an approach–avoidance conflict, as many would suppose, but rather an approach–approach conflict. Most often, procrastinators really want to study, for example, but the competing alternatives may be more attractive, or compelling, or accessible. Furthermore, Quattrone (1985) suggested that people in general may believe that they have less choice or freedom when engaged in activities that are less interesting. This may serve to compound the resistance of procrastinators to their less interesting but "ought to be done" tasks.

Finally, Gollwitzer and Brandstatter (1997) distinguished between goal intentions—"I intend to achieve X"—and implementation intentions—"I intend to perform goal-directed behavior Y when I encounter situation Z"—and have highlighted the importance of well-formulated implementation intentions in accomplishing tasks or reaching goals. This is an extremely useful distinction in counseling procrastinators, because procrastinators tend to be deficient in their use of implementation intentions compared to their goal intentions, more so than nonprocrastinators. Procrastinators will readily say that they intend to get a grade of A in their history course this term, but they are less likely to incorporate into their thinking the steps needed to reach this goal, even when prompted, compared to nonprocrastinators.

DETAILS OF THE PROGRAM

There are usually five sessions, sometimes six, and each session is 1 1/2 hours long.

Session 1

As already mentioned, in the first session I ask the participants to explain in turn why they are here. This can be a time of unease for some individuals, although others present their circumstances with a certain bravado. A few are quick to assure those present that they receive top grades in their schoolwork, or near top grades, despite their procrastinatory tendencies. Although not typically explicitly recognized by each group member at this point, this is their first exposure to what has been a common phenomenon in these sessions, and that is the recognition that they are not alone, that other people also engage in frequent dilatory behavior. I hear this often from group members, a fact that surprised me at first. But it is a continuing and important theme as they begin to deal with their own behavior and with the need to change.

I also ask the students to complete a personality questionnaire within the next 4 days and return it to me. I score the inventories as students hand them in, and I give them a summary of their personality scores the following week. For whatever reason, one or two students in a group, usually male, will not submit the questionnaire before the second session and will not attend the second session or thereafter.

At this point, I introduce the most basic orientation toward change for someone who continually puts things off. It is the most elementary point and is the answer to procrastination: *You must spend more time working on the tasks that are most important.* I stress this simple point over and over again. Of course, to enact this solution is more difficult and more complex, just as in telling the overweight person that to lose weight he or she must eat less and exercise more. Nevertheless, this tenet is the basic starting point, and it is an essential one in getting individuals to begin to think differently and to understand the route of change. This simple statement should not be dismissed as too obvious. It is the essence of change for procrastinators and the solution to their dissatisfaction with themselves.

This "solution" is really the goal, and during the remaining sessions we spend much time discussing how to enact this solution and how to reach this goal. From this point on, I also stress the payoff of this behavior. And it is not higher grades or more courses completed; it is that they will feel better about themselves. Most participants, at this point in time, at least, see this as a very desirable outcome. I wait until the next session to introduce my thesis about what constitutes success in life—that is, the timely pursuit of one's intentions.

Given the limited hours in a day, to spend more time doing what one ought to be doing (based on very specific intentions) involves the acceptance of its corollary: *You must spend less time on less important tasks.* I then ask each student to identify a relatively unimportant activity that he or she spends a lot of time on. Some of the activities put forward are watching television, talking on the phone with friends, visiting and going out with friends, surfing the Internet, and sometimes reading several newspapers daily. I ask the group members if they are willing to give up some of the time they spend on these activities and to commit themselves to this change. Most agree, and I ask for reports in the later sessions.

Of course, the giving up of less important activities is to some degree only, rather than completely, and group members consider the need for balance in their lives. During the academic year, however, the most important tasks involve academic work, and so the balance in students' lives is shifted in that direction. I encourage group members to communicate with their family and friends about these proposed changes in their lives and to seek their cooperation and encouragement.

This discussion often brings us to the end of the first session, although, if time permits, I do like to introduce another topic (otherwise, we do so in the next session). In the context of spending more time on what is more important, I ask the participants to consider what time they wake up in the morning, what time they go to bed at night, and their perceptions of when the weekend begins and ends. We often hear that students wake up in conjunction with when their first class is that day. I stress the need to wake up at the same time each day, including weekends. Regulating when they go to sleep is more difficult, given the great variety in their social habits, study habits, and part-time work schedules, but we consider the obvious: Group members need a certain number of hours of sleep each night. For some students, the weekend begins Thursday afternoon and extends to the first class on Monday. We discuss other interpretations, and I propose to them that during the school term, they are engaged in a 7-day-a-week "job," and that when they form intentions concerning their academic tasks, scheduling should also include the weekend.

Session 2

I open the second session by asking the participants to discuss their behavior in spending more time on more important tasks and spending less time on less important tasks or activities during the past week. It is at this point that I introduce my general thesis that the enactment of their intentions during the past week constitutes success in life. I also ask the group members to discuss how they feel about themselves in reference to the link between their intentions and their behavior in the past week. These are important considerations in the change process. For example, Meichenbaum (1977), in outlining the third phase of the cognitive theory of behavioral change, stated,

> But just focusing on such skills training is not sufficient to explain the change process. For what the client says to himself about his newly acquired behaviors and their resultant consequences will influence whether the behavioral change process will be maintained and will generalize. (p. 225)

At this point in the second session, I distribute the personality results; each participant receives a score for each personality trait assessed and some normative data. I inform them that personality tests do not measure without error. We then go on to consider most, or all, of the personality information by describing one of the traits and indicating by name who in the group scored high, or low, depending on the nature of the characteristic (with high or low generally established as greater than 1 standard deviation above or below the mean).

We start by looking at their scores on the trait procrastination measure. Low scores on this trait indicate group members who are not general procrastinators (there are usually one or two in each group), and I ask them to consider why they signed up for the group. Some are in the group because they procrastinate on only certain aspects of their lives, particularly academic ones, like writing essays. Others indicate that they were mistaken in thinking that they were procrastinators. Others appear to be individuals who sign up for all the self-help groups available in our counseling and development center. Low scorers may remain in the group, and most do.

We next turn to *neurotic disorganization,* a concept that pertains to the inability to focus on the details of everyday life. People who are high on neurotic disorganization are very scattered in their thinking, misplace things, and are forgetful. We start with this characteristic because it is very highly associated with trait procrastination on a broad empirical level (Lay, 1987). This association is paralleled by the relations between state orientation, a concept that is positively associated with procrastination (Blunt & Pychyl, 1998), and cognitive failures (Kuhl & Goschke, 1994). Furthermore, neurotic disorganization may even be a source in the development of the disposition to procrastinate. Effortful, or directed, attention is not always easy and may be fatiguing (Muraven et al., 1998), perhaps particularly for the neurotically disorganized individual. This greater effort involved in directed attention to necessary tasks, and not to tasks that individuals may intrinsically rather be doing, may result in greater aversiveness, and then delay, in the young, developing procrastinator. A large number in the group generally score high on trait neurotic disorganization.

A large percentage of trait procrastinators tend to be very scattered in their thinking and planning. They are known to plan their day, even writing things down in their daily planners, only to forget to look at their daily planner until late that evening. They may set out with the intention of going to the library, by chance meet someone on the way, and forget to go to the library. It is important that those high on neurotic disorganization continuously consider this weakness in trying to counter it. They are in particular need of some of the points considered later in the sessions.

We may next consider the trait characteristic energy level. Typically, a few members in the group score very low on energy level. This is a complex issue, and I suggest that a medical checkup may be in order. I also remind them of the obvious, that their low energy level may be to a large extent psychological and that as they change and enact more of their intentions, and as they begin to feel better about themselves and experience less dejection, their energy levels may improve. We stress later on that they should follow through with their specific intentions at the moment, even when they do not feel like it, are too tired, or are not in the mood, and that getting started will often help them overcome their inertia and put them in the right mood.

There is a measure of trait optimism, and I discuss low and high scores. High optimism is a valued characteristic, but for a procrastinator, optimism may be a dangerous thing (Lay & Burns, 1991). Optimistic procrastinators may be too complacent and too likely to reassess their need to engage in the intended behavior at a given point in time. These individuals tell themselves not only that they will do it tomorrow, or the day after, but also that things will turn out OK, nevertheless. On the other hand, pessimistic procrastinators will likely lack a challenge perspective in approaching their tasks. When I ask those in the group who score very low on optimism why they are so pessimistic, they often say that their lives have offered little reason to be otherwise. At this point, I can only give them hope that as they change their behavior, they will become less pessimistic.

Scores on a measure of stimulus screening are also considered. Low scorers tend to be unable to screen out irrelevant stimuli in the surrounding environment, which has implications for where they should study or engage in other intended behaviors. In contrast, high stimulus screeners can concentrate in crowded, noisy, school cafeterias.

The order of discussion in considering the other characteristics often depends on the pattern of scores in the particular group. One measure is breadth of interest. High scorers are the people who read widely during the school term beyond their academic assignments, read a number of newspapers everyday, and would attend, say, a film on the life of the otter if it were being shown that evening. Breadth of interest is desirable, but not for procrastinators, and these people must pay additional attention to spending more time doing what they ought to be doing.

One popular interpretation of why people procrastinate is that their actions, or lack thereof, are an act of rebellion or a proof of autonomy. Group members who score high on measures of rebelliousness or socially prescribed perfectionism may fit this interpretation. Socially prescribed perfectionism measures the extent to which individuals believe that important others in their lives expect them to be perfect (see chap. 13, this volume). I simply ask individuals to think about the extent to which their pervasive dilatory behavior may be an act of autonomy, albeit a self-defeating one.

Although improved time management will help many individuals complete their tasks, time management, in and of itself, is not the answer in counseling trait procrastinators. Their problems go well beyond time management deficiencies. Nevertheless, I do assess three aspects of time management—setting goals, mechanics regarding planning and scheduling, and perceived control of time (Lay & Schouwenburg, 1993). Setting goals is assessed through questionnaire items like "I review my goals to determine if they need revising." Mechanics is typified by a positive response to the item "I write notes to remind myself what I need to do." Finally, perceived control of time is reflected in the item "I underestimate the time that it will take to accomplish tasks."

Some group members may score low on setting goals, and we discuss this topic. Furthermore, some who score low on goals also score low on a measure of need achievement. Individuals who score low on both appear to have no clear aspirations, academic and beyond. When asked what they want in their lives and why there are in university, they do not know. This is a larger question beyond the purview of a 5-week counseling group, so I simply propose for their consideration that while they are in university, they should accept the typical goals of other students—that is, to learn and to do well in their courses. It is an approach that suggests, "As long as you are here, you should be a good student. If you decide at some point in the future not to continue, then that is another matter to be dealt with then."

In a group of procrastinators, surprisingly few score low on mechanics. But those who do are encouraged to buy a day planner immediately and use it. Most members of the group are low in perceived control of time; this characteristic goes with the territory and hopefully will improve with changes in their behavior. We discuss certain aspects of this characteristic, such as underestimating the time taken to complete a task.

There is a measure of self-oriented perfectionism, or the tendency to demand perfection from oneself (see chap. 13, this volume). Individuals often cite this type of perfectionism in explaining their own procrastinatory tendencies, but it may not be a valid underlying reason. They may consider the excuse of perfectionism ("Yes, I procrastinate, but it is only because I am such a perfectionist") preferable to exclaiming, "Yes, I am a procrastinator, and it is because I lack any strong sense of conscientiousness or obligation." For those few in the group who score high on perfectionism, I present this argument.

There are two other personality characteristics assessed, although neither tends to characterize trait procrastinators or the procrastinators who attend the group. The first is anxiety. If a member of the group scores high on anxiety, I suggest that he or she may want to deal with it in other venues. In addition, I try to be very cautious in pushing anxious students too hard. Finally, self-esteem is assessed, and there are as many in the group who score high as score low on this characteristic.

In all of the personality feedback and discussion, I ask the group members to respond in front of the others to encourage them to think about and discuss how they interpret this information in terms of their self-concept and in terms of their presenting problems. Throughout the discussions, I provide examples of how these characteristics apply to being a procrastinator. Finally, I invite participants to consider their personality feedback further with me afterward individually.

The discussion then moves on to the first basic operation toward change (see Exhibit 4.1). If students are to accomplish the goal of spending more time on what is more important—on what they ought to be doing—they must be willing to spend less time on what is less important—on what they ought not to be doing. How do they move forward on both of these goals? To begin with, and vitally important if they are to succeed, is the idea, *You must spend more time in the right places.* Students must find the best place to work, one that is relatively free of distractions and other things to do, and go there. They must simply spend much more time in these places.

The ideal place will depend on the person and the circumstances. For example, for me, that ideal place is the office. If I bring work home with me, I probably will not attend to it. I am much more productive when I stay late in my office and go to my office on weekends. For students in the group, the ideal place may not be their bedroom or living room or their friend's house. It may be at a desk somewhere, often at the university library or a library close to their place of residence. I encourage students to think about the right places and wrong places to be and to make a concerted and continuing effort to spend more time in the right places. Often, students are limited in their choice of places to work or study and will recognize or agree that they need to alter the nature of some existing place. For example, they may take the television out of their room and put it elsewhere. Any such adaptation often requires cooperation from family members or roommates.

Being in the right place is obviously intended to reduce the number of possible other things to do. In addition, being in the right place can prime the "ought" self and reduce ideal self–actual self discrepancies, promote positive self-identity, provide positive feedback, narrow focus, and prompt intentions (Gollwitzer & Brandstatter, 1997). Procrastinators who want to change must be taught how to get to the right place most of the time and encouraged to do so.

The point of spending more time in the right place is generally well received by individuals in the group, and they readily agree to its importance. I suggest to them that when they are in the right place and begin to wonder why they are there, instead of talking with their friends, they tell themselves that they are there because it is their responsibility, that they are fulfilling their obligations to themselves based on their intentions. This works as both an explanation and as a self-rewarding thought.

Session 3

At the start of the third session, the group spends some time discussing individual experiences in the intervening week. The focus is again on successes and failures in terms of spending more time on the more important tasks and less time on the less important activities.

The next discussion point I introduce to the group deals largely with the formation and expression of intentions regarding tasks that ought to be acted on. I begin with the simple tenet that participants should explicitly state their plans for any short-term period on paper. We then consider the nature of intentions. This is an important consideration, because procrastinators are particularly prone to forming ill-defined and underdeveloped intentions. What is more, for many tasks, they often have no clear picture of what is required and what might possibly go wrong. With this fuzziness in their intentions, they often underestimate the time needed to complete the task, although this underestimation will be only approximate and relatively undefined.

Ask procrastinators about their plans to study for a test in 10 days, and they are most likely to respond with a statement like, "I plan to start studying this week and then do some more next week." They may appear quite content with such a statement, satisfied that they have just stated a plan, although their thoughts about carrying it out may be less hopeful. What is missing, both in their verbal statements to the group and to themselves in formulating an intention, are the details or specifics of these plans. At this point, we discuss the concepts of goal intentions and implementation intentions (Gollwitzer & Brandstatter, 1997). I stress the need to *form highly detailed intentions regarding each task that specify day, time, place, and for how long.* In other words, the student must specify

- the exact time that the activity will begin—that is, the day of the week and the time of day,
- the place where this activity is to occur, and
- the length of time to be spent engaging in the activity.

The next step in our discussion of intentions is to stress, *Write down the details of your intentions and refer to them often on a regular basis.* They "practice" this formation of intentions by thinking of a specific task at hand and writing down the details of their intentions in a day planner or similar tool. In their initial attempts at this exercise, group members often continue to omit important aspects of their plans and to use the phrase "I hope to" rather than "I will."

I believe that what procrastinators lack is conscientiousness, which includes dutifulness, self-discipline, and responsibility (see chaps. 1 and 3 in this volume). To change, procrastinators must become more responsible to themselves and to others. And so, as an orientation toward change, I encourage them to adopt the view that, *Once you have formed intentions regarding some task, you have an obligation and responsibility (primarily to yourself) to act on them.* I again stress, *The ultimate payoff for change is— that you will feel better about yourself.*

Sessions 4 and 5

In session 4, in addition to following up on what transpired spontaneously in session 3, we focus on the enactment of intentions—that is, the timely pursuit of fulfilling one's intentions. There are a number of points to be made in this context. For example, group members often say that, regardless of their intentions, on any given day or at any given time or place, they simply are not in the "right mood" to act on their intentions (e.g., to study for a test). I stress to students that once they start to study, they will feel better and that becoming engaged in the task will put them in the right mood, rather than having to be in the right mood before they begin. This engagement is initiated by the reminder, *Your intentions should override how you feel at the moment.*

I also indicate that it is useful for students to continue to work past some point when they begin to feel tired or bored or simply think it is time to go home. They can tell themselves that they will do just 30 minutes more studying, or writing, or whatever. Very often, students find that an hour passes by without their even noticing it.

In session 4, I ask students to think about the times they have put off even a simple little task and then, when they have finally started or completed the task, have thought to themselves that it was not that bad after all, or that it did not take nearly as long as they had thought it would. Most members of the group can identify with this statement and recognize that it is often a matter of "just getting started." In this context, they are asked to remind themselves frequently that, *Procrastinators tend to overestimate the degree of unpleasantness of a task.* The group discusses the variety of ways to perceive the nature of a task (Vallacher & Wegner, 1987). For example, if an individual has formed the intention of going to the library to read chapter 8 of the psychology textbook at 2:00 this afternoon, he or she may perceive this task as a way to gain acceptance into graduate school, at one extreme, to, at the other, as reading letters on a page that form words and then turning the page and reading more words. I encourage group members to remind themselves, *Work on your task at any level, and think of the task at the simplest level when necessary.* For example, students can ask themselves, "What do I have to do for the next hour? I have to turn pages and read words on the pages," as opposed to "I have to complete school, get top grades, please my parents, and get a good job."

Individuals may be overwhelmed by their many tasks at hand. This is especially the case for procrastinators at certain times, for example, near examination time. This sense of being overwhelmed can be attributed primarily to the fact that procrastinators are behind in the enactment of their intentions. There is so much not done and still so much to do. Thus, group members are encouraged to remind themselves, *Focus on one task at a time.*

Such a focus will not be easy, however, and it is a directive that requires considerable practice.

Much of what transpires in sessions 4 and 5 will depend on what the participants have to say. Members introduce ideas spontaneously, just as in any counseling group, and I try to develop these ideas and encourage the participants to discuss them further. Group members also develop support groups among themselves, and this support plays an important role. I again reinforce the idea that a student's role during the academic term is like a job—and is no different than other jobs. I ask them to think about their dilatory behavior on regular jobs, and they often indicate that they are much more responsible when working for someone else; then, hopefully, they see the connection to their job as a student, when they work for themselves.

We also discuss the role of deadlines in all aspects of everyday life. Deadlines are the great organizer and the great narrower of attention and focus. The goal, for procrastinators, is to move these functions closer to the timelines provided by their intentions and not to drive actions based on their immediacy.

SUCCESS OF THE PROGRAM

Unfortunately, I have not systematically assessed the outcomes of the program. My own view is that some participants succeed, and others do not. This view is based on what participants say during the sessions and what they tell me afterwards. There have been some dramatic improvements, evidenced in terms of both a lessening of dilatory behavior and an improvement in how individuals feel about themselves. Self-esteem and mood appear to become much more positive. Many individuals feel better about themselves and more in control by the end of the sessions.

Some participants demonstrate change in a general self-view and a desire to change further. Recently, when I asked a group how they would sustain their decreases in procrastination over a brief break in the school term, one student who had shown remarkable change in her behavior replied, "Now, for the first time in my life, I realize that this is the way it is supposed to be." Another student, in the final session, asked if one can change all at once, or does wanting to change occur this way, and then actual change occur more gradually. This student had "wandered" for much of his life, but during the final sessions he had experienced some direction. The sessions and his experiences with the other group members had provided him with a desire to change unlike that which he had previously experienced. It was as if a switch had been turned on and he knew the route, but he realized that staying on the path would take practice. These students experienced a critical change in self-concept, becoming less diffuse and more consolidated.

RETENTION AND RELAPSE

The question of retention and relapse also has yet to be systematically assessed. My view is that some participants revert to their old ways once the sessions end, and others continue to exhibit change. Part of this outcome will depend on changes in the extent to which individuals view being more conscientious and more responsible in their lives as a high priority and wanting to feel good about themselves as an equal priority. At the end of the five sessions, this change is very evident in group members who attend regularly. For some, however, the cost may be too high over the long term, and they will experience relapses, only to give these views a high priority again later and once again lower their dilatory behavior. In other words, for some group members who change, the change will be cyclical. It is my hope that the program has allowed many to change over their lifetime and, for others, that the program will stay with them to shorten the length of the down cycles and broaden the length of the up cycles.

5

A STUDENT COURSE ON SELF-MANAGEMENT FOR PROCRASTINATORS

TANJA VAN ESSEN, SARY VAN DEN HEUVEL,
AND MARJAN OSSEBAARD

Since procrastination has become a topic for psychological research, student counselors at various universities in the Netherlands have developed interventions to help students overcome their procrastinating tendencies. Two examples of these interventions, both self-management courses with a cognitive–behavioral approach, were independently developed at the Groningen and Utrecht universities.

In this chapter, we summarize the content and approach of these courses. We begin by explaining the context and organization of the courses, then identify the main goal of the courses and describe the content and process of the programs. Following this, we present the results of outcome-related research. The chapter concludes with a brief discussion of the strengths and limitations of this approach for counseling the procrastinator in academic settings.

CONTEXT AND ORGANIZATION

At the University of Groningen (Academic Assistance Center), as well as at the Utrecht University (IVLOS Institute of Education), various study-related skills courses are offered at a central level that are accessible to all university students. These courses are brought to students' notice through handouts, posters in the various faculties, a Web site, and advertisements in the university newspapers. Students enroll for the courses voluntarily and must pay a small fee to promote the feeling of commitment (Groningen) or to contribute to the cost of the course materials (Utrecht).

During the academic year 2000–2001, at both institutions we introduced a self-management course for procrastinators. These courses, although both used a cognitive–behavioral approach, were developed independently and for different reasons. In Groningen, the course development derived from our experience with task management groups (see chap. 7, this volume). Although task management groups have been quite successful, not all students are attracted by this approach. Some students want to overcome procrastination "on their own," they seem to be "allergic" to imposed rules, or they easily drop out because they fail to meet the strict rules of the group. For this reason, we developed a course program with a different approach.

In Utrecht, the main reason for the development of a self-management course was the relatively poor results of a previous course on time management. The main components of this time management course were study planning techniques, effective goal setting, and monitoring of time-spending behavior. After this course, most students knew well how to make a study plan, but a fair number still had great difficulty in actually carrying the plan out. Therefore, a shift was made from a purely behavioral to a more cognitive–behavioral approach.

GENERAL GOAL OF THE SELF-MANAGEMENT COURSES

The self-management courses at Utrecht and Groningen aim at reducing students' procrastinatory behavior by teaching them to arm themselves against their tendency to procrastinate. This main objective can be broken down into two subsequent goals: (a) helping students gain insight into the why and how of their tendency to procrastinate and (b) teaching students to use different techniques and tactics to better control this tendency. As a side effect, we hope that students will feel more motivated and that their feelings of self-efficacy will increase. That is, students should feel more in control of their own (studying) behavior.

Procrastination can be viewed as an acquired behavior, a habit that apparently did pay off in the past as long as students could get away with it. For many of them, in the present, procrastination is a strategy that does not work very well anymore; the costs have become heavier then the benefits. Acquired behavior can be unlearned as well, although this may require great effort. By means of a fairly short course, we seek to provide students with a few tools and some practice in changing their behavior. Although these students have to work hard at overcoming their own procrastinatory tendencies, the self-management courses are meant to help them on their way.

CONTENT AND PROCESS OF THE
SELF-MANAGEMENT COURSES

We based our treatment programs for procrastinating students on the assumption that individuals' behavior, thoughts, and feelings are interrelated (Ellis, 1994; Ellis & Grieger, 1977; T. W. Smith, 1989). People act, feel, and think at the same time. If they want to bring about change in their actions, feelings, or belief system, they can take any of these three dimensions as a starting point for changing all of them. In the course programs, we use techniques addressing all three dimensions—cognitive, behavioral, and emotive— to help students overcome procrastination.

To meet the goals—of helping students gain insight into their behavior and control their tendency to procrastinate—we made sure that both self-management programs included at least three different components: a rational–emotive behavioral therapy (REBT) component, a study planning or time management component, and an informational component. The sections that follow describe the details and objectives of these different components.

We teach students REBT theory and principles to promote change and reduce procrastination. Developed by Ellis in 1955, the basic idea of REBT is that people generally behave and feel the way they think (Ellis, 1994). That means that people's belief system (thoughts, attitudes, and values) stimulates their feelings and actions (Ellis & Knaus, 2002). This belief system can be divided into rational and irrational beliefs. Rational beliefs are beliefs that hold together logically and result in appropriate emotional and behavioral reactions that further basic goals. Irrational beliefs are undesirable because they stimulate overreactions such as anxiety or depression. Rational–emotive behavioral therapy provides a method of identifying and diminishing irrational beliefs (Ellis & Knaus, 2002). With a healthier—that is, more realistic—philosophy of the world, people are able to behave and feel in ways that are more appropriate.

The REBT component has a quite prominent place in both programs. In Groningen, REBT is considered the most important course component. How and why do we think REBT can be of help and may have a surplus value in comparison with a simple behavioral approach in a self-management course for procrastinators? First of all, REBT provides a multimodal approach (Lazarus, 1971, 1989). Because behavior, thoughts, and feelings are interrelated, it seems reasonable to look at all three dimensions when seeking to bring about change. Rational–emotive behavioral therapy includes techniques in all three dimensions: cognitive techniques (disputing), emotional techniques (e.g., imagery, unconditional self-acceptance), and behavioral techniques (e.g., risk-taking exercises, operant conditioning). Furthermore, we consider procrastination also to be an emotional problem. For example, students often become angry with themselves when they are procrastinating, thereby diminishing the chances of getting to work even more (Ellis & Knaus, 2002). We think that looking for the irrational ideas that produce or maintain negative emotions and changing them are of importance. Finally, REBT is an educative model that is quite easy to understand. The theory is broadly applicable in very different aspects of life. Therefore, the method can be quite appealing to students.

In the Groningen course, we begin by explaining the basic idea of REBT and the ABC components. We explain that people generally feel and behave the way they think. Behavioral or emotional problems mainly stem from, or are maintained by, irrational thinking (beliefs). Tracking down their own irrational beliefs (iBs) and changing them is the thing to do. In preparation, for homework students are instructed to fill in a form as soon as they find themselves procrastinating and then to try to discriminate between the situation (A), their behavior and feelings (C), and their thoughts (B).

In the next session, we discuss this homework, looking for evidence for the REBT theory: Does B (their beliefs) "create" or maintain C (their behavior and emotions)? Then we explain that REBT holds four major irrational beliefs responsible for the existence or preservation of irrational feelings and ineffective behavior:

1. *Musts*. Instead of wishing things, people often tend to demand that things work out the way want them to. By doing this, people create unnecessary pressure and stress for themselves. In addition, this view of the world is too absolutistic and inflexible. Examples of such irrational thoughts include "I *must* do well!" and "It *should not* be this hard!"

2. *Catastrophizing*. Instead of seeing things in their proper perspective, people tend to make bad things worse, even beforehand. When they think that bad things are awful and that they cannot handle them, people are catastrophizing. Examples of this type of irrational thoughts include "It's awful when I fail the exams!" and "It is a big disaster if I make a mistake!"

3. *Low frustration tolerance*. Some people cannot stand the way things go and believe that life is too hard. People with low frustration tolerance seem to easily forget, or do not want to accept, that life has its setbacks and hassles. An example of

such an irrational thought is "I can't stand reading this boring book!"

4. *Human worth rating.* The philosophy that people's worth is reflected in the way they act (e.g., "I'm a worm if I can't stop procrastinating") leads people to put themselves down when they do not act appropriately. By doing this, they diminish the chances that they will act or feel better in the future. Rating oneself or others by their behavior does not take into consideration the complexity and uniqueness of human beings; people are much more than the way they act at one moment in time. We try to teach students what Ellis called "unconditional self-acceptance" and "unconditional other-acceptance": That is, that they try to rate behavior only as good, bad, or (not very) effective and to stop rating human beings as a whole (Ellis & Harper, 1997).

We discuss these four categories of irrational beliefs and how these beliefs can affect people's functioning. We hand out a brochure about the principles of REBT and once more instruct students to fill in the form when they find themselves procrastinating during the next week.

In the next session, we discuss the results of the REBT form, asking for examples of A, B, and C and looking for connections between B and C. After that, we give a demonstration of a full ABCDE of REBT, demonstrating the technique of disputing (D) and of formulating effective new beliefs (E). In disputing irrational beliefs, students are encouraged to look for evidence for their beliefs and to ask themselves, "Where is the evidence that I can't stand it when it is this boring?" and "Why do things *have* to go the way I want them to go?" Examples of effective new beliefs include, "It may be as boring as it is, but I can stand it (although I don't like it)!" and "Things do not *have* to go the way I want them to!" Students hand in their REBT forms for feedback and take new forms to fill in for the next week. After demonstrating a full ABCDE analysis of one of the student forms, we explain the idea of rational–emotive imagery—that is, using imagination in disputing irrational beliefs or rehearsing rational beliefs—and we recommend that students use this technique at home.

Finally, we discuss a somewhat basic irrational idea that seems to be a favorite of procrastinating students: that they need to be inspired, alert, fancy it, or in some other state to start working. We ask how familiar this statement sounds and why it is irrational. As a behavioral disputation, students are challenged to plan a few hours for the next week in which they will study, no matter how they feel. This is a behavioral disputation against the ideas, "I can't work when I'm too tired, uninspired, or sick" and "I need to be inspired in order to begin studying, otherwise I just can't work at all." Students themselves choose how many hours and on what specific days they are going to work. After that, again, we execute a full ABCDE analysis in which students actively engage in finding the main irrational beliefs, disputing them, and formulating effective new beliefs.

In the Utrecht course, the students record and analyze their procrastination experiences in their logs. We introduce the principles of REBT and clarify the theory by counseling one of the students in the group, passing through the different phases of the REBT method. Students are encouraged to track down the irrational thoughts that are hindering them most and to write them down on a card. Later on in the course, we discuss the connection between REBT and the six styles of procrastination distinguished by Sapadin (1997). Students are asked to look through a list of excuses and beliefs characteristic of each style and mark the ones they recognize as typical for themselves. During the course, students practice REBT a few times in twos or threes in order to dispute and replace their most persistent beliefs.

By introducing study planning and time management techniques, we try to give students insight into their own time-spending habits. In the Groningen course, this is preceded by a homework assignment instructing students to monitor how they spend every 15 minutes of their time during a full week. In the next session, students analyze how they spend their time and what areas they are satisfied with and what areas they are not. The group discusses their findings publicly, and we encourage them to use this knowledge in devising their next weekly study plan. In a separate session, we discuss the drafting of study plans. Referring to the principle of discounting, that it is attractive and easy to go for short-term goals, we explain the idea of formulating SMART short-term study plans (see chap. 7, this volume). In addition, we give students time to draft their own long-term plans for studying up to the next exams. In both courses, personal diagrams (see chap. 7, this volume) are used as a monitoring device for the study planning and time management process.

With use of self-monitoring techniques and stimulus control techniques, we also aim at facilitating behavioral change. In the Groningen course, we invite students to reflect on reinforcement principles that they can use in the next week to get to work more easily. We encourage students to inspect their own study behavior, which is divided into three stages:

1. *Before studying* is the stage in which they select an environment that makes studying more likely. For example, some students make a study appointment in the library with a friend. Others make sure they have a clean desk and all their necessary books within arm's reach.

2. *While studying* is when they decide how to handle distractions. For example, students can plan the duration of their break beforehand. They can write down their distracting thoughts and plan to consider these thoughts and difficulties after finishing.

3. *After studying* is when they reward or punish themselves after the work is done or not done. Some students allow themselves to go out with friends after their studying, or they agree to do the dishes for their roommates when they do not finish their studying.

The Utrecht course follows more or less the same line. In addition, the group pays some attention to study methods as well. We discuss the various stages of the studying process (and the corresponding study activities) needed to work through the subject contents effectively and efficiently. Because many students find it very difficult to realistically estimate how much time they will need for study tasks, we dwell on the resources that can support them in this.

The Utrecht course focuses on concentration problems as well. We define what concentration is, and the students report their main sources of distraction, both internal and external. We then present a number of ways to help improve their concentration, partly as a recapitulation of the actions directed at solving the conflict between long-term and short-term objectives. Finally, we take the students through a concentration exercise borrowed from Zen meditation: counting one's breaths to focus one's attention. We underline the importance of using a variety of study activities in order to study as actively as possible, and we reflect on how they can make the most of their energies—for instance, by following their biorhythms and by taking regular breaks.

Finally, in the informational component we discuss background information related to procrastination and present some research results. In this way, we try to arouse intellectual interest and to promote understanding of the possible causes of procrastinatory behavior. Also, we hope that the participants' feelings of self-efficacy will increase; explaining behavior—and thereby diminishing uncertainty—is said to be a powerful tool for increasing self-efficacy or sense of mastery (Frank, 1961, 1976; Frank, Hoehn-Saric, Imber, Liberman, & Stone, 1978). The feeling that one can control one's own situation can be an important condition for facilitating behavioral change.

In both courses, we present the theory that procrastination is a result of a conflict between long-term and short-term goals that results in a discounting curve. People are inclined to go for short-term reinforcement at the expense of their long-term goals (Schouwenburg, 1994). We explain to students that this conflict is a normal phenomenon that is exaggerated in procrastination and that behavioral interventions can influence the parameters of the discounting curve. In addition, we invite students to think of various possibilities to increase the attractiveness of studying for a relatively faraway exam and explain how they can tackle or prevent distractions and temptations that stop them from studying regularly.

Apart from this general theoretical background, in the Utrecht course various other theoretical points of view are adopted. Self-reflection (on present behavior, thoughts, feelings, wishes, and physical sensations) is an important issue for discussion; we present self-reflection as a precondition for changing one's behavior. Starting with a brief summary of the causes and functions of procrastination according to the main psychological theories, Higgins's (1987) theory of self-discrepancy is introduced. According to this theory, an emotional conflict arises when a serious and long-lasting discrepancy exists between the way one sees oneself (actual self) and the way one wishes one were (ideal self) or thinks one should be ("ought" self). This conflict results in negative emotions that vary with the type of discrepancy experienced. We encourage students to use Higgins's theory of self-discrepancy to gain insight into the ways their goal setting and planning behaviors are influenced by what they think they should do or by what they expect other people want them to do. For example, some students realize, week after week, that they can realistically complete only 10 hours of studying, and yet they do not adjust their behavior of planning on 40 hours of studying for the next week. By applying Higgins's theory, students often discover at this point that they are led by their ideals or conscience. This insight helps them to let go of these misleading ideals and start focusing on what they really want or are capable of and to use this as a basis for their goal-setting behavior.

To promote a deeper self-understanding of students' own personal procrastination style, in the Utrecht course we present six different styles of procrastination (Burka & Yuen, 1983; Sapadin, 1997): the perfectionist, the overdoer, the defier, the dreamer, the worrier, and the crisis maker. We discuss the qualities and pitfalls, underlying inner conflict, and benefits of each type of procrastinating behavior. On the basis of this understanding, students design their own personal plan of action for changing the way they think, talk, and act.

Both programs include a few unique features. Unique for the self-management program in Groningen are the "success rounds." In principle, we start every session with an inventory of success experiences in the past week. By doing this, and by asking students how they accomplished these successes, we try to raise their feelings of self-efficacy. We encourage students to shift their attention from any failures of the past week to the things they are satisfied about. Students then can try to repeat this successful strategy in the next week. This is a well-known technique used in solution-focused therapy developed by De Shazer (1982, 1985) and associates.

In contrast, two components are unique to the self-management program at Utrecht. First, there is a motivational focus. Students are encouraged to explore their will and to mobilize the energy required to actually make a change. Second, in Utrecht we added a component addressing the dimension of bodily sensations. By teaching students relaxation and visualization techniques, we try to make them more aware of the effect that their procrastination behavior has on their body (e.g., tension).

DURATION OF THE COURSES

Both self-management programs consist of seven sessions of approximately three hours each and one follow-up session. In the Utrecht course, this implies an introductory session, a block of six weekly sessions, and a follow-up session. The introductory session in the Utrecht course focuses on selection. For that purpose, students fill in two questionnaires that allow us to assess whether the students will benefit from the course. The questionnaires are the Academic Procrastination State Inventory (APSI; Schouwenburg, 1995), which identifies study problems experienced in the past week (e.g., procrastination, fear of failure, and lack of motivation), and an adapted version of a study methods questionnaire developed at Twente University, the Netherlands (Oosterhuis, 1995). On the basis of their results, we develop a personal recommendation for each student either to participate in the course or to seek help elsewhere (e.g., a career counselor, a student psychologist, or a study skills course).

The follow-up session at Utrecht usually takes place approximately two months after course completion. During this session the students complete the APSI for the previous week, and the counselor presents a graph to each of them with their APSI procrastination scores. The students draw their own conclusions and receive feedback from the rest of the group. The session focuses on what went well and what did not and which techniques they have used to tackle their procrastinatory tendencies. Students end the follow-up session by formulating their intentions for the next half-year.

Unlike the program at Utrecht, the Groningen course consists of seven weekly sessions, with no intake session and with a less intensive follow-up session. In the first session, we spend a great deal of time on problem identification, getting acquainted with each other, and explaining the content and goals of the course. The follow-up meeting usually takes place 1 month after the last session, and students complete a form of the APSI (in Groningen students fill in the APSI weekly) and inform each other how they are doing regarding their study behavior. Table 5.1 contains a brief overview of both programs.

EFFECT OF THE COURSES

From October 2000 until the end of 2001, we taught four self-management groups ($n = 34$) in Groningen. and five self-management courses ($n =$

TABLE 5.1
Overview of Self-Management Course Programs in Groningen and Utrecht

Session	Groningen program	Utrecht program
1	Problem inventory Course explanation First study plan Time-use assignment	Introduction Selection of course participants Time-use assignment

2	Time-spending analysis
	Discussion of research
	    perspectives
	Basic REBT
		Time management techniques
		Discussion of causes of
		    procrastination

3	Discussion of ABC of REBT Categories of irrational beliefs Demonstration of ABCDE analysis	Self-discrepancy theory Planning instruction Relaxation exercise Discussion of ABC of REBT
4	SMART study goal setting Long-term planning Explanation of D and E of REBT Full ABCDE analysis	Role-play introducing ABCDE of REBT Discussion of procrastination styles
5	Basics of operant conditioning Application to study behavior Full ABCDE analysis	Personal procrastination style Practicing D and E of REBT Relaxation Visualization exercise Long-term planning

6	Introduction of behavioral
	    disputation
	Full ABCDE analysis
		Discussion of short-term vs. long-
		    term goals
		Weekly study plan

7	Practice in ABCDE analysis References Course evaluation	Discussion of concentration and distraction Concentration exercise Evaluation

Note. REBT = rational–emotive behavioral therapy.

49) in Utrecht. To evaluate the course effects, we conducted some research in both universities, which we summarize in this section.

Student Evaluations

On a quantitative evaluation form consisting of a number of statements and a response scale from 1 = *do not agree* to 5 = *fully agree*, students evaluated what they learned during the course. In Groningen 29 students filled in the evaluation form and in Utrecht 28. Regarding the two main goals of the courses, for students to both gain insight into and actually control their tendency to procrastinate, students claimed that they had a better understanding of their procrastinatory tendency (average rating 4.5 in Groningen, 4.6 in Utrecht). As one student put it,

> It seemed that I used to postpone tasks automatically. Now that I am aware of my behavior and know how I spend my time, I can tackle my

procrastination problem. I am very focused on it now, and I have the will to change.

Students also claimed that they could better control their tendency to procrastinate (average rating 3.8 in Groningen) and that they were better able to set realistic and concrete goals (average rating 3.8 in Groningen, 4.5 in Utrecht).

As for self-efficacy, an intended side effect of the courses, in Groningen students reported that they felt more in control considering their own (study) situation (average rating 4.3). In Utrecht, 71% of the students claimed that they expected to procrastinate less after the course. One student observed,

I have learned a lot. I really feel in control again. This does not apply only to the way I spend my time, but also to my life as a whole (procrastination used to have a large impact on my life).

Moreover, from a number of student statements at both institutions, it is clear that at the end of the course students said they felt better. Some students reported that they had regained their motivation and enjoyed studying more.

Students were also required to rate the perceived importance of the different course components. Providing background information and different theories on procrastination was appraised with an average rating of 3.7 in Groningen and 4.2 in Utrecht. Study planning techniques, like effective goal setting and time monitoring, were considered most helpful in Utrecht (average rating of 4.5). In Groningen, the theory of study planning techniques was rated 3.6 on average, whereas the weekly study plan control was rated 3.9. The explanation of REBT was considered the most effective component in Groningen (average rating 4.2), together with the group discussions on the ABCs (average rating 3.9). In Utrecht, the REBT component was given an average rating of 3.9.

The lowest rated course component in Groningen was the weekly inventory of success experiences (2.9). In Utrecht, stimulus control techniques (3.6) and relaxation techniques (3.7) were identified as least useful.

We saw few differences between the Utrecht and Groningen programs in student appraisals of program components. However, Utrecht students seemed to consider the time monitoring and study planning components as the most powerful tools, whereas students in Groningen appreciated the REBT component most.

Quantitative Research

Students in the self-management courses at both institutions were required to complete the APSI to measure whether their procrastinatory behavior decreased during the course. In Groningen, students filled in the APSI weekly and once more in the follow-up session. As for the second group, a

TABLE 5.2
Average z- Scores for Procrastination During and After the Course

Session	Groningen REBT course	Utrecht REBT course	Groningen non-REBT course	Groningen task management group[a]
1	0.88	1.14	0.72	−0.02
2	0.20	0.32	0.22	−0.11
3	0.07		0.30	−0.11
4	−0.08	0.31	−0.04	0.05
5	0.01		0.02	−0.15
6	−0.06	−0.01	0.09	−0.16
7	−0.22		−0.37	0.09
1-month follow-up	−0.45	−0.50	0.06	

Note. REBT = rational–emotive behavioral therapy.
[a]See chapter 7, this volume, for a description of this course.

measure of perceived self-efficacy, the Academic Competence scale (Kleijn, van der Ploeg, & Topman, 1994), was added. In Utrecht, the APSI was scored at the intake session, every two weeks during the course, and once again in the follow-up session. Academic Procrastination State Inventory scores on both procrastination and self-efficacy were standardized with respect to the test construction norm groups of both scales: average university students of the same age. For comparison, we required students in a parallel task management group in Groningen ($n = 12$) to complete the APSI and the self-efficacy measure on the same weekly basis. Table 5.2 contains the results of these comparisons.

During the seven weeks of the interventions, students' average procrastination scores decreased more than 1 standard deviation. A decreasing trend in procrastination score seemed to continue into the follow-up session. This finding may probably be taken as an indication of a significant effect.

Regarding the perceived self-efficacy scores, the average scores of the course participants increased quite strongly during the course ($z = −0.60$ at session 1, $z = 1.04$ at session 7). This trend seemed to continue into the follow-up session as well ($z = 1.37$ after one month). On the other hand, participants' average self-efficacy scores of the parallel task management group seemed to maintain themselves at a level of about 1 standard deviation above the mean of the original norm group.

Retention and Relapse

During the courses, 15% of the students dropped out in Groningen, and 27% students dropped out in Utrecht. We regret having no information concerning the reasons of those who dropped out. We presume that those students did not get what they expected.

Unfortunately, attendance at the follow-up meetings was quite low at both universities. Only 50% of the students who attended the last course session in Groningen showed up at the follow-up session, although we promised those students 5€ as a reward. About 38% of the students showed up at the follow-up session in Utrecht. This low attendance indicates that we missed important information about the long-term effects of the courses.

GENERAL COMMENTS ON RESEARCH RESULTS

The research results at Utrecht and Groningen were very much alike. After repeated measurements, both self-management programs demonstrated the same tendency: Procrastination scores dropped more then 1 standard deviation in approximately seven weeks. What may account for these results? Can we assume that the results are an indication of the effectiveness of the self-management courses? If so, what specific course components were effective in reducing students' procrastinatory behavior? Or could so-called aspecific factors be of relevance in the self-management courses? Factors such as "expression of emotion," "using a collective language," "explaining behavior," and "giving hope" are said to be important features accounting for part of the success in almost all forms of therapy (Frank, 1976; Frank et al., 1978). Maybe students eventually procrastinate less as a result of these aspecific factors. After all, students who procrastinate often suffer seriously from their procrastinatory tendencies and therefore are highly motivated to change. Just giving hope and letting students express their emotions and explain their procrastination are important components of the courses; the REBT and the time management components may be subsidiary. In Groningen, we tried to find out if REBT contributed to the success of the course.

Self-Management Courses Without REBT

Because of the prominent place of REBT in the Groningen course program, we wanted to find out whether REBT contributed to the effect of our self-management course. To answer this question, we conducted some additional research. As an experiment in Groningen, we started in October 2001 and January 2002 with two parallel groups ($n = 14$). Each time, in parallel with a self-management group, we trained another group that followed a slightly different program. This different program consisted of all the elements of the above-mentioned program, minus the REBT theory and techniques.

Because we wanted to expose the students in this behavioral-only program to the same amount of time and attention, we added relaxation techniques to the program. On a smaller scale, these relaxation techniques were also added to the REBT program. Of course, the groups receiving REBT needed more time every session, but the amount of time spent in the groups with the behavioral-only treatment was, in our opinion, acceptable (approximately 1.5 hours). All groups received the training from the same counselor. Students themselves were not aware of the research condition or group they were assigned to; however, the experiment was not a true double-blind design.

Student Evaluations of the Behavioral-Only Program

Students in the behavioral-only condition used the same evaluation forms as did those in the REBT-based conditions. These students ($n = 11$) were found to support the following statements: "I can actually get myself to work better" (average rating 3.6), "I actually carry out what I planned to do" (average rating 3.6), and "I have a better understanding of the components that can play a part in procrastination" (average rating 4.6).

Regarding self-efficacy, these students stated that they felt more in control of their own (study) situation (average rating 4.2). As far as the perceived importance of the different course components, students found the explanation of general theories and backgrounds of procrastination (average rating 4.2) and the weekly study plan control (4.0) to be most effective. The relaxation component was rated lowest in terms of perceived effectiveness (average rating 2.8).

Quantitative Research on the Behavioral-Only Program

For quantitative evaluation, we used the same format as for the REBT condition. The results are included in Table 5.1. Although the number of participants in this condition was very small, we had the impression that both of the self-management programs, one with and one without REBT, worked equally well in decreasing procrastinatory behavior. Also, students' effectiveness ratings of both courses were very much alike. Up to now, there is no evidence that using REBT theory and techniques has a surplus value in treating procrastination in students.

The dropout rate of the behavioral-only program was 22%, which is slightly higher than that of the REBT-based program. The percentage showing up at the follow-up meeting was also comparable to that in the other condition. Again, unfortunately, we missed important information from students who did not show up.

CONCLUSION

Both self-management courses, in Utrecht and Groningen, showed after repeated measurements the same tendency: Procrastination scores dropped by more than 1 standard deviation in approximately seven weeks. Therefore, we think we can claim that these self-management programs really contributed to reducing students' procrastination.

A side effect of these courses—that students felt more motivated to continue their studies—also seems to have been achieved; students in both courses reported that they felt more motivated, and some admitted that they even liked studying again. Also, students reported that they felt more in control of their study situation.

Answering the question of what course components did or did not contribute to overcoming procrastination is difficult. Creating hope, giving explanations for behavior, and expressing emotions may be powerful tools in reducing procrastination. Students often sign up for for self-management courses when they suffer from their behavior and when they feel demoralized. For them, it is an encouragement to find that they are not alone and to understand that changing their behavior is possible.

However, we believe that other important components of the courses had a beneficial effect as well. Student responses to the questionnaires indicate that providing background information, formulating realistic study plans, and facilitating self-reflection all contributed to the success of the courses. In encouraging self-reflection and in facilitating behavioral change, we think REBT can be of great help. Rational–emotive behavioral therapy enables students to learn to reflect on themselves. They have to take a moment to sit down and think about themselves. This may be the beginning of a long-term process, and the duration of the courses may be too short to demonstrate its usefulness. Besides, REBT involves explicit work at unconditional self-acceptance, in our view a powerful tool in helping students to view themselves in a healthier way and to take more control over their own lives. It is our cautious opinion that with REBT, students may be better equipped in the long run—for example, when faced with setbacks.

The relatively high dropout rate remains a point of concern for us, however. Although not every student might be attracted to a cognitive–behavioral approach, in our opinion the self-management courses are a welcome supplement to other courses we already provide.

6

OVERCOMING THE PATTERNS OF POWERLESSNESS THAT LEAD TO PROCRASTINATION

LILLY J. SCHUBERT WALKER

Procrastination, the act of postponing and delaying needlessly, is a pervasive problem affecting the personal productivity of significant numbers of university students. Estimates vary from a high of 95% (Ellis & Knaus, 2002) to a low of 10% (Hill, Hill, Chabot, & Barrall, 1978). This pattern of avoidance affects male and female students equally and increases throughout their undergraduate years (McCown, Johnson, & Petzel, 1989). In fact, many university students assume that because procrastination is such a common practice, it is simply something with which they must live. The typical outcomes of procrastination are lower grades (Rothblum, Solomon, & Murakami, 1986), course withdrawals (Welsley, 1994), stress (Blunt & Pychyl, 2000), increased health risks (Baumeister, 1997), and interpersonal conflict (Day, Mensink, & O'Sullivan, 2000). In one study, 52% of students reported that procrastination had become a serious problem for which they had sought help (Gallagher, 1992). For 20% to 30% of university students, procrastination is a serious problem adversely affecting academic achievement and quality of life (McCown, 1986; Solomon & Rothblum, 1984). Developmentally, the incidence of procrastination increases significantly during the four years of undergraduate schooling and appears to peak in the mid-20s (McCown & Roberts, 1994).

Because the outcomes of procrastination are serious, practitioners and researchers have sought to understand the factors that produce this pattern. As the chapters in this book demonstrate, the causes of procrastination are as varied as the individuals who procrastinate. Procrastination patterns evolve from situational factors and personal factors. Sometimes people procrastinate because of the nature of the task. They find the workload or assignments to be distasteful, too difficult, confusing, overwhelming, or uninteresting (Blunt & Pychyl, 2000; Senécal et al., 1995). At other times, procrastination is related to a variety of personal characteristics. These include low self-esteem (Beswick et al., 1988), neurosis (Schouwenburg & Lay, 1995), self-consciousness (Ferrari, 1992a), depression (McCown et al., 1987), anxiety (Ottens, 1982), perfectionism (Ferrari, 1992a; Flett, Blankstein, Hewitt, & Koledin, 1992), neuroticism (Schouwenburg & Lay, 1995), disorganization (Schouwenburg & Lay, 1995), low conscientiousness (Lay, 1997), motivational problems (Senécal et al., 1995), learned helplessness (Covington, 1993; McKean, 1994), and irrational thinking (Bridges & Roig, 1997; Ellis & Knaus, 2002). It is clear that both the nature of the work tasks and the attributes of the students interact to produce a pattern of personal avoidance. The interactive nature of these factors produces feelings of powerlessness over one's ability to achieve academic success and be fully in charge of one's life.

To help individuals change their patterns of procrastination, treatment must address the factors that produce the powerlessness they experience. The powerlessness reactions that many procrastinators demonstrate are evident in their negative perceptions of self-worth (Beswick et al., 1988; Ferrari, 1991b; Flett, Blankstein, & Martin, 1995a), irrational thinking (Bridges & Roig, 1997; Ellis & Knaus, 2002; Solomon & Rothblum, 1984), and lack of self-efficacy (Ferrari, Parker, & Ware, 1992; Tuckman & Sexton, 1990, 1992). In exploring the factors that produce powerlessness, researchers have demonstrated that procrastinators denigrate themselves (Musznyski & Akamatsu, 1991), are highly self-conscious (Ferrari, 1991b), make negative social comparisons (Ferrari, 1992a), and lack self-control (Milgram et al., 1988; Rothblum et al., 1986). A therapeutic model that addresses these factors by enhancing feelings of self-respect, building self-confidence, and providing strategies for improving a sense of personal efficacy can reduce the personal powerlessness that feeds procrastination.

COUNSELING MODEL

The counseling approach described in this chapter incorporates clinical experience and research findings into a structured 6-week group psychotherapy series. The goal of this therapeutic approach is to reduce the power-lessness reactions that many procrastinators experience, thus providing a basis for changing avoidance behaviors associated with procrastination in academic settings. The focus of the group counseling sessions is to facilitate the development of cognitive, affective, and behavioral strategies that give the participants greater self-mastery or personal power. *Personal power* is a belief in one's ability to take charge of one's life, develop new habits, and eliminate procrastination patterns. This personal power is evidenced by increased self-worth (Covington, 1993), self-control (Perry, 1991), and self-efficacy (Bandura, 1977, 1986; Haycock, McCarthy, & Skay, 1998). By enhancing participants' feelings of personal power, we anticipate that they will improve their self-management capabilities and reduce their procrastination.

To reduce the negative affect associated with procrastination, the treatment model frames procrastination not as a personality flaw but as a coping process or habit pattern that can be changed. By clarifying the ways group members use procrastination to cope with pressures and manage expectations, they are better able to explore the negative and positive consequences associated with their individual procrastination habit patterns. These insights provide the basis for exploring the complex relationship of personal power to procrastination. This framework for describing procrastination—as a coping process—promotes participants' discovery of strategies that can aid them in developing convictions regarding their ability to exert some personal control over the habits, feelings, or thinking that have previously interfered with their personal productivity and academic success.

Throughout the 6-week group therapy session, students are involved in a discovery process that explores the various dimensions of personal procrastination patterns, thus providing a basis for developing strategies for overcoming feelings of personal powerlessness associated with procrastination. The treatment approach recognizes the complex reactions related to procrastination that students experience (Burka & Yuen, 1983). Sometimes procrastination allows them to think they are capable of high achievement; putting off a difficult or distasteful task protects their sense of self-confidence and allows them to engage in activities they find pleasurable (Silver & Sabini, 1981). At other times, worry, negative thinking, guilt, discouragement, depression, anxiety, and inadequacy adversely affect their ability to succeed personally and academically (L. J. S. Walker, 1988; L. J. S. Walker & Stewart, 2000). The model we use assists participants in understanding the interaction among their feelings, thoughts, personal needs, values, and characteristics, especially as they relate to academic expectations, personal adequacy, and procrastination. The model guides our instruction of group members in strategies for eliminating self-defeating thoughts and reactions associated with procrastination.

The counseling sessions foster participants' increasing awareness of personal efficacy expectations related to their views regarding their own capabilities to change. The counselor guides group members in developing productive actions so that they can experience greater personal control and instructs them in designing practical, attainable, and realistic plans for achieving success. The program promotes rehearsal of specific strategies, encourages practice between treatment sessions, and fosters peer support within and between sessions.

The counseling model uses a two-stage awareness and action approach for developing positive self-esteem and greater personal power. During the initial awareness stage, participants learn to identify their personal procrastination style. Using a system that classifies procrastinators according to whether they are task focused or people focused and whether they have high or low needs for personal power, participants analyze their procrastination patterns and develop enhanced self-awareness of their motivations for procrastination. They explore fears, fantasies, family messages, and factors that fuel the actions and inaction that compose their procrastination patterns. Participants also learn to identify the productive and nonproductive components of their procrastination patterns as they identify their procrastination style.

The counseling model includes four styles of procrastination: perfectionist, politician, postponer, and punisher. These types evolved from clinical interviews (L. J. S. Walker, 1988). They include an adaptation of various Myers–Briggs types of procrastination (Provost, 1988) and view procrastination from dimensions of power needs (i.e., high vs. low) and activity focus (i.e., task vs. people). They are similar to the procrastination types identified by various psychological researchers (Ferrari, 1992a; Lay, 1997; Milgram et al., 1988). These styles help members perceive procrastination as a personal pattern with positive and negative consequences. Because a majority of the individuals who request help for procrastination problems experience negative affect associated with their procrastination tendencies, this program uses these procrastination styles to provide participants with a positive view of themselves and the utilitarian function of procrastination as lifestyle habit.

Perfectionist

Perfectionists have high power needs and are task focused. Time is important to the perfectionist, who is focused on doing everything possible to create future success. Never satisfied with the status quo, perfectionists are dreamers who take control by setting high goals for themselves. Because excellence is important to them, they can have difficulty discriminating the amount of time that should be spent on a specific task versus the amount of time a task requires. Their tendency to spend too much time on each task means that they do not have enough time to perform at the level they expect. Their future focus involves continually imagining possibilities. They have great expectations of what they can be, and their lofty aspirations motivate them. However, the expansiveness of their goals and the lack of concrete plans to achieve these goals can present problems for perfectionists. Although their fantasy world motivates, it can also be an escape pattern that interferes with their success.

Perfectionists dislike the ordinary and fear mediocrity. Their thinking patterns are filled with "should" statements that focus on performing well. Typical thoughts of perfectionists include desires to be more responsible and doubts regarding their own abilities to achieve. Common tendencies are to feel dissatisfied in spite of achieving success and worried about not being as good as they could be.

Postponer

Postponers live for the moment. Their sense of personal inadequacy produces feelings of powerlessness. Avoiding difficult tasks is their primary means of managing their needs for achievement. For them, time is to be experienced and enjoyed. They view the future as an extension of life as they experience it now and often act as if there is no tomorrow. With primary needs for experiencing pleasure, fun, and excitement, they are continually searching for the unusual. Because they fear monotony and boredom, these individuals direct their thoughts to fostering excitement and avoiding responsibility. They often run out of time because of inadequate planning. Typical thoughts include "It's just a small test, I've got lots of time" and "I'll start studying after my favorite television program."

Postponers fatigue and frustrate easily. They have short attention spans that interfere with their ability to concentrate and study for long periods. To improve their academic success, they must learn how to adjust their study strategies to give themselves the diversity and variety they need. Because they lack self-discipline and a sense of personal responsibility, they are more apt to succeed when others direct, structure, or supervise their activities. They are responsive and able to manage immediate demands but have difficulty anticipating future problems or planning for the long term. When given a chance, they will choose fun over studying.

Politician

Politicians have high affiliation needs and a strong sense of personal power. Making time for friends, family, and social encounters is a major priority for politicians. They are motivated by a need to belong and be liked by others. Whenever possible, they will devote time to socializing. Anxious to please others, they often spend time doing what others want them to do rather than what they want or need to do themselves. Because they are drawn to many social situations and are busy doing what they believe will please others, they are overextended and experience time pressures.

Adept at social interaction, politicians perceive themselves as confident and able. However, their self-confidence is invested in the opinions of others. They sometimes wonder if they measure up, so feedback from important people is particularly salient. They fear the criticism or disapproval of others. Typical thoughts include "I'm concerned that I will let others down" and "It's hard to stay focused, especially when my friends want me to go out with them." Because of their need for approval from others, time is not their own. They have difficulty setting limits and choosing their own priorities.

Punisher

"What will be will be" is the fatalistic approach of the punisher. Punishers have no sense of personal power and feel as though they do not measure up to others. These individuals also feel little control over their lives. Often pessimistic, uncertain, and self-critical, they are especially aware of past failures and inadequacies. Their focus on the past negatively affects their view of the future by fueling their idea that it will never be any different.

Inefficient and inconsistent, they are acutely aware of others' capabilities. They often conclude that they are not good enough. Typical thoughts include "I can't measure up; everyone I know is better and more successful than I am" and "Nothing ever works out for me." With their attention on the successes of others coupled with their self-depreciation of their own abilities, negativity and discouragement easily overwhelm them. This mindset leads to feelings of shame and inadequacy and undermines their ability to manage time effectively.

As part of the awareness stage of this treatment approach, participants learn that one of the four personal styles fits them better than the others. Some participants, depending on the situation, observe an overlap between these procrastination styles. If they find an overlap between one or two styles, they are encouraged to further explore so as to identify the situational factors that add to their pattern of powerlessness. This awareness discussion allows group participants to develop a picture of the interplay of needs, feelings, thoughts, and habits with their ability to effectively manage their lives and time. By presenting positive characteristics related to their procrastination pattern, as well as limitations, participants can come to appreciate the positive attributes they possess and acknowledge the strategies they use to deal with situations.

In the second stage of the model, action, participants learn cognitive, affective, and behavioral strategies for maximizing the productivity of their personal style, taking control of their lives, changing components of their style that are not adaptive, and replacing the feelings of powerlessness connected to procrastination with feelings of personal mastery. The action phase supports participants in designing realistic short-term goals related to changing components of their procrastination pattern. The sessions are organized to enhance personal power or efficacy. Thus, participants initially learn cognitive approaches designed to eliminate destructive, self-defeating thinking.

Later sessions focus on affective and behavioral strategies aimed at reducing nonproductive habits that interfere with self-control.

PARTICIPANTS

University students who sought help because procrastination was adversely affecting their academic success were the primary participants in these counseling sessions. All 12 (5 men and 7 women) ranged in age from 20 to 24 years, were self-referred, and reported that they were not succeeding at the levels to which they aspired. Their primary focus was to change their procrastination habits to improve their academic functioning.

One comparison group comprised students aged 18 to 26 years who were enrolled in a study skills program focused on developing improved academic competencies (e.g., study strategies, time management, textbook comprehension, note-taking). They attended six weekly 90-minute sessions. A second comparison group consisted of 19 first-year students aged 18 to 20 who were involved in a student support discussion group. They met for six weekly 2-hour sessions focusing on issues of concern to first-year undergraduates (e.g., adjustment and transition, expectations, coping, relationships).

SESSIONS

This structured treatment program consists of six 90-minute sessions of informational and therapeutic content. Each session includes brief informational components, self-awareness exercises, self-disclosure, personal analysis, group feedback, and homework assignments. The format of each session includes group check-ins, theme-relevant didactic information, group discussion, personal disclosure, problem analysis, homework assignments, and round-robin goal-setting commitments.

Session 1: Discovery

The goals of session 1 are to educate participants about procrastination patterns, explain individual styles of procrastination, and identify common objectives. The session begins by providing students with an overview of the goals of the group series, clarifying the various kinds of procrastination, and identifying individual patterns of procrastination. Students complete the two instruments used in the treatment program, a procrastination scale (Lay, 1986) and the Myers–Briggs Type Indicator (Myers & McCaulley, 1985).

To assist members in discussing their personal procrastination patterns within the framework of these sessions, the counselor provides participants with the descriptions of the four types of procrastination and invites them to select the procrastination type that best personifies them. To ensure equal time for everybody, participants are asked to provide one recent example that demonstrates their personal style. Using probing and open-ended questions, the group leader assists each group member in identifying adaptive and nonadaptive aspects of his or her situation and style. Group members share their feelings about their personal pattern. To further help participants understand the components of procrastination, the counselor formally presents the research findings on the affective, behavioral, and cognitive factors related to procrastination. The counselor then asks participants to identify which components are most personally relevant to their goals with respect to developing greater personal control. Homework for the following week includes keeping a procrastination journal. The goal of this journal is to increase participants' self-awareness of their procrastination style and further clarify the situations in which they procrastinate through a process of self-monitoring.

Session 2: Understanding Personal Patterns

Session 2 commences with a round-robin discussion of insights regarding one's own personal patterns of procrastination as revealed through the writing exercises in the procrastination journal. The counselor distributes a procrastination worksheet to assist participants in analyzing their personal patterns of powerlessness (see Exhibit 6.1). By responding to a series of questions, participants review and examine their activities of the past week. This process of completing the personal procrastination analysis reveals individual differences in completing the procrastination journal. It is quite typical for some individuals to have only one entry and for others to have three or four. The personal reflection stimulated through the counselor's questioning and probing provokes participants to identify the wide range of motivations and reactions associated with their procrastinating behavior. The worksheet assists them in further identifying their procrastination type, clarifying problem areas, expressing current feelings, and delineating behavioral and cognitive components of their pattern. Because many procrastinators have negative feelings regarding their procrastination, a critical focus in this session is helping participants to see the benefits associated with procrastination, along with the problems.

Because beliefs about past performance influence individuals' abilities to complete tasks (Bandura, 1986; Ferrari, 1992a; Tuckman & Sexton, 1990), providing participants with a new framework for viewing their ability to be successful in their efforts to change their procrastination tendencies is a primary objective of this session. The feedback of Myers–Briggs scores and subsequent discussion supports students in their exploration of personal strengths and capabilities, thus reinforcing their belief in their own capabilities. The discussion of Myers–Briggs scores and the four procrastination styles encourages participants to consider their self-perceptions and dissect their needs,

EXHIBIT 6.1
Worksheet for Identifying Individual Procrastination Patterns

---

Name:

Procrastination style: ___ Politician ___ Perfectionist ___ Postponer ___ Punisher

Myers–Briggs type:

Self-description: Indicate characteristics that describe you. Also describe how these characteristics are important for understanding the situations in which you procrastinate.

Three problem areas: Use your recordings in the past week's procrastination journal to describe three major problems you experienced as a result of procrastination.

1. _____

2. _____

3. _____

My procrastination pattern:

Affect: Identify various positive and negative feelings you associate with procrastination (e.g., relief, fear, uncertainty, guilt, hope).

Behaviors: Specify typical procrastinatory actions or activities that you do or do not do (e.g., study at last minute, arrive late, overextend yourself).

Cognitions: Describe typical thoughts associated with procrastination (e.g., "I'll never change," "I can get this done easily if I study all night").

Personal analysis:

Positive outcomes of procrastination (e.g., I feel motivated by deadlines, I enjoy time with friends)·

Negative outcomes of procrastination (e.g., I get lower grades then desired, others find me undependable):

Insights about powerlessness and procrastination (e.g., I feel academically confident when I talk about an assignment, but working on it can produce fear and worry):

Options: Indicate the patterns and problems that you want to change and prioritize them (e.g., improve self-management to reduce conflict with partner):

Control strategies: Specify plans for gaining greater personal power (e.g., I will change my approach to my academic schedule so I can earn better grades):

---

values, actions, typical thoughts, common feelings, and motivations. In discussing the connection between their personality style and procrastination patterns, participants explore avenues that allow them to assert control.

The focus of the session is on helping participants begin to develop greater feelings of personal power. Working in pairs, they brainstorm actions they can take to experience greater control over their lives. The counselor guides the questioning process when necessary to assist pairs who are experiencing difficulty with this discovery process. Each participant is asked to delineate one action that will facilitate greater personal esteem and self-worth. For example, a task-focused perfectionist and intuitive thinker identified her problem area as not doing a library writing assignment until she was certain the idea was a good one. Each time she thought about the paper, she worried more. Her plan included listing several specific writing and research tasks so that "doing" could replace worrying. This example contrasts with that of an extraverted politician, who described feeling over-extended because she was unable to say no to others. Her plan was to reduce the amount of time devoted to volunteering and spend this time at the library studying.

The counselor then leads a general discussion, in which participants reveal at least one activity they do that reinforces their sense of control and personal power. Homework plans focus on strategies for developing goals. Participants learn basic information about delineating goals. Research indicates that successful goals are specific, time limited, attainable, and realistic (Locke, Shaw, Saari, & Latham, 1981; Stark, Shaw, & Lowther, 1989). The counselor guides participants in setting daily and weekly goals using a STAR framework that incorporates these four criteria into a personal plan for gaining greater personal control, changing behaviors, and building increased confidence in their ability to achieve. Goals are designed to foster feelings of positive, productive accomplishment. The session ends with a round-robin exercise in which participants reveal their specific, success-focused goals for the upcoming week.

Session 3: Productive Thinking and Peer Support

Session 3 commences with the usual sharing of successes from the past week. Each participant is encouraged to identify at least one positive accomplishment from that week, as well as the feelings and thoughts they experience as they develop greater personal control. After reviewing positives, participants next identify any difficulties or problems they experienced during the week and describe the thoughts and feelings associated with these situations. This review is followed by a general brainstorming discussion of the typical thoughts and associated feelings demonstrated by procrastinators. Group members categorize these thoughts as being associated with one of the four types of procrastination. This process allows participants to observe the repetitive nature and themes of the thought patterns.

The group leader provides a handout outlining the steps of rational–emotive behavior therapy (Ellis & Grieger, 1977; Meichenbaum, 1977). The counselor explains various patterns of thinking and asks participants to identify irrational cognitions and to suggest ways to replace nonproductive thinking with productive thinking. The participants work in pairs to identify personal examples of procrastination and the typical thinking strategies associated with procrastination. Each partner assumes the role of the problem-solving peer consultant, expert, or teacher. This role of peer mentor is important in fostering a sense of personal confidence in one's ability to teach productive thinking strategies. During this peer-teaching process, the peer consultant focuses on the typical thoughts of the partner and presents options for replacing nonproductive thoughts. Partners then reverse roles and repeat this process. Together they identify productive thinking patterns each will practice during the next week and include this along with their plan for changing one behavioral component of their procrastination pattern. In their journals, students list the cognitive strategies that will help them during the week.

The homework emphasizes thinking strategies along with one behavioral goal. At least once each day, participants are to review their personal list of productive cognitive strategies, record their self-talk, and practice reframing thinking that is nonproductive. They are to keep track of their progress behaviorally and cognitively. Peer support is an integral part of this intervention. Thus, partners agree to contact and assist one another during the week via a meeting or telephone call. Group members are instructed to assume the peer consultant role so that they can explore difficulties, identify thoughts, reinforce productive thinking, and encourage each other. The session ends with a round-robin sharing by participants of individual thinking and behavioral plans for the week.

Session 4: Focusing on Fears

Session 4 opens with the sharing of positive cognitive or behavioral accomplishments from the past week and the peer support activities they provided to each other. This session builds on the previous session by directing participants to recognize fears that fuel procrastination and the thinking connected with these fears. The counselor asks participants to explore the connections between their fears, family messages, needs, and personal avoidance tendencies. Other emotional reactions are also shared. Following this self-disclosure and analysis, individuals use the cognitive reframing model that was introduced in the previous session as a means of reducing the fears they have isolated as influencing their procrastination.

Facing fears and overcoming their influence provides an important basis for gaining greater personal power. The counselor encourages the revealing of strategies for reducing fear with questions such as "What do you do when you feel apprehensive or afraid?" and "Can you imagine what you could do differently in order to feel greater control? The counselor supplements this discussion with other pragmatic strategies that can reduce fear, such as exercise, progressive relaxation, or getting support from others (C. E. Walker, 1975). Then the counselor leads the group in a directed fantasy–relaxation exercise and breathing techniques for anxiety reduction.

The homework for the session reinforces the actions of the previous week; students continue to record progress in reframing thinking and behavioral changes for the upcoming week. In their journals, participants are to record their observations and reflect on the relationship of their thinking patterns to their personal commitment levels. They are encouraged to evaluate the connection of their thoughts to their confidence in their ability to change components of their procrastination patterns. To prepare for the upcoming session, they are asked to select one typical day in the week and to keep a log or diary of all of their activities on that day. After collecting this information, they are to categorize their 24-hour time log into four quadrants (maintenance, studying, social, and renewal) and bring this information to the next session. The session ends with group members enumerating their list of strategies for gaining greater personal control and feeling greater personal power.

Session 5: Taking Time Back

Students begin session 5 by sharing the cognitive strategy that was most helpful to them during the week. Using the information from their time logs, individuals categorize and diagram their typical uses of time. Questions by the group leader encourage participants to discover the fit between time use and their personal priorities—for example, "What does the picture of how you spend time reveal?" and "In order to achieve your life goals, how does your diagram have to change?" Further probing requires participants to clarify the choices they make and determine the influence of those choices on their personal patterns of time use. This session strives to assist participants in integrating the information they learned in previous sessions into a personalized self-management plan. During the general group discussion, individuals identify strategies they use to take greater control of their time. Then individuals who share time use and procrastination patterns are grouped together to focus on a process of problem-solving personal procrastination patterns. Individually, participants complete the four-step problem-solving handout, which consists of identifying a problem, brainstorming solutions, selecting a realistic option, and delineating a plan of action. In small-group discussion, they seek feedback and suggestions for alternatives, thus allowing each member options for revising their plans for improved time management and self-control. The counselor then reviews the plans to ensure that each plan includes affective, behavioral, and cognitive strategies for improved self-management. Group members then contract with one another to follow this plan for the next week. The session ends with each participant presenting his or her self-management plan to the group.

Session 6: Making Changes That Make a Difference

The final session provides an opportunity for individuals to clarify and summarize their progress during the group sessions. It begins as usual with students highlighting their successes of the past week regarding their homework assignments. This reflection is followed by the sharing of specific personal stories around the theme of greater personal control of one's time and self. Participants reflect on the changes they have made, the insights they have developed, and the tools they are using to enhance their feelings of personal mastery and positive self-worth. The counselor directs participants to focus primarily on their accomplishments as well as on their awareness of the typical thoughts and feelings they associate with the improvements they perceive. After individually summarizing the areas in which they have developed some skills and identifying the techniques they prefer to use as core ingredients in their personal mastery plan, they design a brief 1-month plan to reinforce their current success. Group members' plans incorporate their success levels, motivational needs, control strategies, and selection of relevant personal management techniques that they believe they can effectively use. These plans reflect the preferences of the individual, so some emphasize primarily behaviors, others emphasize cognitive approaches, and still others emphasize an integration of the two. All of these plans use the specifics of goal setting learned earlier, which include establishing concrete criteria as a means of measuring success. The session ends with individuals sharing their goals for continuing their personal journey of self-mastery

RESULTS AND DISCUSSION

Throughout the group treatment, the 12 study participants disclosed their ongoing reactions regarding their progress in changing procrastination patterns. As the sessions progressed, group members became more proficient in identifying areas of personal success and using this information to focus their planning to continue their progress. Discussions revealed that individuals experienced enhanced feelings of self-worth and greater confidence in their capabilities to procrastinate less.

TABLE 6.1
Means and Standard Deviations of Procrastination Scale Scores, by Treatment Condition

Group	N	Before treatment		After treatment		Change
		M	SD	M	SD	
Procrastination	12	16.6	3.3	13.0	4.3	−3.6
Study skills	37	9.5	4.7	7.6	4.0	−1.9
Control	19	6.8	3.4	6.5	3.8	−0.3

To evaluate the success of this group treatment, participants' scores on Lay's Procrastination Scale (Lay, 1986) were assessed at both the beginning and end of treatment. The change in participants' procrastination scores before and after treatment was compared with similar scores of students in a study skills group and others in a control group. Table 6.1 contains the means and standard deviations of the scale scores by treatment condition. A Group × Time repeated measures analysis of variance was conducted on the Lay Procrastination Scale scores for all groups. Significant main effects for group, $F(2, 56) = 18.05$, $p < .01$, and, time interaction $F(1, 65) = 17.49$, $p < .01$, were found. A significant Group × Time interaction, $F(2, 65) = 3.39$, $p < .05$, also was found. Post hoc tests indicated that the greatest decrease in procrastination, as measured by the scale scores, occurred for individuals attending the procrastination group.

The evaluation of this counseling approach supports the value of an integrated self-efficacy approach to reducing avoidance and procrastination behaviors. The individuals who participated in the multidimensional therapeutic sessions reported greater decreases in self-assessed procrastination than students who participated in traditional study skills sessions or a student transition support group. The results support the importance of providing procrastinators with affective, behavioral, and cognitive strategies aimed at increasing personal confidence and competence as a significant means of addressing the powerlessness cycle of procrastination.

Although the results indicate the success of this therapeutic approach in reducing procrastination, there are several limitations to this evaluation. The purpose of this study was to evaluate the effectiveness of a treatment approach. Consequently, the sample was nonrandom, and the findings may not be representative of the university population in general. The data lack behavior samples that could assess the extent to which the procrastinating behavior actually decreased. Because the Lay Procrastination Scale is a trait measure, the results of this study would be strengthened if there were long-term measures to assess whether treatment gains were maintained over time. Also, no information was collected on the effectiveness of particular components of the program as they relate to individuals' self-perceptions of personal efficacy. The findings of this study suggest that more research is needed to more clearly understand the precise effects of treatment on the complex interactions among self-confidence, self-esteem, and procrastinators' beliefs in their ability to take charge of their lives, develop new habits, and eliminate procrastination patterns.

7

BEHAVIORAL INTERVENTIONS FOR REDUCING PROCRASTINATION AMONG UNIVERSITY STUDENTS

BRUCE W. TUCKMAN AND HENRI C. SCHOUWENBURG

This chapter describes two different behavioral intervention programs for reducing college students' procrastinating or delaying behaviors. The first intervention, called Strategies for Achievement, is an academic study skills course based on four major psychological strategies. It combines conventional and Web based instruction to provide students with a supportive learning environment. It was developed and used by the first author in the United States.

The second intervention program, called Task Management Groups, consists of formal support groups that enable students to work together in a systematic way to effectively manage their time. Its instructional approach focuses on specific, concrete, measurable, and realistic behaviors. It was developed in the Netherlands and used there by the second author.

Both programs represent behavioral interventions that seek to modify inappropriate behaviors by controlling stimuli in the environment that act as consequences and antecedents (Cullinan, 2002; Kavale, Forness, & Walker, 1999; Mathur, Quinn, & Rutherford, 1996). Behavioral approaches have been used extensively with children and adolescents who have emotional and behavioral disorders to help them alter their dysfunctional behavior in the school setting. A behavioral procedure called *functional analysis* can be used to identify controlling stimuli in the environment and thus indicate what environment changes can be made to modify the behaviors (Gresham, Quinn, & Restori, 1999). Students behaving inappropriately often represent these controlling stimuli as thoughts; hence the importance of changing these thoughts.

Procrastination can be defined as an interactive dysfunctional and behavior avoidance process characterized by the desire to avoid an activity, the promise to get to it later, and the use of excuse making to justify the delay and avoid blame (Ellis & Knaus, 2002). Given these characteristics, it is possible to alter the behavior through behavioral intervention. Indeed, if this behavior is often reinforced (as Ellis & Knaus, 2002, claim) by success after last-minute cramming, which strengthens the belief in this approach as a viable strategy, it would clearly suggest a link between behavior and consequences. Because there is some evidence that procrastination is associated with poor academic performance (B. L. Beck, Koons, & Milgram, 2000) and is a source of personal stress (Tice & Baumeister, 1997) among college students whose lives are filled with deadlines, it would appear to be a difficult behavior to change.

The two intervention programs described in this chapter include specific behavioral antecedents and consequences that are typical of other such programs. The antecedents fall into the following three categories: (a) restructuring the environment, (b) using social influence, and (c) providing training (Cullinan, 2002). Regarding restructuring the environment, likely possibilities for success include giving students frequent tasks or deadlines to make it easier for them to self-regulate, which is a particular weakness of procrastinators (Ferrari, 2001; Tice & Baumeister, 1997). Restructuring the environment also provides procrastinators with greater extrinsic motivation, an important component in guiding their active behavior (Brownlow & Reasinger, 2000). Tuckman (1998) found that procrastinators' achievement level on midterm and final exams was dramatically higher than nonprocrastinators when they were quizzed every week in comparison with having weekly homework assignments, suggesting that the quizzes "forced" procrastinators to do serious studying on a timely basis.

Other environmental structuring interventions to combat procrastination include the provision of benchmarks for self-appraisal (e.g., self-tests with criteria for mastery indicated) and external monitoring (e.g., teachers checking to see if work is in progress). This restructuring can be accomplished either in a totally impersonal way, such as being required to submit preliminary drafts of a paper or having published performance standards, or socially, by peers, which leads to the second category of interventions—social influence.

Social influence interventions include aspects such as conveying expectations (e.g., "I expect you to be able to complete 30 problems by Friday!") and urging (e.g., "I know you can finish those problems on time if you begin today!"). These techniques, reported by Bandura (1986, 1997), can lead to increases in self-efficacy (a quality closely akin to self-esteem), which Ferrari (2000) found to be lacking in procrastinators. Public commitment (e.g., telling a group of people that one will finish a particular assignment by this time next week) is another social technique, used in well-known programs such as Weight Watchers. Another procedure involves sponsorship (e.g., being assigned someone to call if one is thinking of breaking a commitment) as used in Alcoholics Anonymous.

The third category of behavioral intervention, training, consists of teaching procrastinators specific techniques for managing their time and keeping themselves on task. Daily schedules, to-do lists, statements of goals, and daily performance targets are some examples. Training is often combined with environmental restructuring and social influence to maximize the impact of a behavioral intervention program.

There is also the matter of consequences, a sine qua non of behavioral intervention. An important element of consequences is accountability, with external monitoring and performance standards acting as necessary antecedents. Positive versus negative performance outcomes clearly represent consequences, along with social embarrassment and rejection as typical byproducts of social monitoring. Consequences should also have a degree of inevitability, because it is well known that chronic procrastinators become adept at the use of excuses, even fraudulent ones, to minimize or altogether avoid consequences (Ferrari et al., 1998).

Although effective behavioral approaches to improve academic performance may use a single form of intervention, the programmatic approach—using many different forms—is more likely to be effective (Hattie, Biggs, & Purdie, 1996). The two programmatic approaches described in this chapter combine environmental restructuring, social influence, and training and are carried out over a sufficient period of time to help students learn how to minimize dilatory behavior.

STRATEGIES FOR ACHIEVEMENT—A WEB-BASED COURSE

Strategies for Achievement is an elective course offered at the Ohio State University. It has been designed, in regard to both content and form of instruction, to serve as a behavioral intervention to assist students in improving their study skills and motivation, with particular emphasis on helping them conquer procrastination. It carries a grade counting toward a student's grade point average (GPA) and meets for 4 1/2 hours per week for 10 weeks.

Background and Content

The purpose of the course is to teach students a set of learning and motivation strategies that enable them to improve their achievement in college. Between one third and one half of all students who take the course are in serious academic difficulty and were advised to take the course by their academic counselors. At the beginning of the course, entering students take the Tuckman Procrastination Scale (Tuckman, 1991). Scores on this scale indicate that procrastination is a serious problem for a majority of course takers. Indeed, we found that compared with a university-wide sample, course takers scored 26% higher on average. We focus half the course time on motivation and self-regulation, with specific units on overcoming procrastination, building self-confidence, building responsibility, and managing one's life. All four units apply directly or indirectly to conquering procrastination. The remainder of the course deals with cognitive strategies for studying.

The Strategies for Achievement approach to improving students' learning and motivation skills evolved from the achievement motivation model espoused by McClelland in the 1960s (e.g., McClelland, 1965), expanded and updated in its application to include both social–cognitive theory (Bandura, 1977, 1997; Weiner, 1995) and schema theory (Anderson, 1995). It can be considered an educational psychology approach, as it represents the application of psychological theories to solving the educational problem of improving student achievement in college.

The four basic learning and motivation strategies for achievement used in the current approach (Tuckman, 2003; Tuckman, Abry, & Smith, 2002) are as follows: (a) take moderate risk, (b) take responsibility for your outcomes, (c) search the environment, and (d) use feedback. Prior work suggests that the use of strategies such as these increases learners' motivation and subsequent achievement (McClelland, 1979). For purposes of instruction, each strategy is subdivided into two substrategies. The substrategies and abbreviated reminders that accompany each strategy are listed in Table 7.1.

In support of the proposed strategies and substrategies, current theory and research in educational psychology that has directly addressed the issue of increasing student achievement in school is relevant. Garcia and Pintrich (1994) offered a framework for self-regulation at the college level that includes two components—motivation and cognition—and two sources of influence—(a) knowledge and beliefs and (b) strategies. With respect to the motivation component, which is particularly relevant to the issue of procrastination, Bandura (1997) identified ways people can be the agents of their own self-regulation and success based on the beliefs they have in their own capability. Zimmerman (1998) presented a conceptualization of academic studying in terms of underlying dimensions that students can self-regulate, and Zimmerman, Bandura, and Martinez-Pons (1992) showed links from both beliefs in one's ability to self-regulate and grade goals to final grades. Tuckman (1991, 1996, 1998) demonstrated a method for increasing students' motivation to engage in academic tasks, such as studying, and to use self-regulation strategies as an aid to academic productivity. Clearly, self-regulation is an

TABLE 7.1
The Strategies for Achievement Approach

Strategy	Substrategy	Reminder
Take moderate risk—the empowering strategy	Set goals that are challenging but attainable	Go for goal
	Break tasks down into small, manageable steps	Bite-size pieces
Take responsibility for your outcomes—the belief strategy	Believe in your own effort and capability	Think positive
	Build a plan	Plan!
Search the environment— the action strategy	Ask questions	Just ask
	Build models	Visualize it
Use feedback—the reaction strategy	Monitor your actions	Keep track
	Give yourself instructions	Tell yourself

important factor in school achievement and one that requires using all four of the strategies for achievement.

Particular emphasis in the Strategies for Achievement training is placed on Bandura's (1977) concept of reciprocal determinism, or the mutually interactive relationship among thoughts, behaviors, and environmental consequences. This concept involves all four of the strategies and is applied directly in training students to overcome procrastination, build self-confidence, and manage their lives. In addition, Graham (1997) developed an approach for changing students' perceptions of the intentionality of others' actions. This work, combined with that of Bandura and the others described in this section, forms the basis for using the strategies of taking moderate risk, taking responsibility, and using feedback to train students to build self-confidence, take responsibility, overcome procrastination, and manage their lives. The overall approach is operationalized in the course textbook *Learning and Motivation Strategies: Your Guide to Success* (Tuckman et al., 2002).

In the module on procrastination, students are first taught to distinguish between rationalizations for procrastination, such as "I work better under pressure," and real reasons, such as self-doubt. Second, they are taught to recognize the thoughts, feelings, and behaviors that are provoked by potentially difficult situations. For example, an impending math midterm may lead students to think that math is confusing, causing fear and resulting in the tendency to avoid going to class. Third, they are taught to counter the tendency to procrastinate by using the four major strategies for achievement. Finally, they learn how to effectively manage their time by creating a to-do checklist, a self-regulatory procedure that facilitates planning.

In the module on building self-confidence, the four techniques taught to students—regulating emotional level, seeking affirmation, picking the right models, and "just doing it"—are based on Bandura's (1977, 1986, 1997) four sources of self-efficacy information. In teaching students to take responsibility, causal explanations and their properties as described in attribution theory (Weiner, 1986, 1995) are used to show students the importance of focusing on effort as the explanation for their outcomes.

Instructional Model

Instead of instruction in a traditional class setting, the course is taught using a hybrid, Web-based instructional model called Active Discovery And Participation through Technology (ADAPT; Tuckman, 2002b). This model for teaching a Web-based course in a campus-based computer classroom (i.e., a "hybrid") combines the critical features of traditional classroom instruction (i.e., required attendance, a printed textbook, presence of an instructor) with those of computer-based instruction, which include class time spent doing computer-mediated activities rather than listening to lectures, a large number of performance activities rather than just two or three exams, and self-pacing with milestones rather than a lockstep pattern.

The training, in its Web-based format, has 216 learning performance activities in the following categories:

- quick practices (exercises with automatic feedback)
- assignments (exercises with teacher feedback)
- applications (assignments done with a partner)
- self-surveys (self-reflective questionnaires)
- self-assessments (self-judgments of competence on the objectives)
- spot quizzes (end-of-module tests on the objectives)
- online, threaded discussions on the use of the strategies in module content and in a biographical supplementary course reading about an inner-city student's academic experiences
- portfolios (transfer tasks directly involving the application of the strategies to other courses or to life in general)
- papers based on the biographical reading (requiring the application of the strategies to the life of the person described)

All activities other than the portfolios and papers can be submitted only electronically (into a database for grading and feedback) and only from the special lab in which the course is taught. Specific examples of performance activities are listed in Table 7.2.

The instructional purpose for the multiple learning performance activities is twofold: (a) to provide the practice necessary for changing behavior and (b) to provide opportunities for transfer. Practice has been shown to be essential in enabling students to become accustomed to and adept at performing a behavior (Ericsson, 1996). Transfer is much more likely to occur if

TABLE 7.2

Some Examples of the 216 Learning Performance Activities

Type of activity	Description
Quick practice from Managing Your Life module	It's a Saturday night. You're out drinking with your friends. You realize that you've already had as much as you can handle, so you tell them you've had enough and are going home. They start trying to convince you to stay, then start calling you names. You think, "What a sorry bunch of jerks!" and split. Identify instances of *person, behavior,* and *environment* and write them in the order that indicates the sequence of events.
Application from Procrastination: The Thief of Time module	Pick one of the rationalizations for procrastinating listed in Self-Survey 3.2, and write a one-paragraph scenario that illustrates it, including (a) Who is involved? (b) What is the situation? (c) What is the rationalization being used?
Assignment from Believing in Yourself: Self-Confidence module	Describe a specific skill where you have doubts about your own capability. List five negative thoughts you think about yourself in this area. For each negative thought, write an affirmation or positive thought to replace it.
Portfolio from Procrastination: The Thief of Time module	Take the courses for which you are registered this term and create a comprehensive to-do checklist for a 1-week period. Start from today, and list 30 tasks that you have to complete in the next week. Break down each task into 30-minute segments, and include breaks.

training is done in the target context (Hattie et al., 1996). Portfolios and papers present an opportunity for students to apply the strategies they are learning to other subjects and to the life of a person outside of themselves.

Behavioral Intervention Features

The course uses all three behavioral intervention categories to help students conquer procrastination. Clearly, it involves training, insofar as it explicitly teaches strategies for life management and techniques for applying them directly to the area of personal procrastination (e.g., to-do checklist, self-confidence building). The course also provides sufficient opportunities for actual practice and transfer, through the learning performance activities, to enable students to internalize the strategies and techniques and incorporate them into future behavior. Additionally, the course has the attractive feature of being offered as a five-credit letter-graded university course, increasing the likelihood of student attendance, participation, and motivation.

In addition, the course uses many techniques for environmental restructuring in its teaching approach as designed behavioral interventions to help students overcome procrastination. Chief among them are the 216 performance tasks and the deadlines or "windows" that govern their use, all made possible by the technology-driven instructional model. All electronically submitted performance tasks (i.e., all but the 10 portfolios and four papers) have windows, or dates during which students have access to them on the computer. Outside of these time periods, the tasks are inaccessible. This window structure serves as a time management tool; students may not begin before the window opens and then simply rush through the tasks to get them done, nor can they complete them after the window closes, thus denying the possibility of successful procrastination. Because each activity carries a point value for its successful completion (out of a total possible 1,000 points), an opportunity missed is an opportunity lost (especially because computers do not accept excuses). The portfolios and papers also have deadlines, but they may be submitted up to 1 week late, with penalties assessed for late submission.

External monitoring is also a major feature of the instructional model. All performances are reviewed and graded by instructors within the week of their submission, and the grades (as points) are entered into the electronic database for students to review (each has access only to his or her own grades). Feedback is also provided electronically at that time. Consequently, if students are procrastinating, instructors are aware of it very shortly after it occurs, rather than one third or one half of the way through the entire course, as in more traditional instruction.

Finally, social influence is also brought to bear on procrastinators. Instructors hold regular personal meetings with students to urge and encourage them to keep up with the windows and not lose points needlessly. Because instructors are quickly aware of procrastination, they attempt to use their influence to keep it from continuing.

Outcomes

During the 2001–2002 academic year, 252 students took the course. Of these, approximately half were of each gender, one third were minority, and two thirds were freshmen and sophomores. On the basis of data collected from a broad sample of university undergraduates, it is safe to assume that a great number of these students had reasonably strong procrastination tendencies that had adversely affected their academic performance. Indeed, fully one third of these 252 students entered the course with GPAs under 2.2 (on a 0–4 scale), with 2.0 being the minimum requirement to maintain academic status. However, the overwhelming majority showed mastery in the course, with 74% earning grades of A or A–.

For evaluation purposes, these 252 course takers were matched on gender, ethnicity, year in school, and prior cumulative GPA with a sample of students who had not taken the course and we compared the groups on three behavioral achievement measures: (a) GPA for the term the course was taken, (b) GPA for the term the course was taken without the course grade included, and (c) GPA for the term following the one in which the course was

TABLE 7.3

A Comparison of Mean Term GPAs for Students Taking the Strategies for
Achievement Course and Matched Controls Not Taking It

Student group	Same term		Same term without course grade		Following term	
	Mean GPA	SD	Mean GPA	SD	Mean GPA	SD
Course takers	2.97	0.62	2.63	0.79	2.46	0.96
Controls	2.48	0.75	2.36	0.77	2.27	1.04
F ratio	68.69***		7.29**		3.78*	

$*p < .05.$
$**p < .01.$
$***p < .001.$

taken. On all three measures, course takers performed significantly better than their matched controls (Tuckman, 2003). These results are shown in Table 7.3.

These results provide at least indirect evidence that as a behavioral intervention, the course helped students conquer procrastination, insofar as academic achievement, which is normally adversely affected by procrastination, increased. However, further insight into these results can be gained from a consideration of the following finding: Tuckman (2002a) administered the Tuckman Procrastination Scale at the beginning of the course to the 116 students who took the course the first term and then divided them statistically into high, middle, and low thirds. The three groups all had the same prior mean cumulative GPA of 2.4 based on performance in courses that lacked the "antiprocrastination" features of the study skills course. However, in the study skills course, the low procrastinators earned an average grade of 3.6, the midlevel procrastinators 3.4, and the high procrastinators 2.9, the difference being significant at the .01 level. This finding reveals that although all three procrastination groups profited from the course, the worst procrastinators profited the least.

These results suggest that the idea of "conquering" procrastination must be taken in a relative sense, rather than an absolute one. It is more a question of reducing procrastination than of eliminating it, perhaps because of its lengthy reinforcement history, particularly within the academic setting.

TASK MANAGEMENT GROUPS

The second programmatic behavioral intervention approach described in this chapter, Task Management Groups, is offered by student counselors in many Dutch universities. The program is primarily intended for students who find themselves procrastinating at study tasks such as preparing for examinations or finishing final theses. At the University of Groningen, such groups have been organized during the last 12 years. Groups of 12 students on average meet on a weekly basis in sessions of 1 1/2 hours. Students can participate for a period of 1 year, as long as they follow the rules of the group. They enter the group as soon as there is a vacancy and after signing a formal contract in which they promise to follow the rules. The group is supervised by a student counselor, who presents the sessions as a game that can be played only as long as the players strictly obey the rules. Counselors act as games master or host.

Background and Content

The purpose of the group is to get students to follow a regular pattern of studying. Students learn to split up long-term individual study goals into feasible weekly study tasks and to monitor task completion. The drafting of weekly study tasks and the monitoring of their completion are both performed in the group following a fixed routine and very strict rules with respect to task completion and group attendance. These rules include completing one's individual weekly task, attending the group every week, being on time for the group session, and making a required telephone call to one of the other group members to urge them to complete their weekly task.

In each session, the counselor explicitly monitors execution of each rule and notes the results on the personal graph of every group member. Successful observation of each rule is rewarded symbolically with a plus on a performance graph, and a transgression is punished with a minus. Group members who show two minuses in a 3-week period receive a warning, consisting of the obligation to have pluses for the next three consecutive sessions on the rule in question. If during the warning period another minus is received on the relevant rule, the group member is expelled from the group.

Instructional Model

During group sessions, participants are taught to formulate their weekly study tasks in SMART terms; they must list *specific* and concrete activities that are *measurable*, either in number of pages or hours spent on them; *acceptable* to themselves; *realistic* or objectively feasible; and *timed*, or arranged within a concrete schedule of when work on them will occur. Group members mutually assist one another in drafting, discussing, and evaluating study plans in two rounds of exactly 15 minutes each. During these rounds group members work in pairs, with each member having a fixed role of either "booster" or student. The student of the pair drafts his or her weekly plan and reports on the completion of the previous plan. The booster assists actively in drafting the plan in SMART terms and evaluates completion of the student's previous plan. There is no prescription for the size of the planned task, and a student is held responsible for his or her own study progress. Every group member is a student during one 15-minute round and a booster during the other 15-minute round.

After the two planning rounds, the counselor conducts a 10-minute businesslike plenary monitoring round, during which the rule observation results are noted on personal graphs that are displayed publicly on the course room wall. An additional rule during this monitoring round is that excuses are not acceptable. Evaluations are made on the basis of behavior only.

Following the monitoring round, there is a more extensive, 35-minute plenary planning round, also conducted by the counselor, in which all group members present and explain their weekly study plans to the group. Group members may discuss individual plans before formally approving them. After this planning round, coffee and cake are served in a more informal atmosphere to provide a final 15-minute period of relaxation and reward for group attendance.

Behavioral Intervention Features

Task Management Groups efficiently combine all three features of behavioral intervention. They restructure the individual's study environment by splitting up large end goals, which can be demotivating, into manageable weekly tasks and by providing weekly deadlines and feedback on task completion instead of only one deadline and one result at the end of a 6-week period or a 3-month term. Completion of an intended task creates satisfaction and the experience of success. Repeated success experiences make studying a more pleasant activity than before, thus increasing intrinsic motivation.

Being a member of a group means being subject to social influence. The group conveys its expectations to its members—namely, that they will obey the group rules, particularly by completing their weekly study task. Moreover, boosters urge their fellow students by telephone during the week to complete their tasks. The pairing of booster and student can be regarded as an example of sponsorship, providing both the expression of group support and a source of influence on student behavior. Finally, public presentation of new weekly individual study task plans and formal approval of them by the group constitute an instance of public commitment that in the case of violation leads to severe loss of face.

Providing information—that is, training—takes place mainly during the two rounds of booster–student pairs in the form of informal instruction in effective study planning techniques that is provided by the more experienced students in their role of booster. In addition, the games master provides planning materials such as schedules and to-do list formats. The lengthy duration of group membership, with its recurrent episodes of information transmission and feedback, makes the experience a very effective form of training.

Finally, the consequences of group membership, as long as one adheres to its rules, are inevitable. There is a session every week throughout the year at a fixed time where a group member must be present, must report the results of his or her study plan, must be evaluated, and must draft a new plan for the week to come. In this way, study progress becomes visible. In the case of writing a final thesis, for example, there are clear performance outcomes in the form of chapters completed. Such concrete outcomes result in feelings of confidence and of realistic optimism. In addition, group acceptance, or the fear of rejection in case of failure, sustains this growing awareness of competence.

Outcomes

One of the best qualitative outcomes is the fact that Task Management Groups have become popular among students at the University of Groningen. In the past 12 years, more than a thousand students have been group members, and quite a few of them have occasionally published favorable testimonials in the university newspaper. A systematic qualitative evaluation procedure was conducted in the mid-1990s among former group members of three consecutive years ($n = 134$), providing a number of details about the course's outcomes.

To begin with, students joined a Task Management Group because they procrastinated in their academic work (mean score of 4.3 on a procrastinatory behavior rating scale ranging from 1 to 5, with 5 indicating the highest degree of procrastination). Most participants left the group before the maximum period of 1 year was reached because they had attained a satisfactory study rhythm and enough self-confidence (mean score of 3.0 on the procrastinatory behavior rating scale, a significant decrease). Only 20% of the participants left the group because they had breached the rules and only 10% because they had reached the maximum period of 1 year. Another 10% left because they were not satisfied with the group regimen.

The average satisfaction score was 4.0 on a rating scale ranging from 1 to 5. More than 90% of the participants judged that a Task Management Group was a good aid in getting through a studying impasse. After leaving the group, students reported significant changes in their ability to split subject matter into weekly tasks (difference score 1.3 on a rating scale ranging from 1 to 5), draft a long-term plan (difference score 1.0), monitor study progress (difference score 0.9), study regularly instead of only just before examinations (difference score 1.0), and not do things other than studying at times reserved for studying (difference score 0.9). These differences were all significant ($p < .01$).

It would be too much to expect for behavior intervention programs to eliminate procrastinatory behavior altogether. A recent quantitative evaluation of academic procrastination among participants in Task Management

Groups confirmed this. Responses to the Academic Procrastination State Inventory (Schouwenburg, 1995) in each of 7 consecutive weeks revealed that the average procrastination score remained constant at stanine 5. This score indicates a normal base rate of dilatory study behavior corresponding to that of the general student population. It seems clear then, notwithstanding the satisfaction reported by participants of Task Management Groups, that this approach offers a maintenance schedule for keeping dilatory study behavior at an acceptable base rate level, rather than a total cure for academic procrastination. Nevertheless, this behavioral intervention program is no doubt a valuable addition to the intervention methods student counselors use to support and help procrastinating students.

CONCLUSION

We have attempted to demonstrate that the behavior of procrastinating in an academic setting, and its resulting consequences, may be reduced, if not eliminated, by behavioral intervention programs that rely on environmental restructuring, social influence, and training over reasonably long periods of time. Participation in these programs appeared to significantly reduce students' dilatory behavior, largely as a function of the supports provided by each program. The resulting reduction in procrastination enabled participating students to perform better and achieve better academic results. Were the support systems to be continued or entirely internalized by those who have experienced them, long-term reductions in dilatory behavior would be reasonable to expect. Unfortunately, there are at this point no data available on how long lasting or sustainable the behavior change may be, and we recognize that a return to prior levels of procrastination is not out of the question.

The intensity and duration of programs to curb procrastination may be important variables in their success. The two described in this chapter each operated for a considerable number of hours over an extended period of time. It would be desirable to work on ways to incorporate features of both programs into regular university courses or ongoing student affairs activities. Residence halls may be likely candidates for places to locate the elements of such programs.

Finally, it must be noted that participation in these kinds of programs is voluntary and reflects a preexisting degree of motivation to reduce or control the tendency to procrastinate and minimize its undesirable consequences. Questions regarding the effects of such programs on an involuntary basis, or their persistent or long-term impact, remain to be answered.

8

A COGNITIVE–BEHAVIORAL APPROACH IN GROUP TREATMENT OF PROCRASTINATORS IN AN ACADEMIC SETTING

WALTER VAN HOREBEEK, SOFIE MICHIELSEN,
ANNE NEYSKENS, AND ERIC DEPREEUW

This chapter summarizes our practical experience in organizing group training sessions for students with extreme procrastination problems. These sessions are organized within the Psychotherapeutic Student Center (PSC), which is part of the Student Facilities of the Catholic University of Louvain in Belgium and offers a wide range of psychotherapy from different psychotherapeutic disciplines. The PSC is accessible to all university students, and for some years now it has also been open to all higher education students from the Louvain district.

The group procrastination training is delivered by the behavioral therapists of the PSC. Beyond the group training, there is no other individual program for procrastinators, except for non-Dutch-speaking students or students who would clearly be excluded from this group due to personal characteristics (e.g., age of older working students or serious pathology). For these other clients there is an individual coaching program. In the summer term individual coaching for procrastination is also possible.

TARGET GROUP FOR PROCRASTINATION TRAINING

The procrastination training target group consists of students who exhibit extreme study delay problems. We focus on those students who show a large discrepancy between their intentions and their behavior. These individuals seem to approach their study projects with a lot of goodwill and courage, but they do not succeed in responding to these intentions in a timely manner with relevant actions, let alone in persisting in these intentions over a longer period. They do share with other students the intention to pass all their examinations, or at least to graduate, but they have extreme difficulty in putting forward the necessary effort or perseverance to reach their objectives.

It is important to mention that students who almost never study or hardly study at all and who show no motivation do not belong to the target group. As a matter of fact, for this group of students there is no procrastination problem; in other words, there is no discrepancy between intention and behavior. Family or friends of these students often find it hard to understand why these students don't belong to the target group of procrastinators and find it hard to understand why we don't allow them in the program.

The following six criteria, as described by Depreeuw, Dejonghe, and van Horebeek (1996), draw a good picture of the kind of student we have in mind for our training sessions:

1. Students enroll themselves more or less voluntarily in the study project and basically know what is to be expected from them with regard to objectives, standards, and time limits.
2. At a certain moment in time, the student must form the intention to achieve an objective or to avoid something negative.
3. Notwithstanding this intention, the specific task behavior is chronically postponed or delayed. Task-relevant behavior is replaced by or goes together with task-irrelevant behavior.
4. Sometimes, or often, the procrastination behavior, directly or indirectly, shows serious negative consequences.
5. From a learning perspective, we assume that this procrastination strategy gains an advantage (analogous to addiction behavior; advantages are seen from a short-term vs. long-term perspective).
6. Apart from an undeniable procrastination problem, these students frequently have other psychosocial problems (e.g., personality disorder, socioeconomic problems). In addition, the question of whether their study problems are caused by or are a consequence of procrastination is not always clear.

STUDENT CONTACT WITH THE
PSYCHOTHERAPEUTIC STUDENT CENTER

Students usually contact the PSC on their own initiative for a variety of reasons. Students presenting themselves at the PSC get at least one appointment for a 50-minute intake conversation. They are asked to complete an application form that requests some general information, reasons for contacting the PSC, and their expectations.

During the first session, which is held from a psychodiagnostic point of view, we examine the problem involved and sound out the students' expectations about our therapeutic options. From our clinical background, we screen the students for general psychopathological disorders (criteria from the *Diagnostic and Statistical Manual of Mental Disorders*, 4th edition; American Psychiatric Association, 1994). Sometimes more than one intake conversation is needed. After this, we discuss each case in our team, and we formulate a proposal for therapy.

If the student has a potential procrastination problem (apart from other possible problems), during this intake session or later during the weekly team meeting we discuss whether the student will be eligible for group procrastination training. If so, we ask him or her to complete a questionnaire that assesses the extent of the procrastination behavior. We use the VaSEV, also called the TASTE (Test Concerning Abilities for Study and Examination; Depreeuw, 1989; Depreeuw, Eelen, & Stroobants, 1996). This 78-item questionnaire contains four subscales: (a) study valuation (14 items), (b) optimistic self-appraisal or task competence confidence (19 items), (c) test anxiety (30 items), and (d) procrastination or effort avoidance (15 items). According to the test manual, the four subscales of the TASTE are sensitive enough to measure real fluctuations and evolutions in the various constructs. Only students reaching a score at the 80th percentile or higher on the procrastination subscale are admitted to the group program. Consequently, this group includes only extremely high scorers. Once this thorough intake assessment is complete, the student can start the program.

The training sessions are not advertised in any organized way. This is a general policy option rather than a specific arrangement for this group of students. Offering more groups would not be feasible and the sessions are always full, so advertising is not necessary. Of course, these training sessions have been organized already for several years and have a good reputation, and we receive many referrals.

Most students contact the center on their own initiative, but some do so on advice from colleagues, student coaches, fellow students, parents, or others. In exceptional cases, students are "obliged" to contact the center as mandated by, among others, academic authorities (e.g., an application for "tris" or "quater" enrollment in which they have to take the exams of one study-year over again for the third or fourth time). Although taking part in the training itself is not an obligation, we are nevertheless aware of the fact that some participants feel obliged to take part. We try to restrict this as much as possible during the interviews preliminary to the training sessions because we are convinced that participation can be useful only when it is based on students' own free, and preferably motivated, choice.

AIM OF THE INTERVENTION

The aim of the program is to diminish the discrepancy between intention and behavior. This discrepancy can be decreased in two ways, and both approaches are of equal value. On the one hand, the intention can be translated into the desired behavior (i.e., behavior moves closer to intention). On the other hand, the intention will move in the direction of some unstated behavior (i.e., intention moves closer to behavior). It is obvious that there is a strong preference for the first direction. In other words, we try to switch the cycle from procrastination, ignorance, discouragement, and demotivation to the cycle of effort, knowledge, motivation, and self-confidence. The intended result is a reduction in dilatory behavior and a countering of the secondary consequences of procrastination and failure, which include low self-confidence, negative self-image, conflicts at home, increasing social isolation in relation to the age group, and health problems (DeWitte & Lens, 2000).

Overall, the objective of the training session is to give the participants insight into the factors and processes that play an important role in causing procrastination. The approach is designed to guide the students in the self-examination of their motivation and reasons for procrastination. We work on behavioral changes only after having mapped the problematic behavior.

THEORETICAL BACKGROUND

As indicated, our intervention program addresses both motivation and applied behavioral analysis. In the next section we deal with the theoretical concept of motivation and its application in the training program. We discuss attitudes, principles, and techniques that we use as behavior therapists in our interaction with students, both individually during the intake session and later in the group program. Our inspiration for this approach can be found in the work of Miller (Miller, 1983; Miller & Rollnick, 2002) and Prochaska and DiClemente (1984).

In the next section, we explore applied behavioral analysis and changing behavior. Students are stimulated to observe their own procrastination behavior. On the basis of learning psychology, we teach them techniques to handle their dilatory behavior.

Stimulating Motivation With Procrastinators

Following Miller and Rollnick (2002), we define *motivation* not as something that does or does not exist, but rather, in this context, as the probability that someone really wants to engage in personal change and continue with a change process. Motivation can be influenced and in our program is conceived of as the product of interaction between therapist and student.

Beginning with our first contact with the students, we specify in detail that there are two ways to deal with procrastination behavior: either to carry through with a change of behavior by exerting the necessary effort or to grow old with the problem. And both choices are presented as of equal value. Changing procrastinatory behavior takes a great deal of effort, and for many students it is a very difficult and unpleasant process. Unlearning procrastination torments the self. There is less time for pleasant and innocent pastimes and for social activity; one must forgo the current affairs of the day and even put up with an unclean and messy residence. One will probably feel more anxious, be confined to a desk, and spend a great deal of time studying to obtain a higher level of performance, even though the higher level of performance is not guaranteed. Certainly, growing old with the problem can be an attractive alternative.

From the first contact and through all sessions, we underline this freedom of choice between changing and not changing. In most cases, even for those who eventually give up, we have provided a new option in their lives, one that was not there before.

Students who have a procrastination problem often recognize the self-destructive consequences (Baumeister & Scher, 1988) of their dilatory behavior. Nevertheless, for a number of reasons, they cling strongly to this behavior, even as they detest the behavior. We understand this as an intrinsic conflict between their approach tendencies and avoidance that has developed over many years. This ambivalence is understandable, and the outside world often considers it to be an indicator of insufficient motivation. Within this perception, we attempt to convince students more and more about the negative consequences of their behavior and about the fact that it is high time they do something about their procrastination. Essentially, we convey to them that "the time is up!" The more we try to persuade some of them, however, the more they may reply with conditions beginning, "Yes, but. . . ." In this way, these students in the end persuade themselves of the advantages of their troublesome behavior and convince the therapist that they are unmotivated. Our interventions are oriented toward setting into motion a process that will shift the equilibrium in small increments so that change may begin. Instead of arguing, we use the students' resistance to change their perceptions and to propose new points of view.

This change process often goes slowly. "Take your time" is the phrase we often use. The process of changing behavior is rotated over six stages (Prochaska & DiClemente, 1984; Prochaska, DiClemente, & Norcross, 1992): precontemplation, contemplation, decision making, active change, stabilization, and relapse. To motivate also means to anticipate appropriately the students' state of willingness. It is important to know which stage a student is in. It is, for example, useless to try to raise the amount of study hours when a student is in the precontemplation stage.

We make the assumption that participation in the group program does not automatically mean that a student has made the decision to change his or her procrastination behavior. During the first sessions, we do not talk about changes, and we do not discuss time management (the planning of study hours). Rather, we ask, "What are you intending to do? What is your plan?" Within this framework, we submit three further questions to the students that they must ask themselves:

1. Do I really want to succeed this year, and if so, what do I want to achieve through this in my life?
2. Am I prepared to meet, therefore, all the requirements stated by the university?
3. If I study long enough with high intensity, what are the advantages and disadvantages?

Applied Behavioral Analysis

As a theoretical background to situate their procrastination, we offer the students the process model regarding task behavior by Depreeuw (e.g., Lens & Depreeuw, 1998; Vanden Auweele, Depreeuw, Rzewnicki, & Ballon, 1999). The student tries to fit his or her own procrastination behavior into this model. By formulating the problem in terms of task behavior and by emphasizing its processlike nature, the focus is no longer on the static aspects of procrastination. As a result, students gain insight into experiences and thoughts and can now view them in different ways. The problem then becomes easier to handle, and the student recovers control of something that seemed to be unchangeable.

Students have to analyze and evaluate their own pattern of behavior in terms of reasons for procrastination and possible consequences in the future. Within the group, we discuss in detail self-observation with regard to dilatory behavior. From this, we deduce an accurate description of the internal and external procrastination antecedents, of the real procrastination behavior, and of the possible positive and negative consequences.

Together with each student, we put this information in an SORC diagram (see Exhibit 8.1). The S stands for the inventory of all antecedents preliminary to the procrastination behavior, as well as for the context of procrastination (Situation or Stimulus). The R indicates the patterns of be-

EXHIBIT 8.1
Example of Applied Behavioral Analysis of
Typical Procrastination Behavior

SORC Diagram of Task-Relevant Behavior				
S (situation)	**R** (responses)	**C (consequences)**		End result of procrastination
		Short run (−) +S−	Long run (−) −S+	
Study desk Textbook	Read Study	Aversive sensations Fatigue Loneliness	Failure Bad grades	Task-relevant behavior is extinguished.

Note. +S− = A negative stimulus is added. −S− = A negative stimulus is taken away.

SORC Diagram of Task-Irrelevant Behavior				
S (situation)	**R** (responses)	**C (consequences)**		End result of procrastination
		Short run (+) +S+	Long run (−) +S−	
Friends Internet Dirty room	Visiting Surfing Cleaning	Not alone Fun Clean room	Failure Bad grades Interpersonal conflicts	Task-irrelevant behavior becomes automatic.

Note. +S+ = A positive stimulus is added. +S− = A negative stimulus is added.

havior that are actually set or not (Response or behavior). Under C, we collect all possible positive or negative consequences of procrastination and other behavior (Consequence). The O factor refers to all processes taking place within the intrapsychological process ("black box") of procrastination (Organism). In the last few years, more attention has been paid to the O factor, especially from a cognitive–behavioral therapeutic point of view. The basic assumption is that feelings and behavior are the consequences of the meaning (interpretation) an individual gives to a certain situation. So it is not so much the situation that leads to the procrastination behavior, but the student's *interpretation* of the situation. Therefore, we are interested in the cognitions of the student during procrastination.

Starting from the SORC diagram we pass concrete techniques to the students. In the following paragraphs, we discuss successively the participants' study planning (R), stimulus control (S), self-management of consequence (C), and cognitive aspects of procrastination (O).

One of the central techniques in the group program is time management, or study planning. From the third session on, we direct the students in formulating realistic, clear, and specific objectives regarding their time. On a weekly schedule, based within the perspective of long-term planning, students have to describe how much time they will spend on studying and how much on free time. In doing this, they are describing the R component (behavior). Students initially determine their objectives on their own, giving them sole control over the formulation of intentions, although they may modify these intentions after receiving recommendations from other group members and from the counselor. Every week, students report on their results in the preceding week. The weekly score, or amount of hours spent studying, for each student is displayed on a graph and can be seen by the other members of the group. Over time, this graph represents a view of the development and maintenance of change in the students' behavior. Through this approach, the extent of lost hours through procrastination in preparation for examinations (C component) is clearly visible to all participants. In this context, students cannot help but face reality. Through positive change, students become more hopeful, although unfortunately some view a successful week as an excuse to study fewer hours the following week.

We work with self-controlling procedures (see Kanfer, 1975; Thoresen & Mahoney, 1974) regarding both the S component and the C component. Stimulus control of study behavior with procrastinators begins with a clear view of the S component: Where is the place selected for studying? With whom do they study? How is the study place organized? A suitable place to study is emphasized—for instance, a student's home or at the library. When studying on their own does not seem to be easy for them, students are encouraged to study together with fellow students, preferably with nonprocrastinators. Working with nonprocrastinators models for them more realistic expectations and strategies. Changes in the S component will depend on the individual. For some students, studying at home at their desk will be successful only if certain elements of this environment are first removed, such as the computer and Internet access. For other students, the ideal environment may be just the opposite, in which a computer and Internet access are in reach.

Students also map out the C component, or the positive and negative consequences of the current behavior. Procrastinators have available to them many unconditional, attractive activities that are not linked to the intended study behavior. With students who can hardly get around to studying, we prefer to introduce a system of positive incentive (reward) if they succeed in reaching the assumed objective. We prefer to work with rewards (positive result after a desired behavior) rather than with punishments (negative consequence after a nondesired behavior). If appropriate, however, we implement negative consequences, like not being allowed to go to a party, if the number of intended study hours could not be reached.

As noted previously, the O component refers to the whole of the intrapsychological process of procrastination. We do not consider the impact of the whole O component at length, as we believe that this would only encourage the process of procrastination. In the training sessions, we deal with cognitive restructuring. Ellis and Knaus (2002) indicated that irrational, curbing cognitions really do have an effect on procrastination (see chap.

5, this volume). Ellis's rational–emotive therapy (RET) is based on the idea that it is not the situation itself that involves certain feelings and thoughts, but how one thinks about the situation. The aim of RET is to trace and challenge irrational cognitions to arrive at the formulation of logical, real cognitions and feasible or reasonable objectives.

We use the ABC formulation of the RET, as outlined in the handbook of RET (Ellis & Grieger, 1977). Every student writes down a specific study-related situation in an ABC diagram. Under A they write the real, objective situation. Under C they note the emotional and behavioral consequences. Then they trace the Bs, or the beliefs, which comprise the total amount of thoughts, both rational and irrational. The aim is to let the student recognize that C is not the result of A, the situation, but—on the contrary—of B, particularly the way he or she is thinking in a certain situation. After having inventoried the Bs, they then challenge these thoughts. They examine whether these thoughts correspond to reality or whether they were formulated as adequate objectives. The final aim is to achieve new cognitions, increasing the probability that desired behavior and desired feelings occur.

PROGRAM PROCEDURE

The basic program consists of 10 weekly 1-hour meetings (see Table 8.1). The number of participants is limited to seven students. Students of all ages and disciplines and different types of procrastinators are mixed together. The trainers are always psychologists and behavior therapists. After completing the basic program, students may enroll for five more sessions.

As a stepping-stone to the training sessions, we use Depreeuw's process model (see Vanden, Auweele et al., 1999) regarding task behavior. This provides the students with insight into their own functioning, perhaps as a first step toward change. In this model, eight steps play an important part in performance and task behavior: estimating the interest, estimating the opportunities to succeed, formulating purposes, preparing, performing, self-evaluating the performance, making causal attribution, and mastering a three-level learning process.

Because the group program for procrastination behavior is embedded in the services of a psychotherapeutic center, rather than a student counseling center, we look to a greater extent for psychopathology. The distinction made between a psychotherapeutic center and a student counseling center is specific to the situation at the University of Louvain. Even students with personality disorders (Axis II of the *Diagnostic and Statistical Manual of Mental Disorders*, 4th edition; American Psychiatric Association, 1994) take part in the group program, sometimes in combination with other therapy or medical support.

TABLE 8.1
Intervention Program Content

Session	Content
Intake procedure	TASTE test
1	Introduction
	Discussion of group arrangements (e.g., group confidentiality, active cooperation, payment of deposit)
	Examination of the motivations for procrastination
	Explanation of the process model of task behavior
	Assignment of homework:
	Respond to the three motivation questions
	Read the text about the process model on the basis of chapter 9 of Lens and Depreeuw (1998)
	Fill in the process model using examples of proper studying or lack thereof
2	Discussion of preceding week's homework
	Introduction of the circle of behavioral change (Prochaska & DiClemente, 1984); each student situates himself or herself within this circle
	Introduction of the SORC diagram
	Assignment of homework:
	Think about your own place in the circle of behavioral change
	Fill in the SORC diagram on the basis of registration
3	Discussion of preceding week's homework
	Introduction to time management (study planning), including the weekly graph of hours to study and hours achieved per week
	Assignment of homework:
	Read the Study Planning handout and develop a plan
4	Discussion of preceding week's homework
	Introduction to cognitive restructuring (ABC diagrams)
	Assignment of homework:
	Do study plan
	Work out at least one ABC diagram if the planning has not been achieved
5–9	Continuous self-monitoring, evaluation, and adjustment
10	Self-evaluation in group—progress? stagnation? relapse?
	Discussion of arrangements for the future (e.g., avoiding pitfalls, anticipating difficulties)
	Instruction on relapse prevention

PROGRAM EVALUATION

The data we have collected through the years are based on diagnosis and clinical evaluation rather than empirical measures. The main purpose for obtaining data, up to now, has been to evaluate, on an individual basis, the evolution of the students and not to evaluate the program itself. We have several ways of doing this:

- After the training, there is an evaluation discussion in the group. The graph of each student's weekly study behavior is also considered, with increased time spent closer to examinations taken into account.

- In the last session, students complete the TASTE questionnaire for a second time.
- For some students, it is possible to obtain their academic results.

Although the program has been run for several years, we have reliable information only for the last three academic years. This information is reliable but not complete (e.g., in one training students did not complete the TASTE in the last session, and for some students we could not obtain academic results after the training). The data are summarized in the following sections.

CHARACTERISTICS OF THE PARTICIPATING GROUP

During the academic years 1998–1999, 1999–2000, and 2000–2001, nine procrastination training programs were organized. Thirty-two men and 16 women participated. Before the training, these 48 students had an average loss of curriculum years of 1.8 (minimum 0 years, maximum 5 years lost). In Belgium, depending on the specific study program, academic programs take 4 to 5 years of study. The higher education programs take 3 to 4 years. For each academic year, there is a fixed package of courses for which students have to take exams. In general, students can go on to the next academic year only if they pass all the exams of the previous year. If students don't pass every exam in the package successfully, they fail and are not allowed to go on to the next year. This means they have to take the failed courses for a second time and try to pass the exams, and a year is lost.

As depicted in Table 8.2, we can conclude that the participants were appropriate for our target group. The procrastinators had a much higher average score on the procrastination scale in comparison with the other groups and a higher score on test anxiety in comparison with the norm group of university students (but still lower than the test-anxious students).

EVALUATION OF THE TRAINING PROGRAM

Comments by Participants

Thirty-three of the 48 students completed the program. The comments of these 33 participants indicate that they generally endorsed it as a positive experience. They noted that they gained some insight into their own behavior and were given some means to tackle their behavior prob-

TABLE 8.2
Means and Standard Deviations for the TASTE Scales From the
Procrastinators (*n* = 48) in Comparison With Some Reference Scores
From the Test Manual

	VaSEV (TASTE)			
Group	Procrastination	Study valuation	Self-confidence	Test anxiety
Procrastination group (*n* = 48)				
M	51	55	90	56
SD	8.3	12.3	13.7	8.4
University students (norms; *n* = 865)				
M	49	61	70	40
SD	7.5	10.2	16.7	8.8
Highly test anxious students (*n* = 126)				
M	55	48	106	40
SD	6.9	11.1	15.2	9.4

lem, and most of them found the group format helpful (e.g., because of the recognition and support they received). Many found it a surprise, but also a relief and stimulating, that the focus was kept on their own choice to change or not to change and that the focus was *not* from the beginning on time management. The behavior graph was for some students an incentive, and for others a confrontation.

Even students who showed almost no change in effort but attended the whole training program often commented that the training program was very significant for them. Part of this group did enroll for the follow-up set of five sessions.

TASTE Scores

Table 8.3 shows that students' TASTE scores evolved in the direction desired. On average, the scores on the procrastination scale dropped almost to the score of the norm group. As a side effect, we noticed that for the test anxiety scale, there was a change in the direction of less test anxiety. The average scores of the two other scales did not change.

Academic Performance After the Training Sessions

We were able to obtain the academic results after the training of 29 of the 33 students who completed the program. Of those 29 students, 17 passed their examinations.

TABLE 8.3
Means and Standard Deviations on TASTE Scales Before and After the Training Sessions ($n = 26$)

Group	VaSEV (TASTE)			
	Procrastination	Study valuation	Self-confidence	Test anxiety
Intake				
M	52	54	91	57
SD	9.6	14.9	15.1	10.0
After				
M	49	59	82	45
SD	9.5	11.6	19.0	9.6
University students (norms; $n = 865$)				
M	49	61	70	40
SD	7.5	10.2	16.7	8.8

PROBLEMS ENCOUNTERED IN THE INTERVENTION PROGRAM

Students dropped out at many points during the process, including before the first intake conversation, after the first conversation, before the group program started, and during the group program. This certainly reflects the problem of motivation (there are enough reasons to procrastinate, but only a few to stop it). Seen from the circle of behavioral change (Prochaska & DiClemente, 1984), it seems likely that not every student was in the right stage to start with the training or to wait a little longer. For some students, it would probably be better to start the training immediately, whereas for others it might be better to wait a little bit longer. From a practical and maybe diagnostic point of view, correct timing is not easy to realize.

Another common problem is the comorbidity of procrastination with other psychosocial problems. Students suffering from psychopathology but still manageable within a group training program are also provided with individual therapy or a coaching program. This offers two advantages: First, other forms of serious pathology can be kept out of the training sessions, and in this way the level of pathology in the program will not be raised seriously, and second, individual therapy does not get entangled in the pace of an academic year. On the other hand, there are also significant disadvantages. The time investment required is greater, from both the student's and the PSC's point of view Also, there is the possibility that experiences within the procrastination group will have a negative influence on the individual therapy or vice versa.

RELAPSE PREVENTION

After the training session, we discuss each student's evolution in the group. Working in small groups has the advantage that the therapist gains fairly comprehensive insight into each student and his or her progress and difficulties. After the group evaluation, we recommend that students meet with us to talk a few things through again in an individual conversation. After the training, students can decide on their own whether they want to continue in group for the next set of five sessions.

Students learn to handle relapse prevention during the 10 sessions. When they report moments of relapse during the program, we help them learn skills to deal with possible future relapses.

CONCLUSION

The most striking feature of the course results is the relatively high number of dropouts both before and during the training sessions, in spite of all the formal arrangements and the loss of the deposit. Two out of three students who enroll finish the entire training program (33 of 48 in 3 years); 1 of 10 students drops out before the 5th session.

Overall, however, our results indicate that training can be useful to procrastinators. Satisfactory results of the training sessions were reflected in both the TASTE scores and the students' academic performance. From our perspective, at least, it seems a good idea to continue along the same lines. In addition, further research that we are now conducting should help clarify the effects of the program from a more empirical (i.e., less clinical) perspective.

Beginning in academic year 2001–2002, we introduced a few changes to the program. For example, the additional set of five sessions has been replaced by an open follow-up group of "experts," or students who completed a procrastination training in the past. In addition, through the introduction of the 6-month examination system from the academic year 2001–2002, the 10 one-hour sessions will be replaced by seven 1 1/2-hour sessions.

Based on our experience that there are several types of procrastinators, we are thinking of starting the next academic year with groups composed more homogeneously according to type of procrastination, instead of composing groups based on the R component. Further, we think it would be very interesting to provide more detailed questionnaires on personality at the beginning of the session or during the intake process. In that way, we can examine whether there are elements from an evaluative point of view that may optimize the effectiveness of our intervention program.

9

CONSTRUCTIVE CONFRONTATION: COGNITIVE–BEHAVIORAL THERAPY WITH ONE TYPE OF PROCRASTINATING UNDERACHIEVER

HARVEY P. MANDEL

Approximately 15% to 20% of high school and university students show a significant gap between their potential and their performance (Mandel & Marcus, 1988; McCall, Evahn, & Kratzer, 1992). In addition, almost all of these underachievers report that procrastination is a key ingredient in their deteriorating academic performance (Mandel, 1997; Mandel & Marcus, 1988).

This chapter describes a counseling approach for one type of procrastinator, the academic problem (AP) underachiever (American Psychiatric Association, 2000). This chapter describes the AP underachiever and the use of constructive confrontation as part of cognitive–behavioral therapy (CBT). The chapter concludes with a summary of treatment outcome findings and recommendations for future research.

The confrontive CBT approach presented here has its roots in a research program on procrastination and underachievement conducted in the 1960s through the 1980s with university students at the Illinois Institute of Technology (IIT) in Chicago (Mandel & Marcus, 1988; Roth, 1970). Conceptually, procrastination was viewed as a symptom, and the role it served for the student varied among different types of underachievers (Mandel, Friedland, & Marcus, 1996a, 1996b; Mandel & Marcus, 1988).

The IIT research team found that the most prevalent type of procrastinating underachiever at the university level exhibited no significant internal or interpersonal difficulties, learning disabilities, or attentional problems and was generally well adjusted and well liked. More recent research at the Institute on Achievement and Motivation (IAM) at York University in Toronto has replicated this finding in high school students (Glanz, 1988; Mahy, 1995; McKay, 1985; Mitchell, 2003).

FEATURES OF THE ACADEMIC PROBLEM PROCRASTINATOR

The characteristics of the AP procrastinator are strikingly similar to the description by Lay (1988) and Lay and Burns (1991) of optimistic procrastinators. These students express their optimism through good intentions and a strong belief in their ability to change. However, they resist developing detailed plans for change, preferring to remain vague. When confronted, many are able to verbalize effective problem-solving strategies, and they may initiate some of these actions but rapidly abandon them when external forces appear (e.g., the phone rings, friends ask them out). They use these hindrances as rationalizations to explain why they did not follow through on their original plans. They frequently describe themselves as "lazy and unmotivated," implying that in addition to external forces beyond their control, they are also victims of their own temperament. They report mild tension just before exams and approaching deadlines and some disappointment when their report card arrives. Yet they do not get upset for any significant period of time about the continuing pattern of procrastination. And at the beginning of each term, they show renewed optimism and declare their intentions to do better, implying that they have learned valuable lessons about their procrastination.

The male-to-female sex ratio of high school AP procrastinators is approximately 1:1 (Mitchell, 2003), in contrast to the overall male-to-female underachiever sex ratio, consistently reported as 2:1 (McCall et al., 1992). No sex ratio data exist for university AP procrastinators.

A number of researchers have found that AP procrastinators are not lazy and unmotivated (Mandel & Marcus, 1988; Roth, 1970). AP procrastinators do not want to fail. In fact, they are motivated to get by with a minimal amount of work. But they do not want to assume greater personal responsibility or work more in order to achieve higher marks and increase their options for the future. In brief, they are ambivalent about the future and about change.

For the AP underachiever, procrastination appears to be both a manifestation of ambivalence about the future and an immediate solution to that dilemma. Procrastination serves to delay the dependence–independence struggle while allowing the student to continue to believe that he or she really wants to change. Decreasing marks are best understood in teleological rather than causal terms. AP procrastinators do not take ownership of their procrastination and are not terribly bothered by their circumstances. Their procrastination is much more of a concern to their parents and teachers than to AP students themselves.

ACCURATE ASSESSMENT: THE BRIDGE TO COUNSELING

Because procrastination is common to many types of underachievers, a psychological assessment is recommended. At York University's IAM, we include a review of the student's academic history, cognitive testing to assess whether a learning disability is present, evaluation of academic skills and study habits, screening for attentional problems, achievement motivation and personality testing (Mandel et al., 1996a), and a semistructured diagnostic interview (Mandel & Marcus, 1988) that includes an in-depth discussion of school, family, peer relationships, self-perception, moods, and aspirations for the future. The results of the assessment should distinguish among types of procrastinating underachievers. The confrontive CBT presented in this chapter is contraindicated for other types of procrastinators.

CONSTRUCTIVE CONFRONTATION AND
THE AP PROCRASTINATOR

Models, Techniques, and Structures

Effective counseling of the AP procrastinator is predicated on identifying automatic thoughts (i.e., excuses) and linking these to dysfunctional actions (i.e., procrastination). Students can be taught to identify these maladaptive thoughts, and it is the examination of their maladaptive beliefs that exposes their ambivalence about change and provides an opportunity for change. The approach incorporates CBT principles (J. Beck, 1995; McMullin, 2000; Salkovskis, 1996), principles of constructive confrontation (Egan, 1976), and methods of addressing client ambivalence and resistance (Leahy, 2001; Miller & Rollnick, 2002).

Confrontation can be defined as any comment by the counselor that requires and invites an immediate response from the student because the comment focuses on discrepancies contained in the student's thoughts, feelings, and actions. Confrontation is intended to precipitate a degree of dissonance and disorganization in the student and, if done constructively, leads to increased engagement between the counselor and student. If done destructively or ineffectively, defensive student reactions result, including avoidance of the topic, distortion of the content of the confrontation, devaluation of the importance of the topic, or verbal statements of agreement but an absence of follow-through.

For a confrontation to be constructive, the counselor must ensure that he or she confronts in a focused but gradual manner and that the focus remains more on the current situation and less on the distant past, except when discussing long-standing patterns of procrastination. The confrontation must contain a clear invitation to jointly examine the student's ambivalence about change. The counselor's motivation must be to assist in this exploration and not merely to expose the ambivalence.

Factual confrontations are designed to expose a discrepancy about stated facts, as between a statement of intention to act and a lack of follow-through. Experiential confrontations are designed to expose an experiential discrepancy, as between concern voiced by a student and observed lack of concern on his or her part. Confrontations can be phrased to focus on a student's strengths that he or she is not using or on student avoidance or minimization of problems. Ultimately, these confrontations should lead to action-based decisions.

Counseling with AP procrastinators can be conducted in an individual or small group format with about five students per group. Once a group is formed, group membership should be closed and regular attendance expected. Group composition should be homogeneous, consisting of AP procrastinators of approximately the same age. The counseling approach described in this chapter is appropriate for men and women, because male and female AP procrastinators are strikingly similar in their thinking and behavior. Sessions should last for about an hour and be held twice weekly. The groups should continue to meet for at least one school term, or approximately 20 to 25 sessions.

Stages of Confrontive CBT

Contracting

As mentioned, group membership is predicated on a diagnosis of AP. In the initial session, the counselor addresses expectations about confidentiality, frequency of sessions, and attendance. In addition, he or she invites students to present an overview of their academic situation and their expectations about group counseling. By the end of the first session, it should be obvious to members that they share important characteristics, including procrastination and a gap between their stated intentions and actions. The emergence of shared attributes enhances group cohesion.

High school counselors can increase AP procrastinator attendance by involving parents and school administrators as team members who monitor and ensure high attendance rates. In addition, at the IAM we provide seminars for parents of AP procrastinators at the high school level in order for parents to learn more constructive ways of confronting their children (Mandel & Marcus, 1995).

The situation is somewhat different for university counselors who work with AP procrastinators, because involving parents is inappropriate. Universities with special programs for at-risk or probationary students have some leverage to enhance regular attendance.

Exploration of Procrastination Patterns

Exploration of procrastinating behavior occurs over a number of sessions. Initially, students are invited to present a detailed description of their academic status in each course. As students begin to realize the extent to which they share patterns of procrastination, the counselor can begin confrontation about the vagueness with which AP procrastinators describe their course requirements and evolving academic problems. Many AP underachievers are not sure about their course requirements. It is one thing to procrastinate regarding looming deadlines. It is quite another to be ignorant of those deadlines, of the grading system, or of the number, type, value, and dates of tests.

Students are required to complete weekly course data sheets focused on course requirements, deadlines, progress to date, things that still need doing, potential problems, intended versus actual study sessions, and so forth. The counselor asks students to bring the completed forms to each session, and the content (or more often, the lack of content) provides a starting point for a discussion about procrastination and options. AP students will predictably miss some counseling sessions or forget to complete the weekly data sheets. Addressing a missed session or an incomplete data form allows the counselor to highlight the consistency and pervasiveness of the student's procrastination patterns in daily life and in counseling. Often, it is the linkage of significant events in counseling with significant events outside of counseling that increases the salience of the counseling sessions and the likelihood of change.

Requiring students to complete and update their course information sheets on a weekly basis serves two purposes. It provides a model for the students about how to monitor and organize academic responsibilities. It also facilitates the rapid identification of problems either by the counselor or other group members. In conducting this inquiry, the counselor must help students go beyond vague statements in order to achieve a more accurate picture of the realities in each course. A good example of this is contained in the following counseling exchange with a 14-year-old AP student:

> Counselor: So, how are you doing in French?
>
> Student: The thing that really burns me up, in French, is I really put in an effort. But the other students learn and I don't.

> Counselor: So what is your actual average now in French?
>
> Student: It's 52%. It was 57% before the last test.

This student had not answered the counselor's question directly and had left the impression that he had not done well in spite of significant effort. Further inquiry by the counselor revealed a very different fact.

> Counselor: So, it sounds like you had a good attitude in French starting the term and were putting in effort.
>
> Student: *(hesitates)* Well, that's kind of what I said.
>
> Counselor: But that's not exactly what has been happening?
>
> Student: *(pauses)* OK. In the beginning I was doing the kind of job I do in every other class. I wasn't doing so well. I really wasn't getting to my work. But then on the first test I managed to pull a C, so I thought that was kind of good, right? Actually, I didn't feel too encouraged by the C. I mean I was happy about passing and everything, but relative to everyone else it wasn't too good, and I wanted more. So, I kept working at that pace and let's see—I think I flunked a test, yeah, I got in the high 40s on another test, so I was doing pretty bad. Then, all of a sudden, I started to do some French work. Like, we don't get too much homework in French, but I did my homework whenever I had it. I also started participating in class, even though I really didn't know what I was talking about. But the teacher gave out extra marks for participation. So, I managed to grasp some concepts along the way. I was doing pretty good in French. Then my teacher sent home a progress report that I was getting 57%, but she was pleased with my effort. But then I flunked another test. I mean, I was doing good otherwise, but the test just didn't go the way I wanted it to.
>
> Counselor: Now, that was the second test you flunked, right? You got in the 40s on a test before that one, right?
>
> Student: Yeah.
>
> Counselor: What did you do when you got in the 40s? You got the test back and you realized you flunked. What did you do?
>
> Student: *(long pause, subdued voice)* Well, nothing, really.

During a detailed inquiry, AP procrastinators often react with veiled irritability in strikingly similar fashion to the way they react to parent or teacher reminders. These negative reactions must be addressed in counseling, as exemplified in the following example:

Counselor:	So, you said you were going to put in more time on geography.
Student:	(*somewhat annoyed*) Well, I guess it didn't happen.
Counselor:	OK, but what did happen?
Student:	(*sarcastically*) Nothing, I guess.
Counselor:	You know, you sound a bit ticked off with me.
Student:	Not really. (*pauses*) Well, yeah, some.
Counselor:	What is it that I said that upset you?
Student:	I'm not really that upset. It's just, like, you sounded a lot like my parents when they keep bugging me about my homework.
Counselor:	OK, that's fair. But I want to be very clear about something. The only reason I was asking you about geography is that you said you wanted to get to it more.
Student:	(*grudgingly*) Yeah.
Counselor:	And I really don't care whether you do more geography or not. Now, I assume that your parents do care. But I am not your parent. The last thing you need is another parent.
Student:	(*grins*) OK, OK.
Counselor:	So, let me ask you again—do you really want to put in more time in geography? If you really don't, just say so.
Student:	Yes, I do.
Counselor:	OK, let's talk about what has been holding you back from reaching that goal.

One advantage of group counseling over individual counseling is that AP procrastinators are quite adept at confronting the gap between their peers' statements of intention and action, even while being unable or unwilling to see through their own rationalizations. In addition, the AP procrastinator reacts to peer confrontation with less resistance than to confrontations with adults.

Confronting Choices

As mentioned earlier, confronting AP procrastination means exposing the student's ambivalence about change. This includes exploring the choices already made and alternatives not used.

The following excerpt from the seventh week of group counseling provides an excellent example of these issues. The group consisted of four male middle-class White 16-year-old high school procrastinators. One student was from a divorced family, and the other three were from intact families. All had siblings who were achieving in school.

In the previous session, student 1 had made a commitment to study for a history test. In the current session, he reported that early the previous Saturday evening he had taken his younger sister to a party, intending to return home to study. As he dropped his sister at her party, he realized that his sister's friend had a very attractive older sister. As the group responded with roars of recognition, he admitted that he had spent the evening socializing with his new female acquaintance.

Counselor: So, did you have any control over what happened on Saturday?

Student 3: No, not when the hormones kick in. [Student 1]'s fate was sealed!

Student 1: You know, it all happened so fast. I intended to study.

Counselor: OK, that was part of the plan. But it sounds like the plan totally and instantly changed. Now let's assume that nobody in their right mind who found themselves in your situation would go home to study.

Student 2: Right!

Student 3: Not a chance!

Counselor: So there was no force on earth that could have stopped you from getting back to studying on Saturday night. OK. So what was your alternative?

Student 1: You mean simply not to go?

Counselor: No. No. Assume that you're going over to stay for the evening. So, what's the alternative plan beyond Saturday night?

Student 1: (sounding very assured) Oh, to study on Sunday.

Counselor: Oh. So what happened on Sunday?

Student 1: I did!

Counselor: How much?

Student 1: Well, not a lot.

Student 4: (laughing) Well, that's our problem right there!

Student 3: Yeah, and how much is "not a lot," like, you know, 5 minutes?

Student 4:	Hey, I think that we should be talking about why [student 1] was sitting at his desk for an hour and a half on Sunday and didn't do any work.
Student 1:	Well, I sat there and had my notebook open. I started reading the stuff, and it's on seven chapters, and it's the first test we've had.
Student 4:	Let me tell you something about seven chapters. If you have one chapter, it doesn't look so big. But if you have seven chapters, you get this feeling that you're shrinking and that it's overwhelming. From the second that [student 1] said the test was on seven chapters, he was doomed!
Student 2:	Your teacher should call it an exam if it's on seven chapters. And tell your teacher that you should have tests more frequently and not cover as much work on each test. That's absolutely ridiculous, unless these are general questions, in which case it can be on seven chapters.
Student 1:	Yeah, the questions were general, with choices.
Counselor:	Let me say something here. What were we originally focusing on? We're now talking about the composition of the test, right? You know, it's become a constitutional issue—the composition of the test was unfair!
Student 2:	Actually, now that I know the composition of the test, I don't find it unfair. Sounds like you just had to read it and comprehend it, as opposed to reading it and memorizing it.
Counselor:	OK, let's go back to Sunday. [Student 1], what happened when you sat down?
Student 4:	You didn't sit down and say, "holy shit!"
Student 1:	No. I sat down intending to study. So I read the whole thing.
Counselor:	How did you read it?
Student 1:	(looking irritated) With my eyes.
Student 3:	Very quickly.
Student 1:	Yeah, I read it quickly.
Counselor:	OK. You read what quickly?
Student 1:	My notes.
Counselor:	Good. How long did it take you to read your notes? (Students 2, 3, and 4 suddenly became quiet and looked more serious).

Student 1:	*(lowered voice)* In 10 minutes.
Counselor:	And the notes covered how much?
Student 1:	Seven chapters.
Counselor:	Seven chapters, and you read all your notes in 10 minutes?
Student 1:	*(in an irritated tone)* I said I read them. I was reviewing.
Counselor:	OK. By reviewing your notes the way you read them in 10 minutes, was that the best, most effective way of reviewing?
Student 1:	*(grudgingly)* I'd say not.
Counselor:	Thank you. So why did you choose that method?
Student 3:	Because it was the easiest!
Student 4:	Absolutely.
Counselor:	Right? *(student 1 nods affirmatively)* So your intention was to review the material. The method that you chose spoke to how committed you were to really learning the material, how in-depth you were ready to go. And it seems to me that the message is very clear. *(assuming student 1's voice)* "I can say to myself that I want to review it. I can even go over it in 10 minutes. But between you and me it's not the best way to do it. But I'll do it, and then I'll feel OK, because I did it."
Student 1:	*(looks trapped).* Mm.
Counselor:	And you're actually knocking off two birds with one stone. You can convince yourself that you've done your review, and you can say to your parents that you've done it, so they should get off your back. But what you've really done is fooled yourself. You're bullshitting yourself.
Student 3:	We're so good at it!
Counselor:	That's exactly right. And I believe that if we went around the table to talk about the method everyone uses to study, to prepare for tests and to position yourselves to do OK, I believe that we would find that [student 1] is not alone. Although, when you took the test in history, you were alone. *(other students nod in agreement)*
Student 2:	Yeah, [student 1], we would have been there for you if we could have. *(laughter)*
Counselor:	Now, if that's the way all of you want to operate, I guess the conclusion is obvious—you will all be choosing to do

> poorly. And if that's what you want, that's OK with me. Just don't say one thing while doing the opposite. Just don't bullshit yourselves about it.

Group members and the counselor left the session about 15 minutes later in a much more serious mood. In a follow-up interview about 6 months after the end of counseling, student 1 identified the counseling session excerpted previously as a turning point in his life. He reported feeling very uncomfortable, at times angry with the counselor and even with the other students in the group. Yet he realized that he was facing something he had not faced before.

Student 1 has since graduated from high school, completed a college degree, and is now employed in public relations for a large international company. He commented that his supervisor appreciated how well he worked with others and how much everyone liked him. Student 1 stated that his tendencies to procrastinate had lessened significantly, although he still enjoyed putting off some things, albeit more often than not as part of a conscious decision. All of the other group participants also completed high school. Student 2 is enrolled in a university degree program. Student 3 completed two college degrees and is currently managing a small chain of music stores. Student 4 completed college and is running his own business. He is also married, although he recently joked that he couldn't remember whether he had proposed to his wife or she had proposed to him.

STUDENT CHANGE AND COUNSELOR CHANGE

It takes many sessions to expose the ambivalence and to confront the false cognitive assumptions that AP procrastinators use. Invariably, as AP students gradually face the struggle they have been avoiding, the affective tone in the group shifts. Self-doubt and increasing inner tension emerge as uncertainty about the future becomes the focus (Mandel & Uebner, 1971). The counselor must be alert to this shift. The counselor must become more empathic and sensitive about the students' active engagement in daily responsibilities and decisions about the future.

Yet even when these former procrastinators work more consistently, the payoff for their efforts takes longer than many had imagined it would. Disappointment and self-doubt at the slow speed of change are part of this process, and the counselor should address these issues in an attempt to prevent regression to dysfunctional behavior patterns (Miller & Rollnick, 2002).

Termination

The school year contains natural counseling termination points. In dealing with AP procrastinators, however, it is important to schedule several sessions following termination to review the student's marks, explore whether any further counseling is necessary, and help the student identify emerging needs that can be addressed outside of counseling.

Defining Counseling Success

Obvious criteria of counseling success for the AP underachiever include a significant decrease in procrastination and an increase in academic performance. Another and equally important criterion of success is an increasing sense of personal responsibility.

RESEARCH FINDINGS

Successful counseling of the AP procrastinator is predicated on both the accurate identification of this type of procrastinator and the effective provision of confrontive CBT. Studies on university students have shown that the AP procrastinator can be reliably differentiated from other types of procrastinating underachievers using a semistructured diagnostic interview. In these studies, interrater reliability ranged from .80 to .90 (Mandel & Marcus, 1988; Mandel, Roth, & Berenbaum, 1968; Noy, 1969; Roth, 1970; Roth, Mauksch, & Peiser, 1967).

The development of the Achievement Motivation Profile (AMP; Mandel, Friedland, & Marcus, 1996; Mandel, Friedland, Marcus, & Mandel, 1996) has provided clinicians with an objective personality measure that can assist in the identification of the AP procrastinator in high school and university students. In addition, studies on high school students have shown that the AP procrastinator can be distinguished from other types of procrastinating underachievers on the basis of age of onset of the underachievement (Glanz, 1988; McKay, 1985) and family interactions (Ben-Knaz, 2002).

Several counseling studies examined personality change and achievement change in university AP procrastinators. Noy (1969) reported that the greatest personality change occurred when AP procrastinators underwent confrontive CBT, compared with when they received either client-centered or psychodynamic therapy. Although Noy's sample consisted of only 14 students, the study included counterbalancing for treatment effects. The differential counseling effects were large.

In a treatment study of 67 differentially diagnosed underachievers, Mandel et al. (1968) found that there was a significant statistical relationship between personality change and achievement change only for the AP procrastinators. This was not true either for anxious underachieving procrastinators or underachievers described as intensely involved in a quest for self-definition and identity.

Roth et al. (1967) compared changes in grade point average (GPA) of 52 AP university students who had undergone confrontive CBT with the changes in GPA of 52 AP students in a no-counseling control group. The treatment group produced a statistically significant increase in GPA by the end of the semester, and the control group did not. At follow-up, these GPA gains were maintained a semester after the termination of counseling.

Clearly, there are many shortcomings to the research on AP procrastinators. There has been a greater emphasis on establishing the reliability and validity of the AP procrastinator diagnosis than on examining the outcomes of treatment. In spite of significant results, the number of treatment studies is small, and most were conducted over 30 years ago with male university students. In addition, there is little in the way of multicultural research on the AP procrastinator. All of these shortcomings are fertile ground for future research.

10

DIGITAL COACHING OF PROCRASTINATORS IN AN ACADEMIC SETTING

ROBERT M. TOPMAN, DIETA KRUISE, AND SABINA BEIJNE

Considering the high prevalence of procrastination in academic settings and the moderate effect of existing forms of treatment (Ferrari, Johnson, & McCown, 1995), new approaches are needed. This chapter outlines the development and assessment of one such approach.

At Leiden University, in the Netherlands, student counselors searched for new pathways in the counseling of procrastinators in academic settings. Procrastination is often related to anxiety, depression, or more severe forms of psychopathology (Ferrari, Johnson, & McCown, 1995). The new approach is primarily focused not on these factors, but on the question, What does a student need to do to study properly and get satisfactory academic results? The goal of treatment in this approach is not only to overcome procrastination but also to acquire productive competencies and study skills. To do this, we have developed several innovative tools based on the use of modern information communication technology (ICT), which offers opportunities for new approaches to counseling students.

This chapter consists of two parts. In the first part, we describe our Web site, titled Study Support, and its use and users. The development of the Web site is described, with special attention to procrastination. On the basis of positive experiences with the Web site, we started a Web-based project called "Digital Coaching," which we describe in the second part of the chapter. We discuss the theoretical basis and the tools we use to promote a productive style of studying, and we present results of a pilot study.

STUDY SUPPORT WEB SITE: ITS USE AND USERS

Web sites in an academic context not only deliver information on the organization, study programs, and rates but also aim to help students study successfully and solve problems. An overview of self-help Web sites of high schools, colleges, and universities can be found in the Student Counseling Virtual Pamphlet Collection at http://counseling.uchicago.edu/vpc/virtulets.html. The subjects of this collection range from alcohol and substance use to writing. Even a brief perusal of this overview indicates that Web sites are used in many educational settings and offer self-help for a wide range of problems. Procrastination as a specific subject is not mentioned in the collection. Related subjects, however, are listed, such as time management (45 links in September 2002) and study skills (at least 6 useful links for procrastinators, e.g., "concentration and distraction" and "planning").

At the Web site of the Procrastination Research Group (http://www.carleton.ca/~tpychyl/prg/self_help/selfhelpsites.html), nine self-help Web sites (as of March 21, 2002) are listed as links. The Web site itself and the linked sites offer information on procrastination (signs, causes, theoretical background, forms of procrastination) and information on management strategies on a behavioral and cognitive level.

In addition, the Procrastination Support Center at http://all.successcenter.ohio-state.edu/dontdelay/ should be mentioned. The different areas of the Web site provide information and additionally offer the opportunity for interactivity between user and site and between users. Students can share their personal ideas and experiences in bulletin boards. Users can also fill in the Tuckman Procrastination Scale (Tuckman, 1991) and submit it for scoring and interpretation.

Our impression is that most of these Web sites, with the Procrastination Support Center as a favorable exception, use only a limited part of the range of possibilities that the Internet provides. Most Web sites seem to be functioning as a digital kiosk, supplying students with digitalized booklets.

Advantages of the Study Support Web Site

The Study Support Web site (http://www.leidenuniv.nl/ics/sz/so/index.html) at the University of Leiden is intended to deliver support to (procrastinating) students not only through information but also through more interactive exercises, checklists, and questionnaires. The present Web site is the result of development that began in 1997. In developing the Web site, we used an educational software model consisting of three developmental phases (Mirande, 1999).

In the first phase of development, a Web site delivers only noninteractive, static information. Students are informed, for instance, on how to take a test, write or present papers, or improve their time management. The texts function as digitalized booklets. Providing tips and tricks (e.g., instructions and lists of 10 dos and don'ts) is a simple form of support that is nevertheless useful because clinical experience shows that some students, and especially procrastinators, seem to have only vague notions and misconceptions about study activities.

In the second phase of development, interaction between the user and the Web site becomes the main focus. In other words, instead of gathering information in a passive way, the student has to become active. Examples are a Web-based checklist with 10 important points for studying and a checklist about time management. The student responds on a 4-point scale, and the site provides immediate feedback. Another example of an interactive application is the Web-based questionnaire Speaking in Groups (Topman & Kleijn, 1996). After completing the questionnaire, the site automatically presents results and remarks on the scores. These texts and tools are very accessible. Superficial browsing of the texts is hardly possible because action by the student is necessary and feedback is immediate. The active involvement is intended to promote a sense of commitment, which is an important dimension to address in changing the behavior of procrastinators.

In the third phase of development, the interactions between student and Web site can be described as transactional. The system not only offers a questionnaire, scores the responses, and presents an outcome but also gives advice on how to solve problems without intervention by a psychologist. For example, by using the Study Management and Academic Result Test study questionnaire (Kleijn et al., 1994; Topman, Kleijn, van der Ploeg, & Masset, 1992), students can get an overview in about 15 minutes of the strong points and weak points in their approach to and organization for studying. The individual test scores are linked to advice, based on the expert knowledge of psychologists, on how to solve problems concerning academic and test competence, time management, strategic studying, and the appropriate investment of study hours.

These Internet applications seem to be especially useful for procrastinators. In our clinical work, procrastinators often report doubts about seeking help. Many of them have postponed seeking help for a long time. For these individuals, the possibility of having immediate access to a Web site that offers information, personalized feedback, and advice has a substantial advantage in the counseling process. No prior planning is required, such as telephoning the counseling center to make an appointment. In addition, shame about their behavior is not an important factor because they remain anonymous. In sum, the threshold for this kind of support is very low, with the result that the intention to seek help easily leads to the realization of this intention.

The Web site also offers the opportunity to direct questions to student counselors by e-mail. It is possible to explore a file with questions by previous (anonymous) students and to see the answers the student counselors provided. These questions and answers make it more likely that procrastinators will get a realistic idea of the kinds of problems that are suitable for addressing in this forum and the kinds of reactions and solutions that are available. This feature lowers the barriers that procrastinators might otherwise place between themselves and counselors.

Use of the Study Support Web Site

Study Support is intended to be a positive example of the possibilities of the use of the Internet for student support. As a sign of its acceptance, all Dutch universities and many other organizations in higher education in the Netherlands offer links to the site. Beyond its popularity, we wondered whether the Web site has proved useful for students who exhibit high levels of procrastination. To address this question, we conducted a pilot study on the use of the Web site. We asked four questions: Do students notice and use the Web site at all? Do specific topics attract more attention than others do, and if so, what topics seem to be important to users? What are the characteristics of the users of the Web site? Do those who visit the Web site work with the content in a serious way, or are they just superficially browsing?

To answer these questions, we conducted an analysis of data provided by the university computer system. This system records all the hits (i.e., number of visitors) of its Web pages and presents monthly overviews. Therefore, it was possible to monitor the overall number of visitors in a specific period and the number of visitors for specific topics. The results of three Web-based questionnaires were used as an indication of the characteristics of the users.

Trait procrastination was measured by the Dutch adaptation (Schouwenburg, 1994) of Lay's Procrastination Scale (Lay, 1986). Academic and test competence, time management, strategic studying, and average number of hours spent studying per week were measured by the Study Management and Academic Result Test (Kleijn et al., 1994; Topman et al., 1992).

To measure the frequency of test-related thoughts, the site uses the State of Mind (SOM) test (Topman et al., 1992), a thought-listing procedure (Cacioppo & Petty, 1981) in two steps. First, participants are instructed to write down as many thoughts related to tests as possible. Second, the participants are instructed to assess the subjective meaning of these thoughts as positive, negative, or neutral. Following the SOM model of cognition proposed by Schwartz and Garamoni (1986), the SOM ratio (positive thoughts/ [positive + negative thoughts]) is calculated by a computer algorithm.

The SOM model postulates an association between psychological well-being and an optimal balance of positive and negative thoughts (Schwartz & Garamoni, 1986). An SOM ratio of .6 represents an optimal balance of positive and negative thoughts. Too many positive thoughts in relation to negative thoughts can lead to a "positive monologue" and "unrealistic optimism." Too many negative thoughts in relation to positive thoughts can lead to a "negative dialogue of conflict" and can be called "unrealistic pessimism."

This measure was included to examine the possibility that procrastinators have an unbalanced ratio of positive and negative thoughts. In addition, a counselor could respond to any idiosyncratic thoughts listed. After they complete the SOM Test, the site automatically presents students with the results, remarks on their scores and advice about their study problems.

Since the Web site began, data on hits were collected. We analyzed hits for March, April, and May 2001 in detail. During September 2001, an extra counter was installed for the Study Management and Academic Result Test. In addition, during April, May, and June 2002, scores on the Dutch Lay's Procrastination Scale, the Study Management and Academic Result Test, and the SOM Test were sent automatically to the e-mail address of the first author (Topman). We analyzed these three sets of data for this pilot study.

The development of the Web site started in 1997 and attracted in that initial period 75 visitors per month. The number of users per month increased to an average of 2,035 in March, April, and May 2001 and increased further to more than 3,500 in May, June, and July 2002. On the basis of these figures, we concluded that students did notice and use the Web site.

Our second question was whether specific topics attracted more attention than others. We collected data on the number of visitors for the specific elements of the Web site. One of these elements consists of short tips for six problem areas. When visitors are interested in one of these areas, they can click on a title to obtain advice.

The average number of hits per month ranged from 234 to 395. The dos and don'ts of "postponing study tasks" (i.e., procrastination) were clearly consulted most frequently (395 hits per month), followed by "taking tests" (281 hits per month), "study problems" (279 hits per month), "concentration" (263 hits per month), "writing papers" (246 hits per month), and "study stress" (234 hits per month).

The observed interest in overcoming procrastination is further confirmed by the popularity of the topics "well-known excuses for postponing tasks" (266 hits per month), "planning and the use of time" (229 hits per month), and "making an effective plan" (226 hits per month) in that period. Therefore, it can be concluded that topics on procrastination in academic settings were visited relatively often.

Although we now know that procrastination is of much interest to the users of the Web site, we do not know whether procrastinators in particular visit these topics. Some relevant data are available from the Web-based versions of the three questionnaires (Dutch Lay's Procrastination Scale, the Study Management and Academic Result Test, and the SOM Test). A total of 135 university students completed the Dutch Lay's Procrastination Scale and the Study Management and Academic Result Test. Using the Dutch norms of Schouwenburg (1994), we found that 40% of this group had a strong tendency for procrastination (cutoff score 72). The average Study Management and Academic Results Test score for time management was in the second decile, indicating weak time management skills. The average SOM ratio was .45 and indicates an unbalanced ratio with a prevalence of negative thoughts. From these data we concluded that a large percentage of university students who visited the Web site could be characterized as procrastinators.

The last question was whether the visitors just browse the pages. On the Study Support Web site, three sources of information on user effort and possible impact are available. The structure of two exercises on multiple-choice test taking makes it possible to analyze the use of subsequent pages because a page can be visited only if the question on the former page is answered. In the first three pages half of the users dropped out but the rest of the users completed the series of ten pages. These figures from two exercises indicate serious involvement of users in a series of pages that are not particularly intriguing in their own right.

The third source of information is user results on the Study Management and Academic Result Test questionnaire. Comparison of the hits recorded by the computer system at the starting point of the questionnaire ($n =$ 724 in September 2001) and the hits on a second counter in the final part of the Study Management and Academic Result Test gives an indication of the involvement of the users. Of the persons who started the questionnaire, 42% finished the entire questionnaire and received the outcome results.

In summary, nearly 50% of our users can be considered to be active users who are involved in the Web-based exercises and the questionnaire. Whether this conclusion is also true for the specific group of procrastinators (40% of our users) is not clear, as the content of these pages is not specifically related to the subject of procrastination. The relation between the level of trait procrastination of users and their use of the Web site will be studied in a new project. Nevertheless, the Web site is searched by many students who seek advice on overcoming procrastination, and we can assume that procrastinators are equally involved.

In the Netherlands, as elsewhere, there is an ongoing discussion on the differences between numbers of hits and "unique visitors" and the reliability of counters. We found a 10% difference in a comparison of the number of hits measured by the university computer system and those measured by the extra counter. Although this can be considered a rather insignificant difference, we present our figures with some hesitation because of the possible reduced reliability.

The findings on number of hits provided by the university computer system have some serious limitations. More sophisticated counters would be useful to monitor the behavior of users more precisely. These counters, in combination with Web-based questionnaires, will make it possible to analyze the Web-use behavior of procrastinators. Such an analysis could be the basis for "intelligent" Web tools that adapt themselves to the needs of procrastinators.

Overall, the Study Support Web site offers possibilities to inform procrastinators, to interact with them, and to give personalized feedback and advice. Given the low threshold, procrastinators who are not (as yet) inclined to seek traditional help are nonetheless provided with ideas, information, and self-help tools. In this way, the knowledge and expertise of psychologists becomes available to a larger group of people. In addition, the procrastinators who communicate via this Web site might become more inclined to seek further help and more formal counseling as they form more realistic ideas on ways to change.

We believe that it will be important to explore further the opportunities that ICT has to offer procrastinators. Inspired by the high number of visitors and the positive experiences with the Study Support Web site, and considering the high number of procrastinators we see in our practice as student counselors, we started a new ICT project called "Digital Coaching."

DIGITAL COACHING

Theoretical Considerations

A triangular model called the Golden Triangle offers the framework that we used to analyze study situations, successes, and failures during the study process and to find ways for procrastinators to improve. The three factors in this model are self-efficacy expectancies, academic performance, and goal setting. They form a triangular relationship. In a meta-analysis of 14 studies, Locke and Latham (1990) found that on average self-efficacy is related to performance ($r = .39$) and to goal setting ($r = .39$). Goal setting was also closely related to performance ($r = .42$). We describe these factors and their implications for the treatment of procrastination in the sections that follow.

Self-Efficacy Expectancies

Self-efficacy expectancies have been found to be related to academic performance in general (Bandura & Schunk, 1981; McMillan, Simonetta, &

Singh, 1994), to procrastination (Ferrari et al., 1992), and to specific domains of studying such as the level of study goals (Graham, MacArthur, & Schwartz, 1995), writing papers (Zimmerman & Bandura, 1994), and taking tests (Glass et al., 1995; Topman & Jansen, 1984). In addition, self-efficacy expectancies have been related to the tendency to stay in a study skills training program and to improvement in academic performance after the training program had ended (Topman & Stoutjesdijk, 1995, 1998). Thus, self-efficacy expectancies have been found to be highly predictive of performance in a variety of domains.

Through our training groups and an invitation on our Web site, we assembled a list of the debilitating beliefs students express, and we distinguished in an ad hoc categorization three sets of beliefs: One is unable to regulate study behavior, One is unable to process the study material, and One is unable to use the acquired knowledge while taking a test. Procrastinating students in particular often perceive themselves as not able to prepare well or to acquire good academic results.

In the treatment of procrastination, therefore, attention should be given to both the development of self-efficacy expectancies (e.g., "A good study schedule helps me," "I can plan my study schedule like my sports program," "I've always had good marks, so I'm able to pass this test") and the abandonment of beliefs that are pseudological and self-defeating reasons to keep procrastinating.

Performance

Performance increases a sense of self-efficacy, and self-efficacy is related to performance (Bandura, 1997). The importance of academic performance is evident; however, the perception of performance may be as important. In general, students seem to have rather naive ideas about performance or lack of performance and about how to overcome study problems; "just spend more time studying" is an example of such an idea (Topman, Kleijn, & van der Ploeg, 1990). For some procrastinating students, it is indeed as simple as that because many procrastinators underestimate the time needed for completion of tasks (Ferrari, Johnson, & McCown, 1995). Most often, however, the situation is more complicated.

In particular, misattributions seem to be common among students with high scores on measures of procrastination. In comparison with students with low scores, these students tend to attribute test success to external and unstable factors (Rothblum, Solomon, & Murakami, 1986). Furthermore, procrastinators seem to believe in a wide range of unrealistic excuses to justify their behavior (Ferrari, Johnson, & McCown, 1995). Many of these thought patterns can be characterized as cognitive misconceptions about successful performing, which may lead to patterns of powerlessness (see chap. 6, this volume).

To overcome these patterns of powerlessness, self-help tools seem to be useful, because students can process confronting information at their own pace and in relative anonymity. At the same time, the self-help tools can attract the attention and involvement of the student and can correct cognitive misconceptions and increase positive outcome expectancies.

Goal Setting

A third important factor in academic performance is goal setting. Individuals who lack self-efficacy set inadequate goals, which lead to fewer accomplishments. It is not a matter of having high or low goals, but rather of setting realistic goals for oneself that are challenging and at the same time within reach.

An important objective in the treatment of procrastinators is to offer help in formulating attainable subgoals. There are two main reasons for this. In the first place, many procrastinators are unaware of the importance of setting goals. They seem not to be aware that they have already set and reached a lot of goals—for instance, in their preuniversity education, completed university courses, paid jobs, and sports. Attention to these success experiences can help convince these students that setting goals can be useful. Second, procrastinators may often set goals that are vague, unattainable, or unrealistically optimistic. This lack of adequate goal setting is in many cases one of the main reasons for previous failure of planning. This failure strengthens the procrastinators' belief that goal-setting, planning, and time management do not work for them.

Procrastinators therefore have to be taught how to set realistic goals and how to work toward them. In this process, again, a lot of pseudological and self-defeating reasons for procrastination have to be discussed and challenged, and self-help tools can be useful in this regard.

Pilot Study

The goal of our pilot study was to assess the Digital Coaching project with students of the University of Leiden. The participants were 12 men and 11 women with a mean age of 23 (range 19 to 31 years). Students had been enrolled at university in different fields of study for a mean duration of 3 years 6 months (range 1 to 9 years). A total of 13 participants completed the project and filled in both pre- and postmeasurements.

Ten students did not complete Digital Coaching and did not fill in the postmeasurements. Two of these participants discontinued their participation after a face-to-face interview. The interview itself clarified their problems, and they believed that they were able to help themselves. Two students manifested serious psychopathology and had to be treated in individual psychotherapy. Reasons for the other six dropouts remain unclear because these students stopped responding.

Procedure

An advertisement inviting students with procrastination problems to apply to the Digital Coaching project was placed on the Internet site of the University of Leiden. Through a clickable button, students could send an e-mail to show their interest, and in response the procedure was explained. As in the first study, students completed the Dutch adaptation of Lay's Procrastination Scale, the Study Management and Academic Result Test, and the SOM Test.

After receiving the results of the questionnaires, we randomly assigned participants to one of the coaches. We functioned as the coaches in this pilot study, being experienced student counselors and trained cognitive–behavioral psychologists.

In a semistructured face-to-face interview, the coach and student discussed the completed questionnaires and the student's study situation. The main reasons for this interview were to form an alliance and to discuss the procedures in the project.

In the weeks to follow, student and coach communicated via e-mail. Students were asked to complete Web-based time and planning forms every day of the week (see Exhibit 10.1), enabling the coaches to monitor and to provide immediate feedback. The duration of the participation was not set beforehand. Participation in the study was terminated by the student and coach when student and coach were satisfied with the progress established. The experiences of the students were evaluated in a semistructured interview at termination, and students again completed the three questionnaires.

Digital Coaching consisted of general components, which add to its efficiency, and more specific features, enabling tailor-made advice for specific problems related to procrastination. The seven main components, as well as the pages that were developed especially for this project, are described in the following sections.

Clarification of Students' Problems and Their Causes

At the start of the coaching process, the questionnaires and the face-to-face interview were used to identify students' problems and their causes. Depending on individual needs, students were subsequently advised to fill in Web versions of checklists for time management, study circumstances, and test preparation. These checklists provided immediate feedback. If necessary, we used e-mail to stress aspects of behavior, cognitions, and study circumstances related to procrastination.

Providing Information on Productive Study Skills

We provided the students with information on study problems and on how to change to more productive circumstances. Examples of passive and

EXHIBIT 10.1
Web-Based Planning Form

Fill in the activities you plan to engage in during each hour between 8:00 a.m. and 12:00 midnight and categorize your activities as study, leisure, or other.

Hour	Activities	Characteristics		
8:00		○ Study	○ Leisure	○ Other
9:00		○ Study	○ Leisure	○ Other
10:00		○ Study	○ Leisure	○ Other
11:00		○ Study	○ Leisure	○ Other
12:00		○ Study	○ Leisure	○ Other
13:00		○ Study	○ Leisure	○ Other
14:00		○ Study	○ Leisure	○ Other
15:00		○ Study	○ Leisure	○ Other
16:00		○ Study	○ Leisure	○ Other
17:00		○ Study	○ Leisure	○ Other
18:00		○ Study	○ Leisure	○ Other
19:00		○ Study	○ Leisure	○ Other
20:00		○ Study	○ Leisure	○ Other
21:00		○ Study	○ Leisure	○ Other
22:00		○ Study	○ Leisure	○ Other
23:00		○ Study	○ Leisure	○ Other
24:00		○ Study	○ Leisure	○ Other

○ OK: Day overview and save: Check this form and press the button. The data are saved on this computer for your weekly overview.
○ Delete: All data are set to 0. You can fill in the form again.
○ Day overview and no saving of data.
○ Print: Use the print button of your browser to print this form.

Please fill in the form below to contact your psychologist.

Last name

First name

E-mail address

Date

Comment on this day and remarks:

interactive Web pages are "Studying for Dummies" (information on studying and preparing for tests), 10 "Dos & Don'ts" dealing with concentration problems, and an interactive lesson and checklist on studying with attention and coping with distraction.

Teaching of Time Management Techniques

Teaching time management techniques was an important aspect of Digital Coaching. Every day, students were supposed to fill in Web-based time-monitoring forms and e-mail these forms to their coach. In addition, we asked students to consult one of our Web pages (e.g., "Information on Planning and Time Management"), to complete the interactive checklist "Spending Your Time," and to take the interactive multiple-choice test "How to Make a Plan." In general, we gave advice and supported the students' task of setting concrete, explicit, and realistic targets and deadlines and discussed negative experiences with unrealistic targets.

Providing Immediate Feedback

The daily time-monitoring forms were the most important and frequent source of feedback to the student. These interactive forms automatically provide simple and immediate feedback. In addition, the students knew that their coach would see their use of time. The coach gave the students feedback on the completed forms and other assignments as soon, and as frequently, as possible, with a minimum of at least one response a week. Besides this tailor-made feedback by the coach, Web pages and the checklist gave automatic feedback as well.

Changing Thought Patterns and Behavior

Another important goal in Digital Coaching was to change unproductive thought patterns and behaviors. Frequently encountered, for instance, were the unrealistic pessimistic thought "I can't do it anyway" and the unrealistic optimistic thought "I'll manage easily if I start tomorrow." As a rule, such thoughts result in the abandonment or postponement of planned tasks and to discouragement.

The Web page listing "Well-Known Excuses for Procrastination," with the clickable "Comments of the Student Counselor" on these pages, proved useful in attacking unproductive thought patterns and behaviors. Other pages provide students with new, constructive approaches to tasks. A series of interactive Web-based worksheets called "Start" helped the student find answers to four questions:

1. Which study goals do you have in mind?
2. How important are these goals, and what other activities do you have to stop?
3. Are you capable of reaching these goals?

4. Do you believe you can start with the necessary study activities and reach your goals?

Ultimately, Start helps the student to get an overview of tasks to be done, to set attainable goals, and to decide which task to start with. In this way, the student learns to replace unproductive thought patterns using a simple four-question approach. In addition, this approach can help prevent postponement of set tasks and discouragement.

Increasing Students' Commitment

As coaches, we also worked on encouraging students' commitment to their work and performance. We supported the students in making a realistic analysis of experiences of success. The aim was to help prevent a repetition of experiences of failure and to improve their acceptance of personal responsibility for their actions. Proper target setting, feedback on attributions of success and failure, and personal e-mails were used to improve management of the self-defeating patterns of powerlessness (see chap. 6, this volume) and to develop a sense of competence.

Overcoming Anxiety, Shame, and Personal Isolation

We helped the students overcome anxiety, shame, and personal isolation and develop a perspective for the future. We tried to do this while using a supportive and encouraging style in the Web tools and e-mails. The tailor-made e-mails made it possible to adjust our tone and sense of humor to the specific student. The style element is important because it offers a new kind of learning experience. Instead of an internal dialogue, which may provoke anxiety and shame, a more constructive, accepting, and businesslike dialogue is demonstrated as a model.

Setting realistic, attainable subgoals not only is a time management technique; it also prevents a subjective appraisal of the study situation as overwhelming. In this sense, setting goals helps students overcome anxiety. Also, immediate feedback may provide support in setback situations. Student and coach can analyze the situation together and try to find solutions for the problems that have arisen. As a consequence, a setback that previously would lead to discouragement and to the shameful avoidance of study tasks can become a learning experience.

We pointed out to the students that they are not the only people with procrastination problems, a fact demonstrated by the existence of the Digital Coaching project. This realization helps students overcome feelings of personal isolation.

Results

The 23 applicants to the Digital Coaching program scored low to very low on the Study Management and Academic Result Test scales measuring academic competence (third decile), test competence (third decile), time management (first decile), and hours per week studied (second decile). Scores for strategic studying were average (fifth decile). Scores on the Dutch Lay's Procrastination Scale of all participating students were very high (ninth decile). An average SOM ratio of .41 was found, indicating "an internal dialogue of conflict" (Schwartz & Garamoni, 1986), comparable to the low ratio score of highly test-anxious students (Topman et al., 1997).

Thirteen students completed the whole Digital Coaching program and filled in both pre- and postmeasurements. The pretreatment scores of this group did not differ from the pretreatment scores of the whole group of 23 applicants.

In a series of paired-samples t tests, pre- and posttreatment scores were compared. No significant differences were found for the four Study Management and Academic Result Test scales, but the number of hours per week of studying increased from 19 to 23, and this difference is nearly significant, $t(12) = -2.12, p < .055$. Scores on the Procrastination Scale decreased significantly, $t(12) = 4.00, p < .002$. The SOM ratio increased from .38 to .52, indicating a more balanced relation between negative and positive thoughts, and the difference is nearly significant, $t(12) = -2.15, p < .054$.

In the semistructured interview, the aspects of the course mentioned as most effective were "someone watching over you," "justification to the coach," "filling in the time-monitoring forms," "finding out where my time goes," "gathered insights," "goal setting," and "the e-mails." The overall evaluation of students was on the whole positive. The aspect of "someone watching over you" was most often mentioned.

Implications, Limitations, and Recommendations

Although the results varied among participants, in general, a positive effect of the Digital Coaching project was evident. For the counseling practice, the Digital Coaching procedure proved to be both useful and feasible. Several implications of the Digital Coaching study can be mentioned.

In this phase of development, Digital Coaching was not more efficient than traditional counseling. Writing texts, solving initial technical problems, developing skills in responding to e-mails, and above all learning to cope with the inventive excuses of procrastinators was rather time consuming. The estimated time to coach a student was about one hour a week. However, this method offers extra tools to support procrastinators beyond those we normally had in our traditional work. Furthermore, an extra group of students was reached who otherwise might not have come to our counseling office.

The severity of the participating students' problems varied. Because the Internet has a low-threshold access potential, we believe, this study attracted students with a very wide range of problem severity. Procrastination is sometimes embedded in more general and personal problems, and the low-threshold access of the project stimulated them to seek help.

Despite the number of procrastinators at the University of Leiden, and despite their interest in our information via the Web, only 2% of the Web visitors applied to join this study. There are several explanations for such a limited response. One factor may be that the advertisement on the Web did not communicate well enough and did not signal a chance for change. Recently, the rather businesslike text was changed to a more personal, inviting text, and we have the impression that the latter text works better. A second factor may be that procrastinators procrastinate in their decision to seek help. A third factor might have been that digital counseling was an unknown novelty at the university. A meeting organized at the end of the pilot study providing information to student advisors (key figures for students) resulted in an increase in applicants. These participants will enroll in a new study.

The results indicate a statistically significant improvement in the measurement of procrastination. However, the progress students made on a behavioral level seems to be rather modest. Two reasons can explain this discrepancy. First, the number of hours spent studying was difficult to estimate for students at the start of the study. There are indications that they tended to overestimate, and only in the coaching process did the students become aware of their use of time and learn to make more realistic estimations. Therefore, the measures they provided did not change as much as their behaviors. Second, the hours the student spent studying varied throughout the project. In the first weeks of the project, many students had good intentions and made a good start, but their performance then quickly declined as old patterns of procrastination reappeared. Although in this phase students often drop out of training groups, Digital Coaching has the advantage of immediate feedback at this risky moment of demoralization. Encouragement to cope with the tendency to postpone tasks is possible. It is clear that serious improvement in time management and time investment takes a lot of sustained effort from both student and coach.

In the process of coaching procrastinators, a distinction proved to be useful between two types of procrastinators, the "unconcerned" and the "anxious" types. Lay's (1988) distinction between optimistic and pessimistic procrastinators was the starting point for this observation. We found, however, that many students had a time-dependent mixture of optimism (several weeks before the deadline) and pessimism (some days before the deadline). As a consequence of their optimism, they postponed their work, resulting in stress and pessimism when the deadline came into sight and they realized they were too late starting.

For unconcerned procrastinators, an increase in awareness is important. These persons are easily distracted and prone to use every excuse to postpone studying. The two main principles for treatment of this group are confrontation with procrastination and reflection on the consequences of the delays (and the internal causes of it). In this project, a friendly but tenacious coach constantly reminded them. Anxious procrastinators experience procrastination as an internal problem. These students often report a negative internal monologue: "I am afraid, I should study, I am ashamed by my own behavior," and so forth. The main two objectives in treatment of this group are modifying debilitating beliefs and developing self-efficacy. In our project, we helped students replace negative monologues with more constructive dialogues—for instance, "I am afraid to make mistakes, *but* I don't have to be perfect" and "It's alright to make mistakes."

The shortcomings of this study are evident. The number of participants is too small to draw definitive conclusions. Also, the time span offered to participants was too short to help them overcome procrastination completely and to establish a stable pattern of positive study-related cognitions and productive study habits. In retrospect, we underestimated the tenacity of procrastination of the students. Just like the students, the coaches had to learn to cope with their own high expectations and unrealistic optimism.

To conclude, we present some future recommendations. The first obvious recommendation is to conduct a larger study that includes more participants, a control group, and extra clinical measurements. An investigation of the dropouts' reasons for withdrawal is necessary, as well as the development of strategies to prevent dropout. Experiments with a longer time span are recommended for Digital Coaching, including extra attention to the development of self-efficacy expectancies related to the coaching process. It seems to be useful to distinguish the two types of procrastinators previously discussed and to experiment with the application of different sets of tools for each type.

Improvements to Digital Coaching have been suggested, such as the development of extra (interactive) tools and of a personalized feedback system. Also, tools to increase awareness and commitment of the participants, such as a signed declaration of commitment, use of a buddy system, and the use of Webcams, mobile phone messages, and tags and stickers with different types of slogans (e.g., confronting, positive self-statement, self-efficacy enhancing) might also be useful.

11

A PROJECT-ANALYTIC PERSPECTIVE ON ACADEMIC PROCRASTINATION AND INTERVENTION

TIMOTHY A. PYCHYL AND KELLY BINDER

There is a certain irony in our approach to the study of procrastination and its treatment. Although procrastination is commonly seen as a *not doing* problem, our approach psychologically has been to investigate the *not having* with respect to the individual, particularly as it concerns the individual's personality. To be more precise, the *not doing* of procrastination is, by definition, the voluntary delay of an intended action toward some legitimate task despite foreseeable negative consequences and a potentially overall worse outcome (e.g., Ferrari, Johnson, & McCown, 1995; Milgram, 1991, Milgram, Weizman, & Raviv, 1991, see also chap. 4, this volume). This seemingly illogical, voluntary delay is the *not doing* problem that we hope to change. Ironically, what researchers have generally studied in their attempt to understand procrastination, and often what counselors seem to address, are aspects of the individual's personality, particularly higher order traits. For example, procrastination is a problem of having too little of some traits such as conscientiousness (e.g., Lay, 1997; Lay & Brokenshire, 1997; Schouwenburg & Lay, 1995; Watson, 2001) or self-esteem (e.g., Ferrari, 1991b, 1994, 2000) or having too much of traits like socially prescribed perfectionism (e.g., Burns, Dittmann, Nguyen, & Mitchelson, 2000; Flett, Blankstein, Hewitt, & Koledin, 1992; chap. 13, this volume) or fear of failure (e.g., Rothblum, 1990;

Schouwenburg, 1992). We study and try to affect *not doing* by investigating or treating *having* or *not having*.

To be fair, this distinction between *having* and *doing* in personality has more to do with level of analysis, as opposed to whether or not traits affect behavior. A long research literature clearly indicates that traits predict behavior or the *doings* in our lives (at least aggregated samples of behavior; see, e.g., Pervin & John, 1999). However, this same research literature also indicates that personality is relatively enduring. This is particularly true when considered at the highest levels in the taxonomy of traits with such things as lack of conscientiousness. What the *having* and *doing* distinction centers on in more recent personality research is the level of analysis at which we investigate personality. Do we consider broad traits such as the Big Five factors (e.g., John, 1990) and what McCrae and Costa (1999) labeled "basic tendencies" in their five-factor theory of personality, or do we adopt more middle-level units of analysis, such as personal projects (e.g., Little, 1999)?

At the heart of this discussion of the level of analysis is that there are more than just trait measures that we can and should consider in our understanding of problems like procrastination. However, this means that we need to move from a *having* to a *doing* perspective theoretically, something which Allport (1937) identified many years ago. This is the purpose of the present chapter, to move away from traditional trait approaches in our understanding, measurement, and intervention with academic procrastination by exploring units of analysis that capture the *doing* and *not doing* of our lives.

In this chapter, we have kept the focus on how both researchers and counselors can explore the *doings* and *not doings* in the lives of students through personal projects analysis. We invite the reader to put on a new set of goggles or lenses through this unit of analysis with which to view academic procrastination and, in adopting this project-analytic perspective, come to understand academic procrastination within what Little (1987) described as the "muddling through [of] our complex and at times perplexing lives" (p. 612).

The chapter begins with a brief overview of a psychological perspective that is well suited to the study of the breakdown in volitional action known as procrastination. In this section, we review aspects of what has been called a "conative" psychology (e.g., Hershberger, 1988; Little, 1999) and a related cognitive–motivational unit of measurement known as the personal project (Little, 1983). We then discuss an investigation of a treatment program for academic procrastination using an instrument called Personal Projects Analysis (PPA) as an outcome measure.

COGNITIVE PSYCHOLOGY AND COGNITIVE–MOTIVATIONAL UNITS OF MEASUREMENT

The personal project is one of a number of units of analysis that emerged during the 1980s and 1990s in personality psychology (e.g., Buss & Cantor,

1989; Little, 1983; Pervin, 1989). Related units of analysis include current concerns (e.g., Klinger, 1977, 1987), evolutionary tasks or tactics (e.g., Buss, 1986, 1987), life tasks (e.g., Cantor & Harlow, 1994; Cantor & Kihlstrom, 1987), personal strivings (e.g., Emmons, 1986, 1989), and possible selves (e.g., Markus & Nurius, 1986). Although new in a chronological sense in personality research, these middle-level units of analysis share a common focus on a concept originally proposed by Allport (1937)—the *doing* (planful action) as opposed to the *having* (trait) side of personality (Cantor, 1990). As Cantor and Zirkel (1990) noted,

> The "doing" approaches that build upon these middle-level units are diverse in their particulars but share a common perspective, in which the explication of the processes of social behavior involves the integration of motivation, affect, and cognition, and in which careful attention is accorded to behavioral measures . . . that reveal this complex side of personality in action. (p. 152)

It is this integration of motivation, affect, and cognition that makes a middle-level unit of analysis like the personal project appropriate for our exploration of procrastination. As can be noted throughout this book, each chapter highlights the interplay between what students feel, think, and do. And perhaps just as important is that a middle-level unit of analysis such as the personal project captures the dynamic action of person and environment, or the negotiation between person and context. Personal projects are defined and carried out within particular personal contexts (Little, 1999). Projects as mundane as "attend class" to as magnificent as "finally write that magnum opus called my thesis" are all planned and executed or abandoned within a specific context. In this sense, the context can serve as a barrier or a facilitator to the successful completion of any particular project and does not stand apart from our understanding of the person and his or her purposive behavior. And, it is this context that some researchers (e.g., Ferrari & Pychyl, 2000a) have focused on to specify academic procrastination as a situational form of procrastination, as opposed to the more general notion of trait procrastination.

The personal project itself is of interest, as it represents how individuals are negotiating their current life situations. Even a cursory glance at a project list paints a picture of respondents' everyday concerns and provides a glimpse at their forward-looking agenda—what their intentions are and where they are going. Without knowing how individuals think and feel about these projects, however, we have only a partial picture. Individuals' evaluations of their attempts to successfully negotiate these projects, or project appraisal, is central to an understanding of how individuals are functioning in their particular ecosettings. Project appraisal is intimately linked to the PPA methodology, so it is presented through a discussion of how project data are collected and analyzed.

PERSONAL PROJECTS ANALYSIS

Traditionally, PPA is presented as a written self-assessment (although interviews have been used; see, e.g., Omodei & Wearing, 1990; Pychyl & Little, 1998). Individuals begin by generating examples of their current personal projects. Typical projects from student samples include projects such as prepare for my exam, study more each day, go to the gym more regularly, visit the writing tutorial center, lose 10 pounds, reduce my hours of work at my job, visit my parents during the holidays, clean the apartment, and watch less television. Specific sample academic projects elicited in this study included work on math problems, read *Watership Down*, raise my grade point average, keep up with readings on a daily basis, study for finals, do research on the Web, speak to an academic advisor, prepare for a presentation, start viewing Instructional Television tapes, meet with my accounting group, drop geography, register for summer courses, finish Java assignment, make study notes for Spanish, find a tutor, pick up marked assignment, get chemistry notes, improve attendance at lectures, review difficult physics questions, and read remaining psychology chapters.

From this project elicitation list, participants select 10 projects that they list on the PPA rating matrix. This PPA module, as originally defined by Little (1983), organizes the 10 projects as rows and the 19 PPA dimensions as columns in a 10 × 19 matrix. Seventeen of these dimensions are defined as rating scales using an 11-point scale (i.e., 0–10). Two open columns requiring the respondents to indicate "with whom" they engage in this project and "where" they engage in this project complete the matrix. The 17 rating-scale dimensions, considered the standard PPA dimensions (Pychyl & Little, 1998), consist of importance, enjoyment, difficulty, visibility, control, initiation, stress, time adequacy, outcome, self-identity, others' view, value congruency, positive impact, negative impact, progress, challenge, and absorption (see Little, 1983, for a copy of the PPA Project Appraisal Module).

Each dimension in this PPA Project Appraisal Module was chosen on theoretical or pragmatic grounds to reflect potentially important characteristics of personal projects (Little, 1983, 1989). For example, the dimensions of visibility, initiation, and control relate to Little's analysis of the inception, planning, and action stages of projects (see also Gollwitzer & Bargh, 1996). Dimensions such as value congruency, stress, and time adequacy are included because of their hypothesized link with various outcome measures of interest such as life satisfaction, affect, physical health, stress, and depression (Little, 1983, 1999). In sum, the dimensions reflect aspects of broader psychological concern and have salience to both the individual and the counselor.

Based on the theory that guided the choice of dimensions and factor analysis, Little suggested that five factors underlie covariation between the 17 rating-scale dimensions (e.g., Little, 1999, Pychyl & Little, 1998). These factors (with their associated project dimensions) have been labeled Meaning (Enjoyment, Value Congruency, Self-Identity, Absorption, Importance), Structure (Initiation, Control, Time Adequacy, Positive and Negative Impact), Community (Visibility, Others' View), Efficacy (Progress, Outcome), and Stress (Stress, Challenge, Difficulty).

With this necessarily brief theoretical overview of PPA complete, we can now turn to our study that demonstrates the utility of PPA as a method for the investigation of, and potential intervention approach for, academic procrastination. Overall, the question that was posed was simply, Does a typical academic procrastination intervention have an impact on the students' lives as evidenced in their personal projects?

POPULATION COUNSELED AND CLIENT CONTACT

To conduct this study, we enlisted the participation of 50 undergraduate students from our university. Fifteen of these participants belonged to the treatment (or workshop) group. The remaining 35 participants belonged to one of two comparison groups. Students in the treatment group were self-identified procrastinators who sought out counseling in response to a campus poster announcement. The remaining students were randomly selected from the Procrastination Research Group (http://www.carleton.ca/~tpychyl) mass-testing pool based on scoring in the top 30% on the Aitken Procrastination Inventory (API; Aitken, 1982). These students were then contacted by telephone, and volunteers were randomly assigned to one of two comparison groups. The first comparison group ($n = 17$) received PPA as part of the research process, whereas the second comparison group ($n = 18$) did not receive the PPA or any form of treatment. (The PPA was not used as part of the intervention program. Instead, it was used as part of the outcome measures in the study of student procrastination.)

COUNSELING PROGRAM OVERVIEW AND GOALS

The cognitive–behavioral approach of this workshop was based on a previous treatment program offered at Carleton University with the purpose of providing increased insight, skills, and strategies to help students overcome their academic procrastination. As the counselor outlined (Delicate, 1998), her goals in working with procrastination were to (a) change the thinking patterns that sustain procrastination, (b) reduce the often paralyzing feelings of guilt and anxiety, and (c) help students manage their workload by breaking down large tasks into smaller ones and thus prevent feelings of being overwhelmed. These aspects of the treatment were similar to various other cognitive–behavioral approaches (e.g., J. L. Johnson & McCown's Doing It Now program, cited in Ferrari, Johnson, et al., 1995), as well as related treatment strategies and techniques (e.g., Burka & Yuen, 1983; Knaus, 1998).

OVERVIEW OF RESEARCH IN RELATION TO INTERVENTION PROGRAM

All participants completed a battery of measures across four time periods including the Procrastination Assessment Scale–Students (PASS; Solomon & Rothblum, 1984); the Academic Procrastination State Inventory (APSI; Schouwenburg, 1995); two measures of subjective well-being, the Satisfaction With Life Scale (SWLS; Diener, Emmons, Larsen, & Griffin, 1985) and the Positive and Negative Affect Scales (Diener & Emmons, 1984); and a modified version of the PPA instrument (Little, 1983). Which questionnaire a student received during any given period depended on the group and time interval. It should be noted that only the first part of the PASS was scored in this study in order to assess the students' tendency to procrastinate on their academic tasks (not the reasons for this task delay or avoidance). A summarized testing schedule indicating what measures were given, when they were received, and by whom is presented in Table 11.1.

SUMMARY OF INTERVENTION PROGRAM IMPLEMENTATION

This section provides the content and format for both the intervention and research procedure. Note that much of the content overlapped between workshop sessions. This overlap was unavoidable and, in fact, necessary, considering the nature of group therapy. When ideas and concepts are shared, it is not uncommon to revisit previously discussed topics. Some may argue that this is inevitable with respect to cognitive–behavioral approaches given that the aim is to modify preexisting beliefs that are often resistant to change (Kuehlwein & Rosen, 1993).

The treatment group participated in six 2-hour workshop sessions (one presession and five treatment sessions) conducted by a certified counselor at Carleton University during the winter term. The second author cofacilitated the group under the counselor's supervision.

The day before each session, the second author called the students to remind them about the workshop. For those students who missed sessions, a telephone checkup was made to inquire about their reasons for not attending.

Presession

Treatment Component

The counselor outlined the workshop objectives and discussed issues of confidentiality and commitment to the workshop with the participants.

TABLE 11.1
Summarized Testing Schedule for All Groups Across All Time Intervals

Group	Presession (T1)	Session 3 (T2)	Session 6 (T3)	Follow-up (T4)
Treatment	All measures	PPA only	All measures	All measures
Comparison group 1	All measures	PPA only	All measures	All measures
Comparison group 2	All measures except PPA	None	All measures except PPA	All measures except PPA

Note. PPA = the Personal Projects Analysis questionnaire (Little, 1983); T = testing interval. The order of measures was randomized within each session. Two measures of procrastination (the PPA and the Procrastination Assessment Scale–Students [Solomon & Rothblum, 1984]) and three measures of subjective well-being (the Satisfaction With Life Scale [Diener, Emmons, Larsen, & Griffin, 1985] and the Positive and Negative Affect Scales [Diener & Emmons, 1984]) were used in this study.

Research Component

The first session was the first testing interval (T1; see Table 11.1). Every participant was required to complete a consent form. The counselor described the research study and distributed a questionnaire package to be completed before participants left the session. The students in the first comparison group received the five questionnaires described in the previous section, and the students in the second comparison group received all measures except for the PPA.

Session 1

Treatment Component

The counselor explained the purpose and goals of the workshop and had participants introduce themselves to the group. In addition, she explored with participants some definitions of procrastination, together with the pros and cons of task delay. Participants shared personal thoughts and feelings pertaining to their own experiences of academic procrastination. The counselor addressed the issue of taking responsibility for one's own behavior. Following this, students discussed their thoughts and feelings about academia. The counselor introduced aspects of procrastination such as task avoidance, fear of failure (e.g., Rothblum, 1990), and irrational thoughts in an attempt to dispel any cognitive myths (e.g., "I should be productive all the time") and to challenge existing maladaptive thoughts that sustain procrastination (e.g., "If I start earlier, I will have less or no time to do enjoyable things"). Students wrote down their feelings about procrastination, and the counselor distributed exercise sheets to help them replace their preexisting, unfavorable thoughts with more helpful ones. On the first exercise sheet, students documented their thoughts and behaviors and rated their feelings (on a 10-point scale) associated with academic procrastination before, during, and after a chosen task or activity. (The results of these exercises were not a part of this study.) On the second sheet, structured the same as the first, students wrote down helpful replacement thoughts that they generated on their own following tips the counselor gave in the session. Next, they rated their feelings and behaviors associated with these new thoughts relative to the chosen task or activity. At the end of the session, the counselor introduced the implications of anxiety in procrastination and taught participants relaxation exercises (involving visualization) to help minimize this anxiety. Assignments for the following session were to practice the relaxation technique and to continue to use the exercise sheets. The thoughts, feelings, and behaviors that students identified as pertaining to procrastination were revisited throughout the workshop. (No data were collected for this session.)

Session 2

Treatment Component

Session 2 began with a discussion of the previous session's assignment. The group discussed additional cognitive beliefs that sustain procrastination (e.g., perfectionism: "I should be perfect, and if I am not I am worthless"). The counselor also brought up issues around getting started. Reinforcing the content from the previous session, she asked students to brainstorm on how to change their cognitive script (i.e., by developing new statements to replace the old, less helpful statements). Subsequently, students broke up into dyads to help each other find solutions to their individual problems and suggest alternatives to their irrational thinking (e.g., irrational thought: "If I like [a particular subject], I should be good at it, and it should come easy to me"). The counselor then handed out another exercise sheet, adapted from psychologist Neil Fiore (cited in Burka & Yuen, 1983), called "the un-schedule." This sheet contained a blank timetable for the week (weekends included) that divided each day into 30-minute intervals. The counselor asked students to fill in all time slots that pertained to routine activities, such as getting ready in the morning, transportation to and from university, and scheduled classes, as well as predictable activities, for example, appointments and meetings. If they were unsure when exactly a particular activity would be done (e.g., grocery shopping), students were to estimate the time and day they might do it. Finally, they were instructed *not* to record doing any academic work until *after* they had done it. Students took the un-schedule home and, over the course of the week, indicated the actual time spent on any coursework by writing it in the schedule. The purpose of the un-schedule was to provide students with a more realistic view of what their individual schedules were like. This exercise allowed students to make several observations, including when they were studying, how long they were studying, and where else in their schedules they could make time to study. This helped students both to look ahead to see how much of their time was already committed and, hence, see the maximum amount of time left to complete tasks and to look back to see where their time had gone.

Research Component

Session 2 was the second testing interval (T2). Participants who previously completed the PPA (the treatment group and first comparison group) were asked to complete it again. Projects were rated along all project dimensions, as previously done in the presession. No research testing was required for the second comparison group.

Session 3

Treatment Component

In session 3, the counselor introduced the topic of project management and sought feedback on students' use of the un-schedule given in the previous session. The counselor mentioned goal setting in the context of breaking down projects into manageable parts. Each student was asked to choose one project to work on and to team up with a partner to plan how he or she would go about working on it. Participants were instructed to take turns listening to and strategizing with their partners about a specific academic task. In addition, the counselor encouraged students to consider possible self-sabotage statements or circumstances that may be preventing them from reaching their goal. A discussion concerning choice brought up issues regarding control (or fear of losing it), self-actualization, societal expectations, and resentment from the group. The counselor then addressed the issue of low frustration tolerance, and she also elaborated further on concepts such as fear of success as well as of failure (e.g., Rothblum, 1990), the distinction between the two, and comfort zone issues (i.e., using procrastination to be connected to others). Further, she mentioned "thought keeping" in the light of easing the sometimes paralyzing guilt students may be feeling. For example, students were encouraged to avoid using words like "should" or "must" with themselves when trying to overcome procrastination. Another dyad exercise gave students the chance to correct this lecturing or "parental" style that many participants had embedded as part of their cognitive scripts. Students were encouraged to monitor and modify their cognitive scripts and irrational negative self-talk over the course of the week as well as continue to work on the task they chose to focus on with their partner at the beginning of the session. (No data were collected for this session.)

Session 4

Treatment Component

At the beginning of session 4, as in previous sessions, students provided feedback as to how they were feeling, what they were doing, and what obstacles or self-sabotaging (if any) had occurred in the past week. Negative self-appraisals (e.g., "I'm too stupid to finish this"), as well as problem-oriented solutions, were addressed as needed. The group as a whole offered solutions for specific students in need of help. The counselor revisited the issue of project management. To assist students in their progress, she presented the following seven guidelines toward meeting goals:

1. make your task specific and concrete,
2. break your task into small steps,
3. start up,
4. visualize your progress,
5. optimize your chances of completing your task,
6. stick to a time limit, and
7. do not wait until you feel like it.

The counselor introduced the notion of commitment, along with the costs and benefits of procrastinating. For example, she pointed out that some students may be feeling "stuck" because they perceived becoming more productive as a threat (e.g., "No longer procrastinating might mean that people will expect me to continue to do well"). (No data were collected for this session.)

Session 5

Treatment Component

During session 5, the group discussed overall feedback about the workshop, and with the permission of all participants, the experimenter (the second author) audiorecorded the session. Students were asked whether they felt that they had benefited from the treatment and in what way. They were also asked to comment on what they disliked about the workshop and to make suggestions on how to improve it. These tape recordings were used to help the experimenter understand the numerical data and were not systematically quantified or analyzed in any other manner, as the focus was on the outcome measures of procrastination and subjective well-being.

Research Component

Session 5 was the third testing interval (T3). The complete questionnaire package was given to all three groups. However, only the groups that previously completed the PPA were asked to complete it again.

Follow-Up Session

The follow-up session contained no treatment component. This was the fourth testing interval (T4). A follow-up appointment was scheduled in mid-April (approximately 2 weeks after treatment ended). All participants completed the questionnaire package. The treatment group and the first comparison group completed the PPA in the same manner as in session 5. Similarly, feedback was audio recorded for those participants who did not attend session 5. The experimenter provided a debriefing summary to each participant on completion of the questionnaire package.

EVIDENCE FOR THE SUCCESS OF THE INTERVENTION

Given the broad readership of this book, including counselors as well as researchers, we have summarized the results quite generally. Although summarized, this presentation of the results captures the main significant effects, as no significant findings were associated with the measures of subjective well-being (i.e., affect measures or Satisfaction With Life Scale). First, we present the results of the pre- and posttest procrastination scale (i.e., the PASS) to demonstrate the efficacy of the intervention on self-reports of procrastination. We then provide a more detailed account of the PPA data in relation to the intervention.

Reported Problems With Procrastination

At the outset, the three groups, although different in manner of recruitment, were similar in terms of procrastination. In response to the PASS question, "To what extent do you want to decrease your tendency to procrastinate on this task?" the mean pretest scores for the treatment, first comparison, and second comparison groups across all six academic domains were 4.17 ($SD = .57$), 3.87 ($SD = .68$), and 4.07 ($SD = .53$), respectively. A one-way analysis of variance revealed no significant difference between groups at the pretest for this item, suggesting that the three groups were equivalent in their desire to decrease their procrastination.

In order to investigate whether a significant decrease in the prevalence of procrastination would occur over time for the treatment group relative to the comparison groups, the total procrastination score from the first section of the PASS was analyzed using a repeated measures analysis of covariance (ANCOVA) with T1 PASS scores as a covariate. As expected, an omnibus F test yielded a significant difference between groups ($F(2, 46) = 8.18, p < .001$). Follow-up comparisons revealed the mean difference in PASS scores for the treatment group to be significantly less than scores for both comparison groups at T3 ($D = -5.91, p < .003$, and $D = -5.14, p < .01$, respectively) as well as at T4 ($D = -3.83, p < .01$, and $D = -3.21, p < .03$, respectively). In other words, this finding reflected a significant reduction in procrastination for the treatment group relative to the comparison groups, both after treatment had ended and at the follow-up. There was no significant difference between the comparison groups themselves.

Using paired-samples t tests, within-subjects analysis for the treatment group revealed significant decreases in PASS scores for T1 versus T3, $t(14) = 2.85$, $p < .01$, and T1 versus T4, $t(14) = 3.89$, $p < .002$. There were no significant within-subjects differences for the remaining two groups. Taken together, these results suggest that the workshop had some effect in lowering the level of procrastination for the treatment group over and above chance alone.

PPA Results

Project Factors

Scores for each of the 17 scale-rated PPA dimensions were summed across all of the projects, and their respective means were grouped into five factors: Meaning, Structure, Community, Efficacy, and Stress. Using paired-samples t tests for both groups separately, only the treatment group revealed within-subjects significance over time for three PPA factors: Structure, Community, and Efficacy. (An omnibus ANCOVA was not conducted for these factors, which results in an inflated Type I error rate in the data analyses. We did not make a family-wise error correction, as the comparisons were set out a priori based on theory.) The treatment group's appraisal of project structure increased at the end of treatment, $t(14) = -2.76$, $p < .02$, as well as at the follow-up, $t(14) = -3.82$, $p < .002$, relative to before treatment began. Similarly, this group reported project community to be higher at the follow-up, $t(14) = -2.66$, $p < .02$; however, this increase did not occur at the end of treatment (T3). On the contrary, project efficacy increased at the end of treatment, $t(14) = -2.21$, $p < .04$, but not at the follow-up, compared with before treatment. In general, these results suggest that project systems for those students receiving treatment for their procrastination were more structured and visible to others. It also suggests that these students perceived themselves to be more self-efficacious by the end of treatment compared with when they started.

Project Dimensions

Only the underlying PPA dimensions of the three significant factors (i.e., Structure, Community, and Efficacy) from the within-subjects analysis of the treatment group were explored. No significant difference in project dimension appraisals across these three factors was found for the comparison group.

Paired-samples t tests revealed several project dimensions to be significantly different when mean pre- versus posttest scores were compared; these included Outcome, Time Adequacy, Control, and Other's View. We also examined the project dimension Procrastination, given the focus of this study. Relative to the pretest, the Procrastination project dimension appraisals decreased significantly by the end of treatment, $t(14) = 2.15$, $p < .05$.

Procrastination Relapse After the Intervention

Interestingly, the postintervention decrease in procrastination was not significant by the follow-up testing, even though the overall procrastination appraisals at follow-up were lower than before treatment began. In other words, it would appear that the treatment group's ability to decrease their project-level procrastination, or at least their self-reports of their project procrastination, rebounded somewhat after treatment sessions had ended. This may indicate that the treatment effects were not sustainable over time in terms of project-specific procrastination, although participants' self-reports of academic procrastination as measured by the PASS reflect a significant, sustained decrease in self-reported academic procrastination.

The remaining four significant project dimensions, Outcome, Time Adequacy, Control, and Other's View, improved over time. Specifically, in terms of the successful completion of their projects, or project outcome, students appraised their projects as potentially more successful by the end of treatment compared to before treatment began, $t(14) = -3.00$, $p < .01$. However, an improved appraisal of the project dimension outcome was not observed at the follow-up. Similarly, in terms of time adequacy, students considered the amount of time they spent on their projects to be more adequate, but only at T4 relative to T1, $t(14) = -2.55$, $p < .02$, and not T3 relative to T1. The same was found with respect to how important projects seemed to be by relevant people (i.e., other's view), $t(14) = -2.88$, $p < .01$. In other words, the treatment group considered that other people perceived their projects to be more important at the follow-up than at any other time. However, in the case of project control, appraisals were significantly higher at both the posttest, $t(14) = -2.56$, $p < .02$, and the follow-up, $t(14) = -2.75$, $p < .02$, relative to the pretest. This would suggest that treatment may have improved students' sense of control over their projects and that this was sustained through to the follow-up testing at T4.

CONCLUSIONS AND IMPLICATIONS

One of the main objectives of the workshop was to help students decrease their tendency to procrastinate. The results of this research revealed two key pieces of evidence that the treatment had some degree of success in reducing self-reports of procrastination. The first of these pertains to the Procrastination Assessment Scale–Students, where a significant difference between groups revealed a decline in self-reported academic procrastination for the treatment group relative to the comparison groups at both the posttest and follow-up testing intervals. Additionally, the within-subjects analysis for the treatment group indicated that the PASS scores significantly decreased at the end of treatment, as well as at the follow-up, relative to before treatment began. Second, the PPA project appraisals of the procrastination dimension decreased significantly over time for the treatment group on examination of within-subjects analysis; this was not the case for the comparison group. These results indicate that the workshop sessions had a positive effect upon students, reducing their tendency to procrastinate.

The present research used the PPA as an outcome measure of subjective well-being, much as McGregor and Little (1998) did in previous research, to determine the effectiveness of academic procrastination treatment. Although the results revealed no significant differences between groups across project factors (possibly due to insufficient statistical power given the small sample size), the within-subjects analysis for the treatment group revealed that the factors Structure, Community, and Efficacy increased significantly from pre- to posttreatment. Subsequently, the project dimensions associated with these factors were also found to be significant: Time Adequacy, Control, Other's View, and Outcome. At the end of treatment, the appraisals of all four project dimensions increased significantly.

Given that two of the four project dimensions—Time Adequacy and Control—load onto the factor Structure, the results would seem to indicate that treatment did more for improving the individual's ability to structure his or her projects. Evidence of perceived improvement in project structure was also found in the comments of the workshop participants. For example, one participant commented,

> [The workshop content] gives you ideas of what you might try *to do*, and if you get different ideas, something might work for you; some things won't, but at least you have *different things to do* and different things to try. So I liked that, and I'd probably encourage a bit more of that and spending more time on these exercises here, because I found it more powerful *when I do them* here because *I focus on doing them*. [italics added]

Perhaps most significant in this quote (as indicated by the added emphasis) is the participant's own focus on *doing*. From a phenomenological perspective, procrastination is not about *having*, it's about *doing*. The question from this perspective is, What is it that I can *do* in my current personal projects to reduce my procrastination, as opposed to what is it about myself that I can change? As captured in the PPA factor of Structure, the academic procrastination intervention had a clear effect on the students' ability to do things, as it increased their project control and time adequacy appraisals significantly across time. This focus on what students can do in their current projects to facilitate completion parallels Lay's suggestion to students (chap. 4, this volume) that they must find the "right" place to do their work. Just changing the location in which one engages in a project may decrease the likelihood of procrastination by providing more control or structure for the project activity.

This participant's comments indicate that the research project more generally brought the focus back to the *doing* as opposed to the *having* of procrastination. From a project-analytic perspective, we were able to capture aspects of the *not doing* of procrastination and provide the potential for a more effective approach to evaluating and, perhaps, implementing intervention strategies. What remains to be discussed is what could be done differently in future research and intervention from a project-analytic perspective.

FUTURE CONSIDERATIONS

All studies have limitations, and we have identified at least three key shortcomings in the present research that need to be considered: small sample size (an important caveat with respect to the multivariate analyses used); lack of randomization of the participants in the quasi-experimental design (which threatens external validity); and the use of a single, campus-based treatment program. These limitations, among others, lead to a number of suggestions for future research such as tracking specific projects, categorizing different types of projects, adding other PPA project dimensions, and including more objective measures pertinent to procrastination.

One improvement in the experimental design might include incorporating a method of tracking specific projects or groups of projects over the course of treatment. For instance, in one of his studies, Lay (1990) asked students to indicate a deadline for their projects—for example, within 2 months (i.e., short term), beyond 2 months (i.e., long term), or no specific deadline. His results revealed a significant relationship between procrastination, short-term deadlines, and dejection; relative to nonprocrastinators, procrastinators reported higher levels of dejection with respect to short-term deadlines. Given that many academic projects have short-term deadlines, a replication of Lay's methodology may be interesting to examine in the context of procrastination intervention from a project-analytic perspective.

In terms of project type, the notion of project categorization might be useful in providing further exploration of procrastination in relation to the PPA and subjective well-being. For instance, analyzing projects based upon their classification with respect to molarity[1] (e.g., "write the introduction to

---

[1]Molarity is a term used in the analysis of Personal Action Constructs units that describes the level at which a project or life task is identified. In this respect, it shares a similarity to action identification theory (Vallacher & Wegner, 1987). For example, a project phrased at a high level of molarity might be "complete my doctoral studies." The same person might phrase this project at a more molecular level with "make my seminar presentation on Wednesday" or "finish reading the last few pages of the assigned papers for class." Personal projects are generally more flexible in terms of the level of molarity, as life tasks by definition are molar concepts that encompass a series of subtasks in their completion. As opposed to the more socially prescribed life task, personal projects range in molarity depending on the individual's current situation. As Little has often noted (e.g., 1989), personal projects range from the mundane and molecular (e.g., "feed the cat," "grow my nails") to the magnificent and molar projects (e.g., "become a better person," "transform Western thought").

my English essay" vs. "get a good grade in the course") as well as content (e.g., reading projects, writing projects, group projects) may be worth exploring in the future. In research by Elliot, Sheldon, and Church (1997), two dichotomous categories referred to as *avoidance goals* (e.g., "avoid procrastination") and *approach goals* (e.g., "be more conscientious and efficient") were created from the lists of personal strivings students provided during testing. The results revealed that students with a greater proportion of avoidance goals reported lower global subjective well-being over the course of the semester. Furthermore, those students who reported fewer self-regulatory skills were found to have a greater number of avoidance projects, suggesting that the more avoidance goals students had, the more they expected to do poorly on their goals. Taken together, these results support the notion that much may be gained from a project analytic perspective in which various categories of personal projects are explicitly identified, and the project-analytic framework itself may help the counselor intervene at the level of the students' projects to help them maintain their self-regulation.

Future research might also benefit greatly by expanding on the PPA project dimensions used, as the ones in the present study were not comprehensive and may "not capture all of the elements that underlie global appraisals of . . . [project] systems" (Pychyl & Little, 1998, p. 452). Possible dimension additions relevant to academic procrastination may include dejection, anxiety, and commitment, to name a few. Again, drawing on Lay (1990), we have reason to believe there is a link between dejection-related emotions (i.e., exhilarated, hopeful, happy, sad, disappointed, and disgusted) and procrastination. We agree with Lay's conclusion that dejection could be treated as an outcome variable in future research. Likewise, the construct Anxiety may be relevant, given that relaxation techniques are a part of many counseling interventions and may be included as an added dimension of PPA. The inclusion of commitment as an ad hoc PPA dimension may be another good choice, as it is supported by previous research by Pychyl (1995; Pychyl & Little, 1998), who concluded that the likelihood of success with any given project may depend mainly on a student's personal sense of commitment to that project. These ad hoc dimensions, along with others, may serve to capture significant changes within counseling interventions that may not be revealed through typical subjective well-being outcome measures alone.

Finally, future research examining the effectiveness of procrastination treatment should include objective dependent variables, as opposed to self-reports exclusively, as part of the testing procedure. In addition to others' ratings of the individual's procrastination, future research may benefit by using the number of projects that fail to be completed or are submitted past their due date as an objective measure of procrastination.

These reflections on future research indicate that a project-analytic perspective has a great deal to offer in terms of an understanding of and potential intervention with academic procrastination. By moving from a perspective that emphasizes the *having* or *not having* of trait psychology to a middle-level unit of analysis perspective that directly addresses the *doing* and *not doing* in students' lives, we may come to a much better understanding of how academic procrastination undermines students' academic progress and well-being. Given the clear focus of the project-analytic approach on the person in context, we may also be able to develop a more reflexive and relevant approach to counseling the procrastinator in academic settings.

12

A NARRATIVE APPROACH TO PROCRASTINATION IN ACADEMIC SETTINGS

JEAN O'CALLAGHAN

Narrative counselors are particularly interested in the stories clients tell about their problems. These stories can create in the storyteller a sense of self that is defined and limited by such accounts (White & Epston, 1990). The stories students tell about their experiences of procrastination can range from confident accounts popular in youth culture ("I'm so clever, last minute is cool") to stories of self-doubt ("I've got a problem"). A narrative therapeutic approach potentially offers the possibility of helping students to "re-author" their problem stories in order to be less identified with the negative attributes associated with being a procrastinator.

This chapter describes an exploratory intervention study using narrative therapeutic techniques with volunteer self-reported procrastinators in a university setting. The effects of the intervention program are presented, using a qualitative method of analysis, to compare these participants' pre-

I thank the Roehampton Education Development Centre for locating and funding this research. Thanks also to Penny Stribling and Frances Michie, who helped audit this analysis; to Sheila Lauchlan and Fran Hedges for their narrative expertise; to Don Rawson and Diane Bray for their support for this research from the beginning; and, finally, to the participants, whose generous sharing made this research possible.

and postintervention accounts over 6 months of one academic year. First, a brief overview of the psychological relevance of working with procrastinators' storied accounts is given, considering both the psychological and therapeutic perspectives of narrative understanding.

A NARRATIVE APPROACH
TO PROCRASTINATION

A *narrative* is a story-based account within which everyday experience is mainly understood. Stein and Policastro (1984) defined a story as an episode that includes an actor/protagonist and a causal sequence that is structured in such a way as to produce a particular conclusion that has purpose for the narrator. Bruner (1986) characterized this intuitive mode of information processing as "narrative knowing," because it is less under conscious control and more influenced by the emotional tone of remembered experience. Such understanding is within the capacity of children as young as age 3 and supports the development of episodic memory that constructs a personal history and a sense of self that can be recalled in storied accounts (McAdam, 1993; Polkinghorne, 1988).

Counselors have always worked with clients' stories for personal change. More recent trends have identified narrative truth as distinct from historical truth (Schafer, 1992; Spence, 1982). A current approach to working with clients' stories has emerged from the writings of family therapists such as De Shazer (1988), Gustafson (1992), and Parry and Doan (1994). Among the most influential of these are Michael White (1995; White & Epston, 1990) and his associates, who see notions of truth as relative rather than transcendent. Although they consider themselves to be broadly agnostic about mental processes and intentionality, they emphasize the importance of how language is used to construct experience in the stories lived and told. It is White's perspective that mainly informs the intervention program used in this study.

Goals of the Intervention Program

The overall aim of the program was to reduce participants' procrastination in relation to their academic writing by (a) raising their awareness of how they construct meanings about personal experience through stories told, (b) illustrating how "problem accounts" that constrain or restrain them can be reframed through various narrative strategies, and (c) co-constructing more flexible and supportive narratives to facilitate engagement with and completion of writing assignments in a timely and satisfactory manner. These goals broadly aimed to create a new learning experience to address procrastination, similar to other intervention programs described in this volume.

Method: The "Start Write" Program

In this study, I examined participants' pre- and postinterview accounts by means of interpretative phenomenological analysis (J. A. Smith, 1996). Student participants were recruited by posters requesting volunteers to take part in research to investigate "how to get going with your writing." The following selection criteria were used: Participants had to (a) be highly motivated and committed to their degree course; (b) be able to complete academic writing assignments, evidenced by the fact that all were either 3rd-year undergraduates with an honors grade average or postgraduate students; (c) acknowledge an awareness that "nothing was stopping them but themselves"; and (d) be willing to take part in a project that demanded a 6-month commitment of weekly sessions for the first 8 weeks and monthly meetings for the following 4 months. Ten full-time mature students (age range 22–36 years, 2 men and 8 women) completed the program.

All sessions were conducted one on one by the researcher/counselor and audiorecorded. Coursework writing was the focus behavior, having been previously identified as among the most psychologically demanding sustained academic tasks (Zimmerman & Bandura, 1994). Before the start of the program, two interviews explored participants' experience and understanding of procrastination. The final four follow-up sessions were concerned with their long-term experiences of academic writing.

Intervention Sessions

The style of the six-session program was informed by an attitude of collaborative inquiry, such that recounted experiences were explored with a sense of curiosity. Rather than focusing on the problem of procrastination, the therapeutic stance suggested was to focus on participants' hopes and possibilities (White & Epston, 1990). Students were therefore invited to "dis-identify" from their accounts of being a procrastinator through the use of different strategies that questioned these "problem-saturated" stories. The process of re-authoring aimed to help participants develop richer accounts of their experience that included their hidden unvoiced stories of capacity and agency. The key strategies used in each session are briefly summarized in this section.

In session 1, I invited participants to think about anyone in their lives, past or present, whom they considered to be nonprocrastinators. Together we explored the personal qualities identified in terms of how participants defined themselves as different and discussed possible ways of developing such qualities.

In session 2, I used De Shazer's (1988) "miracle question" to uncover more of participants' hidden agency. This strategy invited them to consider the following possibility: "Suppose that when you go to sleep tonight, a miracle happens and the problems that brought you here are solved. But since you are asleep, you don't know that the miracle has happened until you wake up tomorrow. What will be the difference that will tell you that a miracle has happened?" (De Shazer, 1988, p. 78). This exercise encouraged participants to practically consider the behavioral consequences of the solution. The request to provide as much everyday mundane detail as possible about what doing coursework would be like without procrastination led them to generate ideas about small changes that they could easily implement.

Session 3 was concerned with externalizing the problem story, in keeping with Epston's (1989) stance that "the person is not the problem, the problem is the problem" (p. 26). Epston (1989) and White (1995) devised this technique to help the person mentally separate from his or her presenting issues. I invited participants to see procrastination humorously, characterized as a restraining influence that "visited" them, rather than as an intrinsic personal trait. They were understood as responding to a problematic situation rather than "embodying a problem." In this session, the relative influence of procrastination on the life of participants and their influence on "the life of procrastination" were also discussed to expand students' perspective on the issue. Such indirect strategies avoided direct confrontation with the problem, as "fighting back" language could have reaffirmed the "old" story and created further constraints (White, 1995).

Session 4 focused on enhancing participants' awareness of how they "positioned" themselves in conversations with others and their own self-talk, suggesting a sense of "multiple selves" (Davies & Harre, 1990). This exercise illustrated that they had both a repertoire of avoidance, energy-draining talk and a capacity for energizing, inspirational talk that often got lost in their negative appraisals of themselves and others.

In sessions 5 and 6, participants' first stories told about their experiences of procrastination were compared with the co-constructed accounts created in the first four sessions, including their own forgotten inspirational stories. This exercise highlighted, for each student, the capacity to generate diverse accounts. The benefits and constraints of these different storied positions were explored in terms of which "audiences" would accept or reject them. McLeod (1997) noted that in the co-construction of more supportive accounts, it is important for counselors to ensure that clients have access to audiences that will accept these new connections in social conversations. Thus, the process of re-authoring involves finding broader perspectives within which the thoughts, feelings, and actions of the person can be practiced, integrated, and understood. It is therefore suggested that this narrative approach encourages individuals to construct a metanarrative that subsumes their previous stories and story-making strategies into a broader framework of meaning, rather than merely replacing negative accounts with more positive ones.

Qualitative Analysis

Interpretative phenomenological analysis (Macran, Stiles, & Smith, 1999; J. A. Smith, 1996) was used to compare participants' pre- and postintervention accounts of their reported experiences of avoiding or engaging with academic writing. The verbatim transcripts of the first two and the last two interviews of the 12 sessions with each participant were the main focus. I read each transcript case by case and identified any statements that appeared relevant to understanding procrastination. These extracts were excerpted and grouped together to represent important themes. This was an iterative process, during which I made constant comparisons within case transcripts and between participants. After each set of interviews had been analyzed in this way, I produced a summary of all identified themes with supporting quotes for each participant. As a validity check on the analytic process, two colleagues, both qualitative researchers, viewed a random selection of labeled themes and their relevant quotes to ensure a consensus of appropriate labeling. There was discussion and modification of labeled themes where significant disagreement occurred.

In the next stage of analysis, I considered the themes identified in all 10 participants' summary documents to produce a comparison of experiences. Themes that clustered meaningfully together were checked against original transcripts and then grouped into broader domains. This process was also checked by the same two colleagues, as the interpretative process always requires vigilance and yet cannot be excluded (Macran et al., 1999). The process of analysis, therefore, aimed to produce a description of key domains and their constituent themes to illustrate how this group of students constructed their experiences as represented by their accounts.

Narrative Domains and Themes

A distinctly different pattern of themes was evident between participants' preintervention accounts of procrastination and their postintervention reports of how they related to their academic writing. Given the constraints of space, the most important domains and a representative sample of constituent themes are summarized in Table 12.1.

Each domain is explored in this section showing the researcher's interpretative comments and illustrated with participants' verbatim excerpts. Some students are quoted more than others due to the succinct manner in which they captured the essence of the theme being illustrated. All excerpts are coded (by transcript) to ensure anonymity.

Domain 1: Constructions of Procrastinating

Domain 1 was concerned with the central issue of the research, how participants' constructions of procrastination changed as illustrated in the

TABLE 12.1
A Comparison of Pre- and Postintervention Themes Grouped Into Domains

Preintervention themes	Postintervention themes
Domain 1. Constructions of Procrastinating in Academic Writing	
Uncontrollable, automatic process	Just a bad habit, understandable
Associated unsupportive appraisals	Power of self-talk or -conversations
Avoidance as easy comfort	Awareness of rewards of procrastination
Writing should be easy and perfect	Writing is hard work and "good enough"
Intentions lost in emotional needs	Awareness of self-regulation
Domain 2. Sense of Self in Relation to Procrastination	
Negative comparisons with others	
The work is me	I am more than the work
Pressure to perform	Awareness of adult mode and need to care for "child" self
Regressed, resistant "child" mode	Core values evoked by supportive stories
Ashamed and mistrustful of self	Lose "ego" in the zone of the work
Domain 3. Ontological and Behavioral Learning Experiences	
Seldom in right mood or state	Do it differently
Dissociation or time myopia	Do it "badly" with presence
Overwhelmed by task demands	Action inspires action
Overwhelmed by contexts	Sense of embodied regulation

pre- and postintervention themes identified. In one preintervention theme, all participants talked about being "in the grip" of procrastination as an *uncontrollable automatic process*. For example, one student said that "after the last time and that all-night stint, I promised myself it would not happen again, but it did, just the same as before. I just could not get going until the last minute. . . . It's scary, 'cause I don't know what to do about it" (J.1.2).

These experiences created in all participants a sense of dissonance with their intentions. They were aware that their plans to work were "getting lost" without their conscious volition. As one participant put it, "I sit there wanting to write, but instead I play computer games. I know what I really want to do, but somehow I don't do it. I keep doing the useless thing and then feel too tired to start the writing . . . another evening gone!" (T.1.1).

The sense that this process occurred outside of students' conscious awareness was also evident in the *associated unsupportive appraisals* participants constructed about their experience of not doing what they had chosen to do. Procrastination was constructed as a problem account. According to one student, "It's like a mountain looming ahead, and I can't find a path to get up and on top of it, so there never feels a right time to really start" (D.1.2). Another construction of "no gain without pain" illustrated the negative, irrational quality of this thinking: "Oh, I think if I suffer in all the misery of waiting and feeling guilty, then I will be able to pull off this brilliant piece of work at the last minute" (P.2.2).

In contrast to constructing procrastination as misery, five participants reported *avoidance as easy comfort* that allowed them to escape from the anxious and demanding experience of writing by delaying engagement with the process.

All participants reported negative appraisals of their academic writing, with overoptimistic assumptions that *writing should be easy and perfect*, illustrated by this excerpt: "I love planning—but these plans are usually overoptimistic. I expect to write easily and the results to be great! But unfortunately, I have strong memories of previous times when the writing has been difficult and frustrating. So I keep putting off the time when I have to face this anxious feeling" (A.2.3).

Overall, such unrealistic expectations and negative memories compounded with low tolerance for discomfort and feeling out of control with their own process, as illustrated above, allowed their *intentions to get lost in their emotional needs*. This was reported as follows by one student: "In spite of all my resolutions and plans, my feelings rule me a lot of the time. I feel impelled to feel good in the moment . . . and only when the pressure is really on will I break free and do the business" (V.1.6).

The postintervention themes showed qualitative differences for eight of the participants in how they talked about engaging with and completing their academic writing. Procrastination as an uncontrollable problem was reported as less "monstrous" and more contained. White's (1995) questioning strategies did appear to allow the problem to be separated from the person. One student said, "It now feels like *a bad habit and understandable*. I can recognize it, and I have ways of dealing with it. I now see it as a barrier I have to go through and I know what to do, so it's not such a monster, or the monster I made it into because I was so afraid of it . . . even though it was myself" (D.11.2).

Some of these final accounts showed evidence of the narrative techniques being used for self-support and integrated into participants' self-talk and awareness. One student expressed *the power of self-talk and awareness* as follows: "I am more aware of the power of talk, especially how I talk to myself. . . . Before I would constantly barrage myself with put-downs, and now I catch myself doing that in conversations as well. . . always seeing the negative and believing it without question. Now the first thing that comes into my head—I think, oh, maybe that's an old story" (J.12.7).

Awareness of the rewards of procrastination as a coping strategy was recalled by four participants. The awareness of this reward, they reported, facilitated greater separation from the notion of procrastination and its connotations. According to one student, "Even though doing other things was miserable, it felt easier than doing the difficult thing, which was sitting down and doing the work. The thought of the writing felt awful . . . the benefit of easy comfort was such a trap. I'm now amazed that once I've started with enough time, I actually enjoy a lot of the work" (B.11.2).

This notion of "easy comfort" recurred as an important subtheme in terms of the change in participants' awareness of their unsupportive beliefs. The reconstruction of *writing as hard work and good enough* encouraged participants to conclude that the work they produced could be adequately competent. One student stated, "The hard work of doing the writing can be OK when you know what you are doing and that what you want to produce is your best rather than some high-in-the-sky, mega-perfect piece of work! This silly myth I carried around, but because I didn't talk about it to anyone, I believed it" (S.12.3).

Overall, this domain illustrated how participants were "mentally separating" from the notion of procrastination being a personal characteristic to being just a bad habit or a rewarding trap, which could be more easily changed. Changes in appraisals of their writing from perfectionism toward it being a "doable" task indicated a more realistic attitude. Thus, postintervention accounts illustrated a change in participants' understanding toward a more mature *awareness of self-regulation* to support doing their writing.

Domain 2: Sense of Self in Relation to Procrastination

Domain 2 was concerned with participants' self-esteem and self-efficacy, which were central issues in all these interviews. Preintervention themes were mainly concerned with participants' close identification with their work and the pressure to perform. These experiences were associated with the academic context of assessment and comparison with others, and for six participants, their experience was further compounded by early insecurities being triggered. These accounts of constraint or deficit were mainly associated with the sense of self, often with contradictory injunctions such as, "I must be perfect" and "I feel weak and frightened." Such a conflictual stance was evident in the first theme, identified as *negative comparisons with others*, which all participants reported were relevant to some extent. In the words of one student, "I say no to friends 'cause I've built up this backlog of work, and even then I don't do it, so I've no time off. They seem to be able to get work done easily and get great grades and have fun as well. They've got something I haven't got. They are clever or have really strong willpower" (V.1.4). This account positioned this student as different and inferior to her peers, possibly legitimizing procrastination as her only way of working. It also illustrates how labeling herself as a procrastinator limited her to identifying with and behaving consistently according to the negative connotations of this social role—that is, being inefficient and weak willed.

Six participants reported close personal identification with the work. It was so important to them that they could not bear to write unless it was going to be inspired and perfect—*the work is me*. This constraining story was personal because the experience triggered "old stories" of *pressure to perform*.

One student said, "This crock of shoulds . . . all the baggage of stories around the essay are so powerful, I cannot think about it in a way that will allow me to really meet it freshly to work on it" (S.2.5). Stories of episodes were recounted in which parental phrases were remembered: "'Make us proud of you'. . . . Every time I try to write my own ideas, it feels too hot to touch, it's a place of pressure . . . a place I can't cope" (P.2.4).

A related theme that was contributed by these six participants referred to a way of coping that was associated with this early parental expectation and evoked in these students a *regressed, resistant "child" mode*. "If you take the childhood angle, I think there wasn't enough for me. I never had enough space to do my own things . . . the things I wanted to do. Wasn't enough for me, and I seem to be making up for it big time. . . . Never challenge that little girl, she can do what she likes, period. I can't fight her anyway" (B.2.8). Other students stated, "It's like there's a little saboteur inside me who won't cooperate—wants to play or do nothing—and it often wins" (A.1.4) and "I feel like a 6-year-old trying to do adult work." (J.2.6). Participants related this sense of regression to feeling like a child and to anxiety triggered by the pressure to perform. For some, there was a resistant, stubborn "child" who would not cooperate: "If I have to, then I won't," whereas other participants reported that doing repetitive, easy tasks gave them a sense of safety from the threat of the demanding adult task of academic writing. One student said, "I keep rehearsing to be prepared, always needing to be right, but that means I fill my time doing easy repetitive things which feel safe" (T.2.5).

Different strategies for self-soothing these powerful emotions of fear, anger, and frustration were associated with the need for immediate gratification in an indulgent "quick fix" manner that participants reported left them feeling *shamed and mistrustful of themselves*. According to one student, "I never know if I'm going to deliver. It's hard to trust my own word, which makes me feel weak and frightened" (M.1.3).

In the postintervention themes, most participants showed a change in their perceived sense of self as less vulnerable and more resourceful in having both a broader perspective and a more complex appreciation of their functioning. Although therapeutically I was aware of respecting the pain and early injury reported in some participants' first accounts, the focus of the program permitted a stance of respect for them as whole persons with capacities as well as fragilities. The narrative techniques therefore highlighted how they could develop greater self-support strategies to engage with their writing.

The theme *I am more than the work* summed up the change away from participants' close identification with performance in their first accounts. Eight of the 10 talked about having a greater sense of self-acceptance and self-worth. One student stated, "Thinking about what I have achieved in the past—that used to get lost in all the negativity, but I remember some of those episodes now" (S.11.4). In the following two themes, the participants' own words are self-explanatory and are representative of how eight of the cohort experienced change in their sense of self.

They experienced an *awareness of adult mode and the need to care for the "child" self:* "This idea of 'many selves' gave me a way of saying, 'Oh, I can be grown up and businesslike now and do my work with as much efficiency as I can muster . . . and at other times I can have fun in 'child mode'" (B.11.5).

Students also identified *core values evoked by inspiring stories for self-support:* "I now think of that story about the butterfly coming out of the cocoon and remember the phrase, 'The struggle oils the wings for flight.' It inspires me to see the struggle as OK, it's about courage" (V.12.2). "Before, there was me struggling, feeling I had to sort it out by myself. In the conversation suggesting I bring my faith into my writing, it got much more doable. I could pray about it and ask for help and kind of hand it over as part of the service in my life . . . so less about me" (M.11.7).

The theme of *lose "ego" in the zone of the work* referred to five participants' reports that they felt their "ego," or "critical self," was forgotten in the flow of their experience of doing the writing: "When I'm really into it [the writing], I just forget myself in the zone, and I'm not worried about how good it is. I'm really just caught up in the ideas and arguing the point I want to make" (J.11.3). This experience was related to an embodied, experiential awareness when the "self-critic" was out of the way, which is also relevant to the third domain.

Domain 3: Ontological and Behavioral Learning Experiences

Participants also reported specific behavioral differences beyond changes in their way of talking and thinking. For example, they described greater awareness of "being with" and "doing" their academic writing. The preintervention themes mainly concerned experiences of "being," associated with procrastination behaviors of "not doing" (i.e., avoidance and distraction). Low arousal levels, dissociation, and a sense of being overwhelmed by writing tasks and work contexts were among the most common experiences reported.

All participants reported a sense of being *seldom in the right mood or state* to write. They were passively waiting for the "magical, inspirational mood to come" so that they could start. Five participants reported that this feeling of not being in the right mood was associated with managing agitation or anxiety. As one student stated, "I flit from one thing to the next without being able to settle and focus—a flitter, so I don't get deeply into the work" (P.1.8). The repetitive behaviors described above related to "child" self-soothing were similarly reported in relation to coping with the physical symptoms of work-related anxiety. Others used immediate gratification and quick-fix comforts to allay their anxiety, such as eating favorite foods, watching TV, or going out or socializing. Four of the participants reported experiences related to a state of underarousal, low energy, or depressive mood. They found any effort to shift their state too difficult and usually "just gave in to the blob" (M.2.9). Three participants reported experiences of *dissociation or time myopia*. One student said, "I go for ages thinking it will be fine in a kind of dreamy bubble. . . . Then suddenly it hits me what needs to be done, a wake-up call that comes when there is very little time realistically left, and I do it [writing] in a complete blind panic, so I don't remember much about how I did it" (J.2.5).

Another theme identified at an ontological level was a sense of being *overwhelmed by task demands*. One student noted, "There is so much detail to manage when you get into the reading, what to say and what to leave out. I want to include it all, and I know I can't do that" (S.1.4). This sense of feeling "de-skilled" was true for many participants, even though they had been successful at academic writing in the near past. From their accounts, it seemed as though they forgot their previous achievements and were having to start over again to orchestrate their writing experiences.

Overwhelmed by contexts was another prevalent theme associated with ontological experiences of procrastinating. According to one student, "When working at home for a whole day, I actually get lonely, and I'm glad if someone phones me or I pop out for something. I think it's the silence that bothers me" (D.1.7). Two participants talked about moving their study furniture to try to feel better about their working space. A more extreme example of generating a last-minute context in which the work could get done was reported by another student: "On my last courses, I've had to get into this tunnel of focus to do an essay in a last-minute, mad rush. I don't eat or sleep until it's done. It's such a painful place to go, but it's the only way I know of managing this procrastination" (A.2.5).

The postintervention themes were concerned with participants' experiential learning over the 6-month period, reported by them as partly influenced by the conversations in sessions and mostly influenced by their own innovations in practically changing their behavior. The theme *do it differently* was an important source of evidence of participants' creativity in developing their own ways of orchestrating new activity repertoires to support their work. One student remarked, "Baby bites! That has been the big learning for me. Before I would do things all or nothing, and that put me off starting. Now I chunk it into baby bites, and I can get going and keep going. I can also stop and get back to it later" (S.11.5).

Four participants reported that the experience of changing from familiar work contexts helped (i.e., physically working in different places to get away from old negative associations). One student said, "I find if I work at home, I find so many things to do. Even the library at college—I see people to chat to. So I go to the British Library; that has this work atmosphere where I can be free to focus on what I want to do" (P.12.3).

For participants who felt de-skilled, *doing it "badly" with presence* facilitated their separation of different tasks involved with their academic writing. "Play mode" allowed them to just play with ideas without anxiety, and then, at a separate time, "edit mode" supported their evaluation of the work when they had to be in a businesslike adult mode.

A number of participants found from their experimentation that *action inspires action*. This theme is best captured in the following quote: "I've played the piano for years, and I realized that I had all these rituals to prepare myself bodily and mentally to get myself grounded to play. Now I've begun to devise ways of getting the right body–mind feeling of being ready to do the writing, which really helps. . . . I call it straight-back mode" (T.11.4). This way of orchestrating his behavior indicated a more "mindful," reflective, deliberate approach to his work, in contrast to previous "mindless" avoidance activities.

There was also some evidence that the narrative intervention strategies directly supported new ways of behaving and being. Five participants found the miracle question helpful, as illustrated by one student: "I now have parts of the day that can be miracle time, so even if I've had a bad morning, the afternoon can still be a miracle afternoon" (D.11.2).

The theme *sense of embodied regulation* sums up the postintervention changes reported by participants. Differences in actual bodily experiences— for example, feeling grounded, having a "straight back," and having a sense of boundaries (i.e., being able to start and stop)—supported the generation of new memories of good experiences. These changes, participants reported, gave them a greater sense of trust in themselves to be able to get into the right body–mind state for engaging with the demands of their work. It was evident that beyond the changes in their storied accounts, embodied experiential learning was important in these participants' change process.

Overall, eight of these 10 participants reported that they had completed the academic year with their coursework submitted on time and meriting satisfactory grades. One participant completed her degree with honors but still reported high anxiety rather than satisfaction with the whole process. One other participant did not complete her course and only submitted one essay.

In summary, comparing the pre- and postintervention accounts for the majority of these participants, it could be concluded that the experiences of procrastination reported were concerned with their cognitive, emotional, and behavioral misregulation. The changes reported by this group of students involved a learning process toward greater self-regulation that was evident in changed behavior as well as in the narrative reconstructions of themselves and their writing.

DISCUSSION

The main aim of this exploratory study was to help student procrastinators to reconstruct their experiences toward greater self-support to engage with academic writing. Despite the participants' diversity of ages, courses of study, and personal circumstances, they all reported a broadly similar range of experiences with procrastination before the intervention. The majority reported greater regulation and satisfaction with their academic writing 4 months after the program ended.

Preintervention accounts indicated that academic procrastination was reported as a complex, heterogeneous phenomenon, with identified issues being in general agreement with the extant quantitative research literature. Variables highlighted were associated with high anxiety and dejection-related emotions (Lay, 1990), self-esteem issues (Ferrari, 1994), perfectionism (Ferrari, Johnson, & McCown, 1995), self-regulation in terms of under- and misregulation (Baumeister et al., 1994), and behavioral automaticity (Gollwitzer & Bargh, 1996). There was also corroboration with the therapeutic literature in terms of participants' reported descriptions of "child ego states" (Berne, 1964) and experiences associated with narcissistic style issues in adulthood, suggested by memories of parental pressure to perform. Such memories could indicate early developmental attachment deficits in empathic attunement (Burka & Yuen, 1983; Kohut, 1971). These personality features have also been identified in research on self- and emotional regulation (Kuhl, 2000).

Postintervention findings broadly indicate that the reparative experiences involved an educative process of unlearning and relearning. This learning was supported by participants' use of the narrative strategies of the program and their experiential learning, which facilitated the development of new skills and more flexible metanarratives. These metanarratives could be described as personally generated "action repertoires" that included an embodied "felt sense" experience (Gendlin, 1996), evidence of "flow experience" (Csikszentmihalyi, 1992), and mindfulness (Kabat-Zinn, 1994) to support engagement with the perceived difficult task of academic writing. Such postintervention experiences qualitatively contrasted with participants' previously reported "mindless" experiences of procrastination. It is suggested that the added value of their metanarrative perspective was evident in the ways participants restructured their experience by using a wider frame of reference—cognitively, affectively, and experientially—to orchestrate themselves and their academic work. This process of change, it is proposed, was partly supported by the features of narrative outlined in the introduction to this chapter.

Owing to the tacit, automatic experience of procrastination these students reported, using an intuitive approach to work with storied accounts was probably a sensitive and an appropriate intervention. Furthermore, owing to participants' core values, inspirational stories, and previous experiences of agency being stored in narrative episodic memory, this level of processing enabled participants to have easier access to their hidden capacities than the use of a more conscious, rational counseling approach.

In addition, as evident in the postintervention accounts, the narrative strategies used offered participants a radically different way of understanding how they create meaning through language. This perspective enabled them to talk differently by developing a more ironic stance toward their own and others' discourse. Questioning their taken-for-granted assumptions and disidentifying from unsupportive problem accounts of procrastination enabled them to focus on their hidden capacities for *being* and *doing*. This finding broadly agrees with the proposal in chapter 11 in this volume that working with procrastinators is more concerned with capacities for *doing* differently than with *having* a labeled trait.

Yet the limits of narrative need to be acknowledged, as highlighted by the case of two participants for whom this intervention did not offer any significant help with changing their perceptions or behavior. The work with one participant indicated possible significant early trauma. McLeod (1997) advocated that sometimes respectfulness to the stories as told may be therapeutically important, particularly where early trauma is identified. It was also clear that for the highly anxious participant, a "talking cure" was not sufficient to generalize to new behaviors. Possibly a more experiential, behavioral therapy or a multimodal model such as that described in chapter 9 in this volume might have been more helpful. These examples suggest that a narrative way of working may be more suited to a nonclinical population of students.

Briefly considering the benefits and constraints of the method of analysis used, interview data potentially offer greater access to participants' understandings of their experiences than data derived from the more structured approach of questionnaire studies. There is always the difficulty of interpretation, which is more in the foreground in this qualitative form of research. Interpretative phenomenological analysis aims to present a description of the phenomenon being investigated, but given the researcher's subjective interpretations, it is acknowledged that certain issues are highlighted and others may be missed in presenting this construction of procrastination from these participants' accounts. Nevertheless, such studies have a distinct contribution to make in representing the complexities involved in the "lived experience" of being a procrastinator, as illustrated in the data described in this chapter.

In conclusion, the particular form of narrative counseling presented here may be worthy of note for counselors working with procrastination in academic settings. Students are usually considered articulate clients; therefore, working with their storied accounts potentially offers an appropriate model for short-term, solution-focused counseling.

13

DESCRIPTION AND COUNSELING OF THE PERFECTIONISTIC PROCRASTINATOR

GORDON L. FLETT, PAUL L. HEWITT,
RICHARD A. DAVIS, AND SIMON B. SHERRY

There is little doubt that readers of this volume will reach the conclusion that procrastination is a complex phenomenon and that there is substantial heterogeneity among procrastinators. Clearly, not all procrastinators are alike. The purpose of the current chapter is to focus on one particular type of procrastinator—the perfectionistic procrastinator. The first segment of our chapter examines descriptions and accounts of perfectionistic procrastinators. The second segment examines how different dimensions of perfectionism relate to indexes of procrastination. The final segment of the chapter discusses issues involved in the counseling of perfectionistic procrastinators, along with an analysis of factors that may make it difficult to provide effective counseling to clients who are perfectionistic procrastinators.

DESCRIPTIONS OF THE PERFECTIONISTIC PROCRASTINATOR

Historically, a number of authors have observed the link between perfectionism and procrastination (e.g., Burka & Yuen, 1983; Hamachek, 1978;

Hollender, 1965), and descriptions of personality problems such as obsessive–compulsive personality disorder note the co-occurrence of perfectionism and procrastination (see American Psychiatric Association, 2000). Ellis and Knaus (2002) suggested that one type of procrastinator endorses irrational beliefs that represent a blend of self-criticism and perfectionism. Dilatory behavior, self-criticism, perfectionism, and distress all stem from the endorsement of absolute irrational beliefs (see also Ellis, 2002). Pacht (1984) also discussed the link between perfectionism and procrastination in his presidential address to the American Psychological Association. Pacht related the case study of a student who suffered jointly from procrastination and perfectionism and, as a result, was unable to complete his dissertation.

Perhaps the most detailed case account of the link between procrastination and perfectionism was provided by Flanagan (1993). Flanagan described the case of Mr. G, a "26-year old single attorney crippled by lifelong problems of procrastination and indecision" (p. 824). Mr. G had been treated unsuccessfully with a variety of approaches before being assessed. Flanagan (1993) concluded that the root of Mr. G's difficulties was the pernicious belief that he had to be perfect.

Ferguson and Rodway (1994) also illustrated the link between perfectionism and procrastination as part of their case descriptions of nine clients who received cognitive–behavioral treatment for problems attributed to extreme perfectionism. Six of the nine clients, including two people with extreme procrastination, were assessed as having problems with perfectionism and procrastination.

These case studies are useful to the extent that some common themes can be detected. For instance, one common theme that emerges is the tendency for perfectionistic procrastinators to suffer from debilitating levels of fear of failure. This fear of failure is either associated with or a byproduct of feelings of personal inferiority, inefficacy, and low self-acceptance. Moreover, some authors (e.g., Burka & Yuen, 1983) have suggested that perfectionism precedes the procrastination; that is, the dilatory behavior is a response to the perceived inability to meet impossible high standards of perfection.

PERFECTIONISTIC PROCRASTINATION VIEWED FROM A MULTIDIMENSIONAL PERSPECTIVE

The first task for counselors when confronted with a client who appears to be a perfectionistic procrastinator is to administer multiple measures of procrastination and perfectionism to determine which aspects of these constructs are involved. It is now generally accepted that the perfectionism construct is multidimensional. Various conceptualizations of perfectionism are briefly outlined in the following paragraphs.

Frost, Marten, Lahart, and Rosenblate (1990) developed the Frost Multidimensional Perfectionism Scale (FMPS) to assess six dimensions of perfectionism. These six dimensions are high personal standards, concern over mistakes, doubts about action, organization, parental expectations, and parental criticism. These six dimensions emerged after Frost et al. wrote new items and culled other items from existing unidimensional measures of perfectionism. Initial and subsequent research with the FMPS has shown that the subscales assessing concern over mistakes and doubts about actions are the subscales that are associated most consistently with measures of distress (Frost et al., 1990). These factors are also associated with procrastinating for reasons involving fear of failure and task aversiveness.

Hewitt and Flett (1991) simultaneously developed another multidimensional perfectionism inventory. This inventory is also called the Multidimensional Perfectionism Scale (MPS), but it has some content that is quite distinct from the Frost version. The Hewitt and Flett MPS consists of three trait dimensions that assess self-oriented perfectionism, other-oriented perfectionism, and socially prescribed perfectionism.

Self-oriented perfectionism includes having a strong motivation to be perfect, setting unrealistic self-standards, compulsive striving, and an all-or-none type of thinking whereby only total success or total failure exist as outcomes (Hewitt & Flett, 1991). Although self-oriented perfectionism has been characterized by some authors as adaptive, this perfectionism can be associated with psychological distress when negative life events are experienced (Hewitt, Flett, & Ediger, 1996) and when self-oriented perfectionists find themselves in highly challenging and competitive situations, such as is the case for medical students (see Enns, Cox, Sareen, & Freeman, 2001).

Other-oriented perfectionism involves a tendency to have exacting standards for other people. The relevance of this perfectionism dimension to interpersonal relationships is quite apparent, in that other-oriented perfectionism is viewed as a stable interpersonal tendency to demand perfection from others and to be extrapunitive and hostile toward others. The presence of other-oriented perfectionism may generate a great deal of stress and interpersonal conflict.

Socially prescribed perfectionism is arguably one of the most deleterious dimensions in terms of its negative implications for personal well-being. It is defined as the perception that others demand perfection from oneself. Individuals with high levels of socially prescribed perfectionism are highly sensitive to criticism, and they have a strong need for approval (Hewitt & Flett, 1991), yet they perceive that approval is not forthcoming from significant others because perfection is expected. This dimension is linked with negative affectivity in various forms (Hewitt & Flett, 1991) and related deficits such as a lack of constructive thinking (Flett, Russo, & Hewitt, 1994) and negative appraisals of problem-solving ability (Flett, Hewitt, Blankstein, Solnik, & Van Brunschot, 1996).

Which of the perfectionism dimensions on the multidimensional inventories are most likely to apply to extreme procrastination? Stöber (1998) reported findings on perfectionism and procrastination as part of his comprehensive psychometric analyses of the FMPS (Frost et al., 1990). A sample of 184 students were administered the FMPS and the Tuckman Procrastination Scale (Tuckman, 1991). Stöber reported that procrastination was associated with doubts about actions and concern over mistakes, which are both recognized as maladaptive aspects of perfectionism. Procrastination was associated negatively with organization, as might be expected, and there was no significant association between procrastination and personal standards, high parental expectations, and high parental criticism.

A related investigation by Stöber and Joormann (2001) examined perfectionism and indexes of worry and pathological worry in 180 students. They found that worry measures were associated robustly with both procrastination and a joint perfectionism factor consisting of concern over mistakes and doubts about actions.

Empirical research on procrastination and perfectionism as conceptualized by Hewitt and Flett (1991) has underscored the usefulness of a multidimensional approach. Initial research in this area was summarized in a previous chapter by Flett, Hewitt, and Martin (1995). Collectively, past research has indicated that self-oriented perfectionism either is unassociated with procrastination or is associated negatively with procrastination after using statistical techniques that take into account the positive intercorrelations among the three MPS dimensions. Other-oriented perfectionism is not relevant to an understanding of procrastination. However, small but significant positive associations have been detected between socially prescribed perfectionism and procrastination (see Flett, Blankstein, Hewitt, & Koledin, 1992; Martin, Flett, Hewitt, Krames, & Szanto, 1996). Parenthetically, both socially prescribed perfectionism and self-oriented perfectionism are associated with fear of failure (Flett et al., 1992).

More recently, Onwuegbuzie (2000) investigated the association between the MPS (Hewitt & Flett, 1991) and the Procrastination Assessment Scale for Students (PASS; Solomon & Rothblum, 1984) in a sample of 135 graduate students. The PASS provides measures of overall procrastination in academic settings, as well as subscale measures of procrastination motivated by fear of failure and procrastination motivated by task aversiveness. Onwuegbuzie found that self-oriented and other-oriented perfectionism were not correlated significantly with overall procrastination in academic settings, but there was a positive association between socially prescribed perfectionism and procrastination in academic settings ($r = .24$, $p < .01$). In addition, fear of failure was associated jointly with socially prescribed perfectionism ($r = .33$, $p < .001$) and self-oriented perfectionism ($r = .22$, $p < .05$).

This link between procrastination and socially prescribed perfectionism is in keeping with results reported by Burns, Dittmann, Nguyen, and

Mitchelson (2000). Burns et al. found that a measure of "negative perfectionism" was associated significantly with procrastination. They observed that many items from the negative perfectionism subscale were derived from the concept of socially prescribed perfectionism, so the findings are in accordance with past evidence linking socially prescribed perfectionism and procrastination.

PROCRASTINATION AND PERFECTIONISM FROM A COGNITIVE PERSPECTIVE

In addition to examining perfectionism and procrastination at the trait level, the advent of new cognitive measures makes it possible to also examine perfectionism and procrastination at the cognitive level. Recent research in our laboratory has supplemented past research on negative automatic thoughts (e.g., Hollon & Kendall, 1980) by showing that there are identifiable individual differences in the frequency of thoughts about perfectionism as well as the frequency of thoughts about procrastination.

Measures such as the Multidimensional Perfectionism Scale (Hewitt & Flett, 1991) and most procrastination measures focus on stable individual differences in personality traits. In contrast, automatic thoughts measures assess thoughts and images in conscious awareness that are often experienced in response to perceived or actual stressors that presumably have activated underlying cognitive structures (i.e., schemas). Existing measures of automatic thoughts tend to assess retrospective accounts of the frequency of thoughts experienced during the previous week, so these measures focus on cognitive states rather than traits (see Hollon & Kendall, 1980).

A measure of automatic thoughts involving perfectionism was developed following observations that certain perfectionists ruminate obsessively about the need to attain perfection (Flett, Hewitt, Blankstein, & Gray, 1998). Flett et al. created the Perfectionism Cognitions Inventory, which is a 25-item measure of the frequency of automatic thoughts involving perfectionistic concerns such as "I should be perfect" and "My work has to be flawless." These perfectionistic thoughts are a byproduct of the ideal self-schema, and perfectionists are especially likely to experience these thoughts while ruminating about their inability to attain perfectionistic standards. Research with the Perfectionism Cognitions Inventory has shown that high scores on this scale predict significant levels of distress, even after partialing out variance attributable to the trait dimensions of perfectionism such as socially prescribed perfectionism (see Flett et al., 1998).

Subsequent research tested the related notion that certain procrastinators are plagued by automatic thoughts that reflect their dilatory tendencies. Regarding this possibility, it should be noted that the original Automatic Thoughts Questionnaire (Hollon & Kendall, 1980) includes items that make specific reference to a tendency to delay. In the light of these observations, Stainton, Lay, and Flett (2000) created an 18-item measure of the frequency of procrastination cognitions. Respondents indicate the frequency with which they have experienced such thoughts as "Why didn't I start earlier?" and "No matter how much I try, I still put things off." According to Stainton et al. (2000), item content was based on "counseling experiences with troubled procrastinators, and on a general understanding of the procrastination construct" (p. 301).

The existence of these new scales makes it possible to investigate perfectionism and procrastination from a cognitive perspective. Recently, we conducted a series of studies that investigated the link between perfectionism and procrastination cognitions and explored the role of procrastinatory cognitions in psychological distress. Our first two studies examined the link between procrastination cognitions and the trait MPS dimensions (Hewitt & Flett, 1991). The initial study was conducted with a sample of 210 university students. They were administered the MPS (Hewitt & Flett, 1991), the Procrastination Cognitions Inventory (Stainton et al., 2000), and Lay's Procrastination Scale (Lay, 1986). The three MPS dimensions were not correlated significantly with trait procrastination in this sample. Thus, previous findings showing a link between socially prescribed perfectionism and scores on Lay's Procrastination Scale (see Flett, Hewitt, & Martin, 1995) were not replicated in this sample. However, socially prescribed perfectionism was associated with procrastination cognitions, $r = .23$, $p < .01$.

In study 2, the link between the MPS and the Procrastination Cognitions Scale was evaluated further in a sample of 88 undergraduates. Self-oriented perfectionism was associated with procrastination cognitions, $r = .25$, $p < .05$, but a more robust association was obtained between socially prescribed perfectionism and procrastination cognitions, $r = .38$, $p < .001$.

Finally, our third study went a step further by including the Procrastination Cognitions Inventory, the MPS, and the Perfectionism Cognitions Inventory (Flett et al., 1998). Analyses of data from 94 undergraduates confirmed the link between socially prescribed perfectionism and procrastination cognitions, $r = .33$, $p < .01$, but a stronger association was obtained between the measures of perfectionism cognitions and procrastination cognitions, $r = .52$, $p < .001$.

An important issue is whether the link between perfectionism and procrastination is simply due to their mutual association with distress and low emotional stability. Consequently, we also tested whether the link between perfectionism and procrastination could still be detected after controlling for trait neuroticism. The participants in our third sample also completed the 50-item measure of the five-factor model developed as part of the International Personality Item Pool (2001). Low emotional stability (i.e., neuroticism) was associated to a similar degree with elevated scores on the perfectionism cognitions measure, $r = -.29$, $p < .01$, and the procrastination cognitions measure, $r = -.29$, $p < .01$. Note, however, that when partial correlations were computed, the two cognitions measures were highly associated, $r = .44$, $p < .001$, even after taking into account their shared variance with low emotional stability. These data imply that there is a substantial association between automatic thoughts about perfectionism and automatic thoughts about procrastination.

Recommendations for Counseling Perfectionistic Procrastinators

This research on automatic thoughts points to the need for cognitive interventions with perfectionistic procrastinators. However, not only do perfectionistic procrastinators experience negative automatic thoughts, it is also the case that both perfectionism and procrastination have been linked with dysfunctional attitudes (Flett et al., 1995a; Sherry, Hewitt, Flett, & Harvey, 2003) and irrational beliefs (Ellis, 2002; Ellis & Knaus, 2002). Thus, once the counselor has been able to establish which cognitive factors are contributing to the distress of perfectionistic procrastinators, then multifaceted interventions involving cognitive–behavioral treatment strategies can be used.

The first goal will be to control and ameliorate the experience of frequent negative automatic thoughts. Our findings suggest that there are times when perfectionistic procrastinators inundate themselves with intrusive thoughts, and this is a form of cognitive interference that may hinder their ability to attend to new material. These individuals stand to benefit by learning thought-stopping procedures and by becoming more cognizant of the situations that tend to elicit these thoughts.

The second goal will be to remove dysfunctional attitudes or irrational beliefs and replace them with more adaptive thoughts using established cognitive interventions (see A. T. Beck, 1976; Ellis, 1994). Dysfunctional attitudes involve a central focus on the need to attain perfection, and interventions must include a central focus on these thoughts (Hirsch & Hayward, 1998). However, it is also the case that both perfectionism and procrastination are associated with dysfunctional attitudes about the need to attain social approval (see Flett et al., 1995a; Sherry et al., 2003). Thus, when seeking to remove dysfunctional attitudes, it is important to remain cognizant of the excessive desire that perfectionistic procrastinators may have for obtaining approval and avoiding disapproval.

Irrational thoughts can be treated with rational–emotive behavioral therapy (see Dryden, 1995; Ellis, 1994). Ellis (2002) provided a number of useful suggestions when it comes to the treatment of extreme perfectionism. He observed that a central issue that underscores debilitating forms of perfectionism is the irrational importance attached to being perfect. In addition to focusing explicitly on the importance of perfection, rational–emotive techniques can be used to improve the perfectionistic procrastinator's level of self-acceptance, perhaps by removing feelings of inferiority (see Dryden, 1995).

Addressing the Fear of Failure

It was noted earlier that fears of failure are very salient among perfectionistic procrastinators. Ongoing research in our laboratory continues to indicate that perfectionistic procrastinators have elevated levels of perfectionism cognitions, procrastination cognitions, socially prescribed perfectionism, depression, and fear of failure. Their fears are very "self-conscious" in that they are focused on possible shame, a loss of self, and an uncertain future.

Given the extensive fears and distress experienced by perfectionistic procrastinators, general cognitive–behavioral interventions should be supplemented with other interventions that are implemented to decrease fears and subjective feelings of anxiety. Ferrari, Johnson, and McCown (1995) outlined established techniques that can be used effectively to reduce the anxiety experienced by procrastinators. These techniques include visualization with relaxation training as well as systematic desensitization to address the anxiety associated with looming deadlines. We also concur with their general suggestion that all procrastinating students should be screened, and it is essential to administer measures of anxiety and depression to identify those students who would most benefit from interventions designed to reduce anxiety and depression.

Problem-Solving and Stress Inoculation Training

Perfectionism and procrastination are two personality constructs that tend to reflect a negative self-concept, a diminished sense of personal efficacy, and lack of satisfaction with the self (see Flett, Blankstein, & Martin, 1995a; Martin et al., 1996). One indirect way of improving the self-confidence and sense of self-efficacy of procrastinating perfectionists is to provide them with explicit training in problem-solving skills, study skills, and stress inoculation training. Just as it is the case that procrastination is associated with deficits in coping and problem solving (see Flett, Blankstein, & Martin, 1995a), a growing body of literature indicates that certain dimensions of perfectionism are associated with maladaptive forms of emotion-oriented coping and problem solving (see Hewitt & Flett, 2002). Moreover, perfectionists experience elevated levels of stress and stress reactivity (Hewitt & Flett, 2002).

Given the stated link between perfectionism and elevated levels of stress generation and stress reactivity, perfectionistic procrastinators are good candidates for stress management or stress inoculation training or other forms of treatment that focus directly on teaching coping strategies. Treatments focusing on problem-solving and coping skill enhancement may be quite beneficial in reducing stress reactions and the accompanying symptoms, as well as fostering increased levels of self-efficacy. However, it should be recognized that perfectionism is a deeply ingrained core vulnerability factor, and the negative impact of this intransigent personality style is the true source of the stress experienced by individuals. Certain perfectionistic procrastinators may require more intensive psychotherapy that emphasizes the core issues in perfectionism. This involves an intensive course of treatment that focuses on the motivations for and the precursors or sources of perfectionistic behavior. As noted by Hewitt and Flett (2002), these precursors are often interpersonal and involve core needs of the individual (i.e., need to obtain respect, caring, and love and to avoid censure, humiliation, or punishment) that propel perfectionistic behavior in an effort to establish an acceptable identity.

It should be evident from this discussion that there can be several challenges associated with the counseling and treatment of perfectionistic procrastinators. We conclude by discussing some of the inherent difficulties in more detail.

CHALLENGES IN COUNSELING PERFECTIONISTIC PROCRASTINATORS

The previous section included an outline of various interventions that can be used to treat perfectionistic procrastinators. How likely is it that these interventions will prove successful? We believe that it is exceptionally difficult to provide effective counseling and treatment to perfectionistic procrastinators for various reasons. As we discuss in the next section, the first concern involves the willingness to seek help.

Unwillingness to Seek Help

Perhaps the overarching counseling issue is whether perfectionistic procrastinators are actually willing to seek help for their problems. Research in our laboratory has been focusing on the likelihood that perfectionists have a negative orientation toward seeking help. Although our research has focused on perfectionism rather than procrastination, Flett, Blankstein, and Martin (1995a) concluded that a negative orientation toward seeking help should also be evident among procrastinators who engage in self-concealment and who fear negative evaluation.

Our research on perfectionism and the unwillingness to seek help is focused extensively on a recently identified aspect of the perfectionism construct known as perfectionistic self-presentation. Over the years, we have noticed that certain perfectionists are unduly concerned with creating an impression of flawlessness (see Hewitt et al., 2003). That is, regardless of whether they have high or low trait levels of perfectionism, certain individuals are preoccupied with creating a social image of being perfect, and these people will go to great lengths to not display or reveal their mistakes, flaws, and shortcomings. Our work with a new measure known as the Perfectionistic Self-Presentation Scale (PSPS) has found that this personality style has three dimensions reflecting the need to appear perfect, the need to avoid appearing imperfect, and the need to avoid disclosing imperfections to others. This research has also confirmed that perfectionistic self-presentation predicts unique variance in psychological distress, over and above the variance attributable to the dimensions assessed by our MPS (Hewitt & Flett, 1991).

Our initial research on perfectionistic self-presentation and procrastination indicates that perfectionistic self-presentation is associated with procrastination, especially among men. For instance, we examined this issue in a recent unpublished study by administering the Procrastination Cognitions Inventory (Stainton et al., 2000) and the PSPS (Hewitt et al., 2003) to a large sample of 257 women and 123 men. The results for women indicated the presence of small but significant correlations between the measure of procrastination and all three PSPS subscales (rs ranging from .18 to .24). Stronger associations were detected for men, with procrastination being associated with all three PSPS dimensions, including the need to avoid disclosure of imperfections ($r = .30$) and the need to avoid appearing imperfect ($r = .40$). Future research should explore whether perfectionistic self-presentation contributes to the greater reluctance of men, relative to women, to seek counseling.

Our findings are in keeping with Flanagan's (1993) case study of Mr. G. This case study included extensive evidence of perfectionistic self-presentation. Examination of Mr. G's daily record of dysfunctional thoughts confirmed that Mr. G was characterized by a need to avoid appearing imperfect and a sense of being an impostor. Flanagan (1993) noted that Mr. G's daily thought record was

> filled with statements such as "I've let so much time go by, I can't afford to make mistakes," "The best I can do is keep up appearances of having it together," "I'm a fraud," "I'm fooling myself as well as everyone else," and "I can't get by alone." (p. 826).

Flanagan achieved success with Mr. G by using a schema-based therapy that focused on identifying these thoughts, teaching him to reframe his automatic thoughts, and using homework assignments to develop competencies.

Perfectionistic self-presentation is relevant to the counseling of perfectionistic procrastinators in many respects. For instance, people who engage in perfectionistic self-presentation are generally unwilling to engage in the types of self-disclosure that are central to treatment progress, and this problem is exacerbated in group therapy settings. As for the willingness to seek help, our ongoing research on perfectionistic self-presentation has confirmed that this personality style is associated with an unwillingness to seek help for personal problems involving a lack of mental health. The overarching hypothesis that guides this research is that the unwillingness to disclose imperfections to others has negative implications in terms of the perfectionist's general orientation toward seeking help.

We have conducted several studies of the link between perfectionism and negative help-seeking attitudes in university students. For example, Nielsen et al. (1997) administered the MPS (Hewitt & Flett, 1991), the PSPS (Hewitt et al., 2003), and the Attitudes Toward Seeking Professional Help Scale (Fischer & Turner, 1970) to a sample of 184 students from the University of British Columbia. The help-seeking measure consists of four subscales that assess recognition (i.e., recognition of personal need for psychological help), stigma tolerance (i.e., tolerance of the stigma associated with psychological help), interpersonal openness regarding one's personal problems, and confidence (i.e., confidence in the mental health professional).

Analyses of the trait MPS dimensions showed that socially prescribed perfectionism was associated with the help-seeking measures, but stronger associations were obtained with the measures of perfectionistic self-presentation. The unwillingness to disclose imperfections was associated with less stigma tolerance, $r = -.43$, $p < .001$, less interpersonal openness, $r = -.43$, $p < .001$, reduced recognition of the need for help, $r = -.29$, $p < .001$, and less confidence in the mental health professional, $r = -.23$, $p < .01$. Moreover, regression analyses predicting overall scores on the help-seeking measure showed that a predictor block comprising the perfectionistic self-presentation variables accounted for an additional 13% of unique variance, even after taking into account variance attributable to demographic factors (including help-seeking history) and trait perfectionism.

Although most of our research in this area has focused on university students, perfectionistic self-presentation is also associated with negative help-seeking tendencies among adolescents. DeRosa (2000) conducted her doctoral dissertation research on personality factors and help-seeking attitudes in adolescents. The participants were 132 adolescents in high school who completed the PSPS (Hewitt et al., 2003), the Depressive Experiences Questionnaire for Adolescents (DEQ-A; Fichman, Koestner, & Zuroff, 1994), and a 22-item instrument created by Garland and Zigler (1994) to assess adolescents' willingness to seek help for psychological problems from professionals in the school setting. The DEQ-A assesses self-criticism and dependency. It was found that the unwillingness to disclose imperfections was associated with more negative help-seeking attitudes ($r = -.36$, $p < .01$). Self-criticism was not associated with help-seeking attitudes, but dependency was associated with more favorable attitudes.

Unfortunately, the research conducted thus far on help seeking has not included a procrastination measure, and examination of the broader psychological literature reveals limited research on the role of procrastination in help seeking. It is quite plausible that a substantial proportion of procrastinators who are also characterized by elevated levels of socially prescribed perfectionism and perfectionistic self-presentation will be especially unwilling to seek help, and these individuals will try to cope with difficulties on their own. Certain procrastinators may never seek help of any sort.

Reluctance to Change Perfectionistic Standards

Ferrari, Johnson, and McCown (1995) indicated that the subset of procrastinators who do seek help are individuals who tend to have very serious adjustment problems. If these students are perfectionistic, then the counseling process may prove to be quite challenging and difficult. One problem associated with counseling perfectionistic procrastinators who do seek help is that their perfectionism is an inherent part of their personal identities, and these individuals may be quite unwilling even to consider the possibility that they need to give up their perfectionistic standards. This unwillingness to change or alter standards will be especially evident among those who either perceive that their perfectionism has been rewarded at various times or report that they use their perfectionism as a coping strategy (see Hirsch & Hayward, 1998).

Ferrari, Johnson, and McCown (1995) observed that some perfectionistic students being treated for procrastination tend to resist psychoanalytic interpretations of their difficulties. Resistance is even greater when it comes to giving up standards. A. T. Beck and Freeman (1990) discussed the unwillingness to change within the context of the case study of Mary, a computer programmer who was suffering from perfectionism and procrastination. They noted that Mary's "compulsive personality traits had been rewarded in school and at home. Teachers always remarked on her neat, perfect work, which resulted in receiving many awards at graduation" (A. T. Beck & Freeman, 1990, p. 7). However, as an adult, Mary was unwilling to change her perfectionistic standards even though these standards were no longer being rewarded, and "attempts to change her hypervalent schemas were met with great resistance. She wanted surcease from the stress that she felt, but did not want to give up rules and standards that she considered important" (A. T. Beck & Freeman, 1990, pp. 86–87). The authors noted that it is vital to include an explicit focus on the anxiety aroused as standards are challenged and relinquished.

All-or-None Approach to Counseling

A third challenge associated with counseling perfectionistic procrastinators is that perfectionists often take an all-or-none approach to life goals and outcomes (see Burka & Yuen, 1983; Missildine, 1963). This all-or-none approach is likely a reflection of more general cognitive biases such as the tendency to overgeneralize negative outcomes to all aspects of the self (see Hewitt & Flett, 1991).

Given this extreme orientation, perfectionistic procrastinators will benefit from self-regulation training that is focused on setting more modest and appropriate goals. It is particularly important that perfectionistic procrastinators learn to set more appropriate goals in terms of the recovery process and that they recognize that they are engaged in an extensive process where even small improvements in functioning are to be cherished. As noted by Hirsch and Hayward (1998) in their description of a perfectionist known as Mr. R, perfectionists in treatment seek dramatic changes and related forms of self-improvement, and they must learn not to regard modest improvements as failures.

CONCLUSION

Our analysis of the association between procrastination and perfectionism has highlighted the complex nature of perfectionistic procrastinators. Our summary of the existing research indicates that perfectionistic procrastinators suffer from an excessive concern over mistakes, socially prescribed perfectionism, and an abundance of negative automatic thoughts about themselves, including automatic thoughts involving themes of procrastination and a personal inability to be perfect. Moreover, it seems evident that perfectionistic procrastinators are overly concerned with impression management issues and may be characterized by perfectionistic self-presentation. Counselors are advised to use a combined approach that involves cognitive–behavioral techniques and skills training, but there should also be a focus on interpersonal concerns that may undermine the alliance between the client and counselor.

Systematic research has not been conducted on the counseling of perfectionistic procrastinators, though various authors have provided helpful observations about relevant issues of general importance that should be considered. For instance, Ferguson and Rodway (1994) reported that procrastination had a negative impact on the counseling process because perfectionistic procrastinators were often late for the counseling sessions. They attributed this tendency to unrealistic goal setting and scheduling too many tasks at once. Counselors should address both of these maladaptive tendencies. Of course, an alternative possibility is that the tardiness of these individuals is a reflection of their general unwillingness to disclose their imperfections.

Finally, in closing, we would like to suggest that the level of perfectionism expressed by the counselor is another important consideration. Freeston, Rheaume, and Ladouceur (1996) suggested that one way to facilitate improvement among perfectionists is for therapists to take a relaxed approach to homework assignments. This modeling of a nonperfectionistic approach to the evaluation of tasks will be especially appreciated by perfectionistic procrastinators who are highly sensitive to negative evaluations from others.

In summary, we have provided a descriptive overview of the characteristics and nature of perfectionistic procrastinators. Relevant case studies were presented and recommendations for counseling were outlined. We hope that these suggestions will prove helpful in alleviating the distress experienced by perfectionistic procrastinators.

III

EPILOGUE

14

PERSPECTIVES ON COUNSELING THE PROCRASTINATOR

HENRI C. SCHOUWENBURG

The development of counseling programs in various academic centers in North America and Europe for students who procrastinate is in its initial stages. To a large extent, these intervention methods have been developed independently of one another, and little communication about these programs has followed. Thus, there was an important need to describe these different programs in one collected volume. The preceding chapters in part II were intended to serve this purpose. In this final chapter, I highlight a number of common and uncommon themes found in the various intervention approaches described. In addition, I discuss various implicit views in the interpretation of procrastination, such as procrastination as mainly a behavioral problem, procrastination as mainly a cognitive problem, procrastination as mainly a motivational problem, and the similarity of procrastination with addiction and with personality disorder. As a next step, I try to combine these views into a comprehensive theoretical notion of the nature of procrastination. On the basis of this theoretical perspective, and supported by research findings, I conclude by outlining a recommended or more ideal intervention program.

General Themes Across the Intervention Programs

The intervention methods described by the contributors to this volume have been drawn primarily from the current mainstream in psychotherapy. As a consequence, a presentation of cognitive–behavioral interventions is integral to most programs described. Thus, behavioral methods and the reframing of unproductive thoughts form main themes in these interventions. Based on a content analysis of the diverse programs, however, three general higher order themes emerge. Each of these themes involves a general purpose.

The first general theme involves the promotion of habit in working regularly. This is done by introducing self-regulation training. Such training typically includes the use of stimulus-control techniques to protect studying behavior from the influence of distractions and the subdivision of large and vaguely formulated goals (e.g., passing an exam, completing a paper) into a series of well-defined, concrete, attainable, and acceptable subtasks (e.g., tasks for the day or week ahead). In addition, self-regulation training promotes the use of time management techniques in setting deadlines, allocating time, being in the most conducive or "right" place to work on the task, and monitoring progress. Overall, the aim of this self-regulation training is to reduce the gap between (vague) intentions and (concrete) behavior. Consequently, this type of training is directed at the core of the procrastination problem and is probably a very effective component of intervention programs for students who procrastinate.

A second purpose common in the various intervention programs described is to enhance feelings of self-efficacy. In most intervention programs (e.g., those described in chaps. 4, 5, 6, 8, 9, 10, 11, and 13), this enhancement is attempted by identifying and reframing the negative, unfruitful, and irrational thinking patterns that sustain procrastination. This approach is largely based on the conviction underlying rational–emotive behavioral therapy (REBT) that thoughts, behaviors, and feelings are interrelated in such a way that changing thoughts may constitute a prelude to changing behavior.

Finally, in most counseling methods, group influence is used in a variety of ways. To begin with, the group members provide support to each other in their recognition of a common problem. In addition, many programs incorporate the imitation of peer models in overcoming dilatory behavior. Both of these elements serve to enhance a sense of self-confidence and challenge in group members. Group support and disapproval also serve to commit individuals to the successful execution of work plans. As most students are of an age in which they are typically very sensitive to social approval, gaining prestige or losing face are powerful reinforcers in promoting behavioral change.

Some Uncommon Themes Within Specific Intervention Programs

Uncommon themes refers to the more or less unique features of separate counseling approaches. Although relatively unique, they may be attractive and useful to other counselors in developing their own intervention programs. Lay's approach in chapter 4, for example, relies heavily on personality feedback on different trait measures. Other uncommon themes refer to a storytelling perspective on procrastination (O'Callaghan, chap. 12); the consideration with group members of various personal procrastination styles, allowing individuals to identify with one style or another (van Essen et al., chap. 5; and Walker, chap. 6); the self-destructive nature of procrastination (van Horebeek et al., chap. 8, and Pychyl & Binder, chap. 11); concentration problems (van Essen et al., chap. 5); resistance to behavioral change (Mandel, chap. 9, and Flett et al., chap. 13); and enhancing feelings of self-respect and better feelings about themselves in general (Lay, chap. 4, and Walker, chap. 6).

Most of these idiosyncratic additions to the more general themes outlined above may initially stem from the particular theoretical perspective adopted by the counselor. Their purpose may be to sustain or magnify the effectiveness of the more general components of the intervention program. There is as yet, however, insufficient evidence that this is really the case. Nevertheless, because of their apparent appeal to both counselors and clients, unique or idiosyncratic additions to any program may improve its attractiveness, which, in turn, may have a beneficial effect on the motivation to change.

VIEWS ON THE PROBLEM OF PROCRASTINATION

Different underlying interpretations of the nature of the procrastination problem seem to be implicit in the counseling approaches proposed in this volume. By the nature of the treatment, such interpretations may be either rather optimistic or more pessimistic. Optimistic views seem to share the conviction that relatively easily modifiable characteristics, such as behaviors, cognitions, and motivations, lie at the base of the procrastination problem. Relatively pessimistic views, on the other hand, seem to acknowledge the strong resistance to change in procrastinators by stressing the addiction-like aspects of procrastination or even the notion of a personality disorder underlying procrastination. I discuss these major emergent views in more detail in the following sections.

Procrastination as (Mainly) a Behavioral Problem

Counselors who focus on the control of dilatory behavior may view procrastination as mainly a behavioral problem. In this view, students are observed procrastinating when instead they should be studying. As a result of this view, the target of intervention is simply to decrease the rate of procrastination, or the percentage of time spent procrastinating, and to increase the rate of studying. It should be noted that this view may also be adopted by counselors who recognize other interpretations of the procrastination problem, but who may regard the modification of behavior as the only feasible route given the limitations of a short intervention program. In interventions based on this view, counselors use the standard toolbox of the behavior therapist, including (a) instructing, (b) modeling, and (c) conditioning.

In line with this approach, instruction in time management and planning techniques and subsequent modeling are elements of some interventions proposed. Operant conditioning methods are also used in rewarding short periods of studying, and classical conditioning is adopted by promoting associations of working hours with studying. Conditioning of this sort, however, requires repeated practice. Therefore, very short interventions may possibly fail at conditioning the intended study behavior.

A relatively pure example of this approach can be found in chapter 7 by Tuckman and Schouwenburg. As can be concluded from their chapter, a purely behavioral approach to counseling the procrastinator is aimed not at "curing" but at decreasing the frequency of unwanted behavior. Such counseling approaches provide, as it were, nothing more than a "maintenance schedule" for "normal" procrastination (see chap. 1 for a discussion of "normal" procrastination).

Procrastination as (Mainly) a Cognitive Problem

Counselors who view procrastination as mainly a cognitive problem believe that people procrastinate because they have wrong thoughts or beliefs about their work, its conditions, and its consequences. They share, as Burka and Yuen (1983) phrased it, a "procrastinator's code" consisting of a mixture of absolutistic demands on the self to do well at almost anything and of low frustration tolerance showing itself in the demand on the task at hand that it should be performed smoothly and without too much effort (see also Ellis & Knaus, 2002).

A common characteristic of such beliefs is that they are unrealistic. Therefore, the target in purely cognitive interventions is to change this procrastinator's code. The most frequently accepted road to changing unrealistic beliefs may be REBT, as applied in chapter 5 by van Essen and colleagues and chapter 8 by van Horebeek and coauthors. Interesting variants of this approach are described in chapter 6, by Walker; chapter 9, by Mandel; chapter 11, by Pychyl and Binder; and chapter 12, by O'Callaghan.

What can be the expected outcome of such cognitive approaches to counseling the procrastinator? Empirically, such approaches show that they produce some decrease in dilatory behavior given the limited number of sessions (see chap. 5 by van Essen et al. and chap. 11 by Pychyl & Binder). This seems, however, not to result in a dramatic improvement. There is no real indication of "cure" in this type of counseling approach, although, as I note later in this chapter, this may well be in part a reflection of the lack of meaningful outcome-related research as well.

Procrastination as (Mainly) a Motivational Problem

The view that procrastination should be interpreted as a motivational problem results from the observation that procrastinators do not seem to be just lazy and unmotivated, but actively engaged in, and obviously interested in, activities other than the task they put off. These other activities usually lie in the sphere of leisure or pleasure, such as socializing, watching TV, or surfing the Internet.

Counselors who adopt this explanation tend to include the complete context of the behavior involved. They regard this context as a choice situation in which each option has a certain motivational force. In an academic setting, the motivational force for studying is simply less than the motivational force of one of the other options. The observable result is dilatory behavior with respect to studying. This explanation amounts to a combination of self-control theory (see chap. 1 of this volume) with current expectancy value theory of motivation, as formulated by Schouwenburg and Groenewoud (1997) and by Steel (2003).

Procrastination as (to Some Extent) an Addiction

Counselors who view procrastination as an addiction will focus on their clients' persistence of and relapse in exhibiting high levels of dilatory behavior (see West, 1991). Psychological theories of addiction (McMurran, 1994; Robinson & Berridge, 2003) attribute such behavioral tendencies to the fact that in addictive behavior, the overall balance of costs and benefits favors a positive outcome of the addictive behavior. In addicts, this will produce a diminished control over the behavior, impaired self-regulation (see chap. 1 of this volume), and finally lowered self-efficacy expectations. A combination of low self-efficacy expectations with maintained positive outcome expectations may lead to the adoption by the addict of defensive tactics, such as unrealistic optimism about possibilities to change the behavior.

Such a point of view, which is, in essence, compatible with a motivational problem view on the nature of procrastination, seems to apply strikingly to procrastinators. In fact, Ainslie (1992) pointed to this similarity already (see also Pychyl, Lee, Thibodeau, & Blunt, 2000), and some schoolteachers may find this point of view revealing when applied to their procrastinating students.

Viewing procrastination as an addiction acknowledges the difficulties in overcoming procrastinatory tendencies completely. Counseling approaches based on this view will therefore aim not at "curing," but at a certain acceptable level of control or at maintenance of dilatory behavior at a "normal" rate. The intervention of task management groups, presented in chapter 7 by Tuckman and Schouwenburg, combines elements found in various self-help approaches to addiction, such as restructuring the environment, training students in more adaptive behavior, addressing the role of social influence, and being responsible for one's behavior. This type of intervention may thereby be considered as a representative of this view. The addiction perspective is also acknowledged in chapter 8 by van Horebeek et al.

Procrastination as (Possibly) a Personality Disorder

There seems to be a certain personality structure underlying procrastination, both in academic and in other settings (see chap. 3 by van Eerde), to be characterized as extremely low Conscientiousness, defined by such characteristics as aimlessness, unreliability, laziness, carelessness, laxness, negligence, and hedonism. Procrastinators may share these characteristics with people who are impulsive (McCown, Johnson, & Shure, 1993). In fact, empirically, Ferrari (1993) found strong correlations between procrastination and impulsiveness.

Personality disorders are rigid patterns of personality traits resulting in insufficient adaptation of the person to changing circumstances and, as a consequence, in vast and recurrent problems in relationships, work, and social functioning (American Psychiatric Association, 2000). Personality disorders, however, are not discrete instances of psychopathology, but should be viewed as exaggerations of normal personality traits (Millon, 1994). Although not explicitly distinguished in the *Diagnostic and Statistical Manual of Mental Disorders* (*DSM–IV–TR*; American Psychiatric Association, 2000) classification, chronic procrastination could be viewed as a personality disorder involving an exaggerated level of trait procrastination or low Conscientiousness.

Treating personality disorders is a holistic enterprise, like psychotherapy, and cannot be limited to separate deficits. As a consequence, based on a total picture of the personality for each patient in terms of strengths, excesses, deficits, and dysfunction, many different kinds of treatment decisions must be made (Sanderson & Clarkin, 1994). Modern treatments for personality disorders are focused on specific aspects of the disorder, and the selection of specific techniques depends on the nature of the problem and the reactance level of the particular patient. In addition, other decisions involve the breadth of the treatment goals (e.g., treatment of simple or habitual symptoms vs. complex symptom patterns), the depth of the patient's therapy experience (determining, for example, the patient's level of defensiveness or his or her capability to handle disturbing material), and the degree of the therapist's directiveness (Sanderson & Clarkin, 1994).

TOWARD A MORE COMPREHENSIVE VIEW

In sum, there can be little doubt that procrastination is a behavioral problem, a problem of *not doing* (see chap. 11 by Pychyl & Binder) what one intends to do. It is also clear that procrastinators share unrealistic thoughts about their work and themselves. Yet viewing procrastination by students as mainly a cognitive–behavioral problem, which could be modified in a limited number of counseling sessions, might be too simple.

Another outstanding feature of procrastinators is that they find the tasks they postpone aversive and that they lack self-efficacy with respect to study task completion (see Blunt & Pychyl, 2000, and chap. 2 by Ferrari in this volume). This points to a motivational problem (see Steel, 2003).

A further characteristic of procrastinators is personality. As demonstrated by van Eerde in chapter 3, procrastinators share extreme low Conscientiousness, as well as related traits such as lack of self-discipline, distractibility, lack of organization, low need for achievement, lack of self-regulation, and impulsiveness (Steel, 2003; see also chap. 2 by Ferrari). Because of these extreme characteristics, it may be appropriate to speak of personality disorders, and this would imply that treatment should be prolonged and intensive, a requirement that is not met in the intervention methods proposed in this book.

Finally, because of the persistence of procrastination and frequent relapse after treatment, the perspective of addiction may add to our understanding of the procrastination problem. For counseling purposes, this perspective draws attention to a need for prolonged treatment in which counselors must be prepared for frequent episodes of relapse.

A more comprehensive view on the nature of procrastination, therefore, would imply that we understand procrastination as a motivational problem, with both behavioral and cognitive components firmly rooted in personality and with addictive features. Such a view could pave the way for a more realistic counseling approach that will probably be closer to long-term psychotherapy than to short-term behavioral interventions.

AN "IDEAL" INTERVENTION PROGRAM

Although the intervention programs presented in this volume do show some effect, this effect might be increased considerably if the intervention was focused more strongly on the main causes of student procrastination, as represented in a motivational view on the nature of the procrastination problem. That is, such an ideal intervention program should connect more closely to both theory and research findings in stressing

1. the relatively low value of the long-term task,
2. the relatively low expectancy in individuals to complete such a task successfully,
3. the relatively long delay in obtaining reward for completing this task, and
4. the procrastinator's relatively high sensitivity to the effects of this delay.

In this final section of the chapter, I outline the components of such an "ideal" counseling program as well as related issues such as client identification, treatment duration, and the assessment of outcomes.

Components

Interventions based on the extended motivational view outlined above would be directed at (a) improving self-regulation (setting goals, monitoring progress, and managing time), (b) enhancing self-efficacy (promoting success experiences, disputing unrealistic beliefs), and (c) protecting goal behavior from distractions. Meta-analysis–based research findings show strong support for such intervention targets (Steel, 2003).

Such intervention goals have a firm theoretical basis in the combination of self-control and expectancy value theory. They are aimed at increasing the value and expectancy components of motivation and at decreasing the delay before a reward for goal behavior is obtained. In fact, behavioral approaches such as the one presented in chapter 7, by Tuckman and Schouwenburg, and cognitive approaches such as the one presented in chapter 5, by van Essen and her colleagues, can be shown to differentially affect each parameter in this motivational theory.

For example, the subjective value of an activity that is easily procrastinated on could be increased by making explicit personal needs and goals, such as intellectual curiosity and the need for achievement, and by stating concrete long-term goals as well as specific short-term goals. This could be supplemented by adding small tangible external rewards to goal attainment and by attempting to argue away one's feelings of aversiveness toward the task at hand through self-talk.

In addition, success expectancy could be enhanced by increasing the client's awareness of the small, everyday successes that can be obtained by working according to concrete and feasible short-term plans in a suitable working environment and with an allocation of sufficient time. By additional monitoring of the progress of the long-term task, through the use of step-by-step plans and subsequent evaluation of each step, clients may acquire a sense of general self-efficacy that in the long run may result in an increase in specific success expectancies.

No doubt, the "royal road" to decreasing the delay following which a reward for goal behavior will be obtained is to split up a large long-term task into a series of small short-term tasks. Because of the discounting mechanism proposed by self-control theory, this will automatically result in increased levels of motivation for the task at hand. In addition, sensitivity to delay can be managed by applying a variety of self-help techniques, such as establishing fixed working hours, committing oneself to task completion with the help of one's social environment, and guarding oneself against distractions during working hours.

In a combined expectancy value and self-control motivational theory of procrastination, the perceived value of a behavioral alternative, its success expectation, its delay in obtaining reward, and the person's sensitivity to delay are all seen as proximal causes of procrastination. Each of these proximal causes, however, may be influenced by other factors that represent relatively distal causes of procrastination and are therefore expected to correlate only relatively weakly with procrastination. An example may be the role of unrealistic thoughts. It can be seen easily that such thoughts may influence success expectancies and, in some cases, also perceived value. Thus, unrealistic thoughts may be viewed as distal causes of procrastination and would be expected to correlate only weakly with procrastination. This, in fact, seems to be the case (Steel, 2003). Consequently, in spite of its attractiveness due to current mainstream psychotherapy, intervention approaches that focus primarily on reframing unrealistic thoughts might not be very fruitful.

The effects of this multitarget approach to counseling procrastinators, however, still do not seem to go beyond the ones discussed in the preceding section. This may be due, in part, to the short duration of interventions like the one presented in chapter 5 by van Essen and her colleagues. Such interventions are intended as a takeoff or beginning point for change, and not as therapy. Given the personality structure involved, and given the more or less addictive nature of procrastination, tangible change would require much longer periods of treatment.

Identification of Procrastinators

Although procrastination may be reduced to a motivational problem in individuals excessively low in the personality factor Conscientiousness, this is only a very general way of stating the problem. First, motivational problems are always complex, because at any time of the day, there are several "motivations" or action tendencies present simultaneously. Each of these motivations has its own value, success expectancy, and delay. Furthermore, values and expectancies are themselves probably compounds that may be influenced by other, more distal variables. Second, Conscientiousness, the major personality factor that determines one's susceptibility to delay, is only one out of five orthogonal personality dimensions. This implies that low Conscientiousness will manifest itself in conjunction with other, unrelated personality factors, each of which may have its own extreme or pathological form.

Consequently, an approach in which clients are allowed to identify themselves as procrastinators and then subjected to a more or less general intervention might not be the most effective strategy to help them. A preliminary thorough assessment of clients and their problems and, as a second step, a series of well-weighed treatment decisions could be a much more effective procedure. In this volume, both Mandel (chap. 9) and Flett et al. (chap. 13) seem to follow this line of thought, Mandel by meticulously identifying "pure" low-conscientiousness procrastinators and Flett et al., although not presenting a counseling program, by focusing on procrastinators who are also perfectionists. In other programs, procrastinators are identified by completing a trait procrastination scale (described by Lay in chap. 4 and Walker in chap. 6), without excluding other factors like anxiety avoidance, however. This might imply that these interventions were also applied to clients who may have attributed anxiety-based avoidance behavior (see chap. 1) to trait procrastination. In other programs, in which procrastinators are self-identified volunteers (e.g., chap. 5, by van Essen et al.), the intervention may be applied to clients with relatively low levels of trait procrastination as well. The presence of both hypothetical subgroups should be excluded to improve possible treatment effects.

Treatment Duration

If procrastination in academic settings is only a special case of general procrastination (see Ferrari's chap. 2), and if procrastination strongly involves one's personality (see van Eerde's chap. 3), counseling approaches as presented in this volume seem to be too short to reach dramatic levels of improvement. It must be noted, however, that most of the approaches presented in this volume do not pretend to be more than a starting point for improvement. Nevertheless, as a starting point, focusing on middle-level units of analysis and the *doing* aspects of personality such as personal projects (see chap. 11 by Pychyl & Binder) may be a more effective way of introducing attempts at behavior change than thinking about procrastination as a matter of personality.

Effect Assessment

With the exception of a few approaches presented in this volume (chap. 5 by van Essen et al., chap. 11 by Pychyl & Binder), no outcome assessment used a dependent variable designed for measuring change, such as Schouwenburg's (1995) Academic Procrastination State Inventory (APSI) or the Personal Projects Analysis instrument (see chap. 11 by Pychyl &

Binder). Other procrastination scale scores, such as Lay's (1986) Procrastination Scale and the Tuckman (1991) Procrastination Scale, are by definition not very sensitive to change. Consequently, they should be applied in long-term comparisons only.

For identifying change in the short term, intervention programs should use the APSI, which was designed for week-to-week evaluations, or the Personal Projects Analysis instrument. I would argue that the latter instrument, as it also allows for identifying intention–behavior discrepancies, should be used more frequently to assess the effects of the intervention.

With few exceptions, systematic, quasi-experimental outcome research studies are still largely lacking. In this regard, the research Pychyl and Binder present in chapter 11 is clearly a step in the right direction. To the extent that more thorough and rigorous outcome-based studies are conducted, attention should also be focused on measurement during and well after the treatment program.

Finally, the need for improved outcome research can be illustrated by the outcomes of simple pretest–posttest procedures, as, for example, in chapter 5 by van Essen et al. Such procedures provide good illustrations of a "hello–goodbye" effect, in which the pretest score for procrastination is relatively high and the posttest score relatively low, but where scores at intermediate moments do not diminish very much and follow-up scores, too, do not show impressive differences. Such effects are clearly not sufficient to demonstrate the effectiveness of an intervention and underscore the need for proper quasi-experimental outcome research.

In sum, although most of the counselors presenting their approaches to counseling procrastinators in an academic setting did their best to show that their approaches are effective, the effects shown are not very large, and there seems to be little evidence of a long-lasting or stable effect on behavior. Overall, this improvement seems to be only partial and is not yet assessed with methods that reach rigorous academic standards. Given the recent beginnings of counseling practices for procrastinators, for state-of-the-art outcome research it is clearly too early.

Yet one should not be unrealistic about the overall aim of a counseling intervention for procrastinators. Probably this aim is not more or less than to reduce exaggerated procrastination to normal levels. Because of the enduring nature of traits, this may require much time, and as most of the intervention methods proposed in this volume are short, their effectiveness in treating procrastination as a personality disorder will be limited.

CONCLUSION

Procrastination is an important problem, both in daily life and in the academic setting. A society that is based on deals, deadlines, and achievement will find it hard to tolerate procrastination by its members. On the other hand, people who suffer from procrastination chronically not only produce dilatory behavior frequently but also are tormented by feelings of low self-esteem and lower subjective well-being (e.g., see chap. 2 by Ferrari). In short, procrastination makes both society and the procrastinator unhappy.

Counseling procrastinators, therefore, is a needed and worthy pursuit. Luckily, a number of counselors, in both North America and Europe, have taken the initiative to design counseling methods for procrastinators, especially for procrastinators in academic settings. This book presents a first overview of their work. Although their results are promising, much refinement remains to be done. Psychological counselors and other colleagues in the field of counseling are invited to join in these efforts.

REFERENCES

Ainslie, G. (1992). *Picoeconomics: The strategic interaction of successive motivational states within the person.* Cambridge, England: Cambridge University Press.

Aitken, M. (1982). *A personality profile of the college student procrastinator.* Unpublished doctoral dissertation, University of Pittsburgh.

Ajzen, I. (1985). From intentions to actions: A theory of planned behavior. In J. Kuhl & J. Beckman (Eds.), *Action control: From cognitions to behavior* (pp. 11–39). Heidelberg, Germany: Springer.

Allport, G. W. (1937). *Personality, a psychological interpretation.* New York: Holt.

American Psychiatric Association. (1994). *Diagnostic and statistical manual of mental disorders* (4th ed.). Washington, DC: Author.

American Psychiatric Association. (2000). *Diagnostic and statistical manual of mental disorders* (4th ed., text rev.). Washington, DC: Author.

Anderson, J. R. (1995). *Cognitive psychology and its implications* (4th ed.). New York: Freeman.

Bandura, A. (1977). Self-efficacy: Toward a unifying theory of behavior change. *Psychological Review, 84,* 191–215.

Bandura, A. (1986). *Social foundations of thought and action: A social–cognitive theory.* Englewood Cliffs, NJ: Prentice Hall.

Bandura, A. (1997). *Self-efficacy: The exercise of control.* New York: Freeman.

Bandura, A., & Schunk, P. H. (1981). Cultivating competence, self-efficacy, and intrinsic interest through proximal self-motivation. *Journal of Personality and Social Psychology, 41,* 568–598.

Baumeister, R. F. (1985). Two kinds of identity crisis. *Journal of Personality, 53,* 407–424.

Baumeister, R. F. (1997). Esteem threat, self-regulatory breakdown and emotional distress as factors in self-defeating behavior. *Review of General Psychology, 1(2),* 145–174.

Baumeister, R. F., Heatherton, T. F., & Tice, D. M. (1994). *Losing control: How and why people fail at self-regulation.* San Diego, CA: Academic Press.

Baumeister, R. F., & Scher, S. J. (1988). Self-defeating behavior patterns among normal individuals: Review and analysis of common self-destructive tendencies. *Psychological Bulletin, 104,* 3–22.

Beck, A. T. (1976). *Cognitive therapy and emotional disorders.* New York: International Universities Press.

Beck, A. T., & Freeman, A. (1990). *Cognitive therapy of personality disorders.* New York: Guilford Press.

Beck, B. L., Koons, S. R., & Milgram, D. L. (2000). Correlates and consequences of behavioral procrastination: The effects of academic procrastination, self-consciousness, self-esteem, and self-handicapping. *Journal of Social Behavior and Personality, 15,* 3–13.

Beck, J. (1995). *Cognitive therapy: Basics and beyond.* New York: Guilford Press.

Ben-Knaz, R. (2002). *Family interaction in differentially diagnosed academically-able male adolescent underachievers.* Unpublished doctoral dissertation, York University, Toronto, Ontario, Canada.

Berne, E. (1964). *Games people play: The psychology of human relationships.* London: Penguin Books.

Berzonsky, M. D. (1989). Identity style: Conceptualization and measurement. *Journal of Adolescent Research, 4,* 268–282.

Berzonsky, M. D., & Ferrari, J. R. (1996). Identity orientation and decisional strategies. *Personality and Individual Differences, 20,* 597–606.

Beswick, G., Rothblum, E. D., & Mann, L. (1988). Psychological antecedents of student procrastination. *Australian Psychologist, 23,* 207–217.

Blunt, A. K., & Pychyl, T. A. (1998). Volitional action and inaction in the lives of undergraduate students: State orientation, procrastination, and proneness to boredom. *Personality and Individual Differences, 24,* 837–846.

Blunt, A. K., & Pychyl, T. A. (2000). Task aversiveness and procrastination: A multidimensional approach to task aversiveness across stages of personal projects. *Personality and Individual Differences, 28,* 153–167.

Boice, R. (1992). *The new faculty member.* San Francisco: Jossey-Bass.

Boice, R. (1993). New faculty involvement of women and minorities. *Research in Higher Education, 34,* 291–341.

Boice, R. (1995). Developing teaching, then writing among new faculty. *Research in Higher Education, 36,* 415–456.

Bridges, K. R., & Roig, M. (1997). Academic procrastination and irrational thinking: A re-examination with context controlled. *Personality and Individual Differences, 22,* 941–944.

Brownlow, S., & Reasinger, R. D. (2000). Putting off until tomorrow what is better done today: Academic procrastination as a function of motivation toward college work. *Journal of Social Behavior and Personality, 15,* 15–34.

Bruner, J. S. (1986). *Actual minds, possible worlds.* Cambridge, MA: Harvard University.

Burka, J. B., & Yuen, L. M. (1983). *Procrastination: Why you do it, what to do about it.* Reading, MA: Addison-Wesley.

Burns, L. R., Dittmann, K., Nguyen, N. L., & Mitchelson, J. K. (2000). Academic procrastination, perfectionism, and control: Associations with vigilant and avoidant coping. *Journal of Social Behavior and Personality, 15,* 35–46.

Buss, D. M. (1986). Can social science be anchored in evolutionary biology? Four problems and a strategic solution. *Revue Européenne des Sciences Sociales, 24*(73), 41–50.

Buss, D. M. (1987). Selection, evocation and manipulation. *Journal of Personality and Social Psychology, 53,* 1214–1221.

Buss, D. M., & Cantor, N. (Eds.). (1989). *Personality psychology: Recent trends and emerging directions*. New York: Springer-Verlag.

Cacioppo, J. T., & Petty, R. E. (1981). Social psychological procedures for cognitive response assessment: The thought-listing technique. In T. V. Merluzzi, C. R. Glass, & M. Genest (Eds.), *Cognitive assessment* (pp. 309–342). New York: Guilford Press.

Cantor, N. (1990). From thought to behavior: "Having" and "doing" in the study of personality and cognition. *American Psychologist, 45,* 735–750.

Cantor, N., & Harlow, R. E. (1994). Social intelligence and personality: Flexible life task pursuit. In R. J. Sternberg & P. Ruzgis (Eds.), *Personality and intelligence* (pp. 137–168). New York: Cambridge University Press.

Cantor, N., & Kihlstrom, J. F. (1987). *Personality and social intelligence*. Englewood Cliffs, NJ: Prentice Hall.

Cantor, N., & Zirkel, S. (1990). Personality, cognition, and purposive behavior. In L. Pervin (Ed.), *Handbook of personality theory and research* (pp. 135–164). New York: Guilford Press.

Carver, C. S., & Scheier, M. F. (1998). *On the self-regulation of behavior*. Cambridge, England: Cambridge University Press.

Cattell, R. B. (1965). *The scientific analysis of personality*. Harmondsworth, England: Penguin Books.

Clark, J. L., & Hill, O. W. (1994). Academic procrastination among African-American college students. *Psychological Reports, 75,* 931–936.

Costa, P. T., Herbst, J. H., McCrae, R. R., Samuels, J., & Ozer, D. J. (2002). The replicability and utility of three personality types. *European Journal of Personality, 16,* S73–S87.

Costa, P. T., Jr., & McCrae, R. R. (1992). *The NEO Personality Inventory—Revised*. Odessa, FL: Psychological Assessment Resources.

Covington, M. V. (1993). A motivational analysis of academic life in college. In J. Smart (Ed.), *Higher education: Handbook of theory and research* (Vol. 9, pp. 50–93). New York: Agathon.

Csikszentmihalyi, M. (1992). *Flow: The psychology of happiness*. London: Rider.

Cullinan, D. (2002). *Students with emotional and behavioral disorders*. Upper Saddle River, NJ: Prentice Hall.

Davies, B., & Harre, R. (1990). Positioning: The discursive production of selves. *Journal for the Theory of Social Behaviour, 20,* 43–63.

Day, V., Mensink, D., & O'Sullivan, M. (2000). Patterns of academic procrastination. *Journal of College Reading and Learning, 30*(2), 121–134.

Delicate, M. (1998, June). *Overcoming academic procrastination*. Paper presented at the annual conference of the Canadian Association of College and University Student Services (CACUSS), Ottawa, Ontario, Canada.

Depreeuw, E. A. (1989). *Faalangst: Theorievorming, testconstructie en resultaatonderzoek van de gedragstherapeutische behandeling* [Test anxiety: Concept building, test construction and an outcome study of the behavioral therapeutic treatment]. Unpublished dissertation, University of Leuven, Belgium.

Depreeuw, E. A., Dejonghe, B., & van Horebeek, W. (1996). Procrastination: Just student laziness and lack of motivation or is the challenge for counselors more complex? In M. Phippen (Ed.), *Culture and psyche in transition: A European perspective on student psychological health* (pp. 43–50). Conference papers presented at the 25th Annual Training Event and Conference Association for Student Counselling, Brighton, England.

Depreeuw, E. A., & De Neve, H. (1992). Test anxiety can harm your health: Some conclusions based on a student typology. In D. Forgays, T. Sosnowski, & K. Wrzesniewski (Eds.), *Anxiety: Recent developments in cognitive, psychophysiological, and health research* (pp. 211–228). Washington, DC: Hemisphere.

Depreeuw, E. A., Eelen, P., & Stroobants, R. (1996). *VaSEV, Vragenlijst Studie- en Examenvaardigheden* [TASTE, or Test Concerning Abilities for Study and Examination]. Lisse, the Netherlands: Swets & Zeitlinger.

DeRosa, T. (2000). Personality, help-seeking attitudes, and depression in adolescents. *Dissertation Abstracts International, 61*(6-B), 3273.

De Shazer, S. (1982). *Patterns of brief family therapy.* New York: Guilford Press.

De Shazer, S. (1985). *Keys to solution in brief therapy.* New York: Norton.

De Shazer, S. (1988). *Clues: Investigating solutions in brief therapy.* New York: Norton.

DeWitte, S., & Lens, W. (2000). Procrastinators lack a broad action perspective. *European Journal of Personality, 14,* 121–140.

Diener, E., & Emmons, R. A. (1984). The independence of positive and negative affect. *Journal of Personality and Social Psychology, 47,* 1105–1117.

Diener, E., Emmons, R. A., Larsen, R. J., & Griffin, S. (1985). The Satisfaction With Life Scale. *Journal of Personality Assessment, 49,* 71–75.

Dryden, W. (1995). *Practical skills in rational emotive behaviour therapy.* London: Whurr.

Eerde, W. van. (1998). *Work motivation and procrastination: Self-set goals and action avoidance.* Unpublished dissertation, University of Amsterdam, the Netherlands.

Eerde, W. van. (2003). A meta-analytically derived nomological network of procrastination. *Personality and Individual Differences, 35,* 1401–1418.

Effert, B. R., & Ferrari, J. R. (1989). Decisional procrastination: Examining personality correlates. *Journal of Social Behavior and Personality, 4,* 151–156.

Egan, G. (1976). Confrontation. *Group and Organizational Studies, 1,* 223–243.

Elliot, A. J., Sheldon, K. M., & Church, M. A. (1997). Avoidance personal goals and subjective well-being. *Personality and Social Psychology Bulletin, 23,* 915–927.

Ellis, A. (1994). *Reason and emotion in psychotherapy* (Rev. ed.). New York: Carol Publishing.

Ellis, A. (2002). The role of irrational beliefs in perfectionism. In G. L. Flett & P. L. Hewitt (Eds.), *Perfectionism: Theory, research, and treatment* (pp. 217–229). Washington, DC: American Psychological Association.

Ellis, A., & Grieger, R. (Eds.). (1977). *Handbook of rational–emotive therapy.* New York: Springer.

Ellis, A., & Harper, A. (1997). *A guide to rational living.* Hollywood, CA: Melvin Powers Wilshire.

Ellis, A., & Knaus, W. J. (2002). *Overcoming procrastination* (Rev. ed.). New York: New American Library.

Emmons, R. A. (1986). Personal strivings: An approach to personality and subjective well-being. *Journal of Personality and Social Psychology, 51*, 1058–1068.

Emmons, R. A. (1989). The personal striving approach to personality. In L. A. Pervin (Ed.), *Goal concepts in personality and social psychology* (pp. 87–126). Hillsdale, NJ: Erlbaum.

Enns, M., Cox, B. J., Sareen, J., & Freeman, P. (2001). Adaptive and maladaptive perfectionism in medical students: A longitudinal investigation. *Medical Education, 35*, 1034–1042.

Epston, D. (1989). *Collected papers.* Adelaide, South Australia: Dulwich Centre Publications.

Ericsson, K. A. (1996). *The road to excellence: The acquisition of expert performance in the arts, sciences, sports, and games.* Mahwah, NJ: Erlbaum.

Eysenck, H. J. (1970). *The structure of human personality.* London: Methuen.

Fee, R. L., & Tangney, J. P. (2000). Procrastination: A means of avoiding shame or guilt? *Journal of Social Behavior and Personality, 15*, 167–184.

Feist, G. J. (1998). A meta-analysis of personality in scientific and artistic creativity. *Personality and Social Psychology Review, 2*, 290–309.

Ferguson, K. L., & Rodway, M. R. (1994). Cognitive behavioral treatment of perfectionism: Initial evaluation studies. *Research on Social Work Practice, 4*, 283–308.

Ferrari, J. R. (1991a). Compulsive procrastination: Some self-reported characteristics. *Psychological Reports, 68*, 455–458.

Ferrari, J. R. (1991b). Self-handicapping by procrastinators: Protecting self-esteem, social-esteem, or both? *Journal of Research in Personality, 25*, 245–261.

Ferrari, J. R. (1992a). Procrastinators and perfect behavior: An exploratory factor analysis of self-presentation, self-awareness and self-handicapping components. *Journal of Research in Personality, 26*, 75–84.

Ferrari, J. R. (1992b). Psychometric validation of two procrastination inventories for adults: Arousal and avoidance measures. *Journal of Psychopathology and Behavioral Assessment, 14*, 97–110.

Ferrari, J. R. (1993). Procrastination and impulsiveness: Two sides of a coin? In W. G. McCown, J. L. Johnson, & M. B. Shure (Eds.), *The impulsive client: Theory, research, and treatment* (pp. 265–276). Washington, DC: American Psychological Association.

Ferrari, J. R. (1994). Dysfunctional procrastination and its relationship with self-esteem, interpersonal dependency, and self-defeating behaviors. *Personality and Individual Differences, 17*, 673–679.

Ferrari, J. R. (2000). Procrastination and attention: Factor analysis of attention deficit, boredomness, intelligence, self-esteem, and task delay frequencies. *Journal of Social Behavior and Personality, 15*, 185–196.

Ferrari, J. R. (2001). Procrastination as self-regulation failure of performance: Effects of cognitive load, self-awareness and time limits on "working best under pressure." *European Journal of Personality, 15*, 391–406.

Ferrari, J. R., & Beck, B. (1998). Affective responses before and after fraudulent excuses by academic procrastinators. *Education, 118*, 529–537.

Ferrari, J. R., & Emmons, R. A. (1995). Methods of procrastination and their relation to self-control and self-reinforcement. *Journal of Social Behavior and Personality, 10*, 135–142.

Ferrari, J. R., & Gojkovich, P. (2000). Procrastination and attention: Factor analysis of attention deficit, boredomness, intelligence, self-esteem, and task delay frequencies. *Journal of Social Behavior and Personality, 15*, 185–197.

Ferrari, J. R., Johnson, J. L., & McCown, W. G. (1995). *Procrastination and task avoidance: Theory, research and treatment.* New York: Plenum.

Ferrari, J. R., Keane, S., Wolfe, R., & Beck, B. (1998). The antecedents and consequences of academic excuse-making: Examining individual differences in academic procrastination. *Research in Higher Education, 39*, 199–215.

Ferrari, J. R., & Olivette, M. J. (1993). Perceptions of parental control and the development of indecision among late adolescent females. *Adolescence, 28*, 963–990.

Ferrari, J. R., Parker, J. T., & Ware, C. B. (1992). Academic procrastination: Personality correlates with Myers-Briggs types, self-efficacy, and academic locus of control. *Journal of Social Behavior and Personality, 7*, 495–498.

Ferrari, J. R., & Pychyl, T. A. (2000a). *Procrastination: Current issues and new directions.* Corta Madre, CA: Select Press.

Ferrari, J. R., & Pychyl, T. A. (2000b). The scientific study of procrastination: Where have we been and where are we going? *Journal of Social Behavior and Personality, 15*, vii–viii.

Ferrari, J. R., & Pychyl, T. A. (2004). *Regulation failure by decisional procrastinators: Awareness of self-control deception.* Manuscript submitted for publication.

Ferrari, J. R., & Scher, S. J. (2000). Toward an understanding of academic and non-academic tasks procrastinated by students: The use of daily logs. *Psychology in the Schools, 37*, 359–366.

Ferrari, J. R., Wolfe, R. N., Wesley, J. C., Schoff, L. A., & Beck, B. L. (1995). Ego-identity and academic procrastination among university students. *Journal of College Student Development, 36*, 361–367.

Fichman, L., Koestner, R., & Zuroff, D. C. (1994). Depressive styles in adolescence: Assessment, relation to social functioning, and developmental trends. *Journal of Youth and Adolescence, 23*, 315–329.

Fischer, E. H., & Turner, J. I. (1970). Orientations to seeking professional help: Development and research utility of an attitude scale. *Journal of Consulting and Clinical Psychology, 35*, 79–90.

Flanagan, C. M. (1993). Treating neurotic problems that do not respond to psycho-dynamic therapies. *Hospital and Community Psychiatry, 44,* 824–826.

Flett, G. L., Blankstein, K. R., Hewitt, P. L., & Koledin, S. (1992). Components of perfectionism and procrastination in college students. *Social Behavior and Personality, 20,* 85–94.

Flett, G. L., Blankstein, K. R., & Martin, T. R. (1995a). Dimensions of perfectionism and procrastination. In J. R. Ferrari, J. L. Johnson, & W. B. McCown (Eds.), *Procrastination and task avoidance: Theory, research, and treatment* (pp. 113–136). New York: Plenum.

Flett, G. L., Blankstein, K. R., & Martin, T. R. (1995b). Procrastination, negative self-judgments, and stress in depression and anxiety: A review and preliminary model. In J. R. Ferrari, J. L. Johnson, & W. G. McCown (Eds.), *Procrastination and task avoidance: Theory, research, and treatment* (pp. 137–167). New York: Plenum.

Flett, G. L., Hewitt, P. L., Blankstein, K. R., & Gray, L. (1998). Psychological distress and the frequency of perfectionistic thinking. *Journal of Personality and Social Psychology, 75,* 1363–1381.

Flett, G. L., Hewitt, P. L., Blankstein, K. R., Solnick, M., & Van Brunschot, M. (1996). Perfectionism, social problem-solving ability, and psychological distress. *Journal of Rational–Emotive and Cognitive–Behavior Therapy, 14,* 245–275.

Flett, G. L., Hewitt, P. L., & Martin, T. R. (1995). Dimensions of perfectionism and procrastination. In J. R. Ferrari, J. L. Johnson, & W. G. McCown (Eds.), *Procrastination and task avoidance: Theory, research, and treatment* (pp. 113–136). New York: Plenum.

Flett, G. L., Russo, F. A., & Hewitt, P. L. (1994). Dimensions of perfectionism and constructive thinking as a coping response. *Journal of Rational–Emotive and Cognitive–Behavior Therapy, 12,* 163–179.

Frank, J. D. (1961). *Persuasion and healing: A comparative study of psychotherapy.* Baltimore: Johns Hopkins University Press.

Frank, J. D. (1976). Psychotherapy and the sense of mastery. In R. L. Spitzer & D. F. Klein (Eds.), *Evaluation of psychological therapies* (pp. 47–56). Baltimore: Johns Hopkins University Press.

Frank, J. D., Hoehn-Saric, R., Imber, S. D., Liberman, B. L., & Stone, A. R. (1978). *Effective ingredients of successful psychotherapy.* New York: Brunner/Mazel.

Freeston, M. H., Rheaume, J., & Ladouceur, R. (1996). Correcting faulty appraisals of obsessional thoughts. *Behaviour Research and Therapy, 34,* 433–446.

Frost, R. O., Marten, P. A., Lahart, C. M., & Rosenblate, R. (1990). The dimensions of perfectionism. *Cognitive Therapy and Research, 14,* 449–468.

Gallagher, R. P. (1992). Student needs surveys have multiple benefits. *Journal of College Student Development, 33,* 281–282.

Garcia, T., & Pintrich, P. R. (1994). Regulating motivation and cognition in the classroom: The role of self-schemas and self-regulatory strategies. In D. Schunk & B. J. Zimmerman (Eds.), *Self-regulation of learning and performance* (pp. 127–253). Hillsdale, NJ: Erlbaum.

Garland, A. F., & Zigler, E. F. (1994). Psychological correlates of help-seeking attitudes among children and adolescents. *American Journal of Orthopsychiatry, 64,* 586–593.

Gendlin, E. T. (1996). *Focusing-oriented psychotherapy.* New York: Guilford Press.

Glanz, B. (1988). *The ages of onset of academic underachievement in differentially diagnosed high school students.* Unpublished masters thesis, York University, Toronto, Ontario, Canada.

Glass, C. R., Arnkhoff, D. B., Wood, H., Meyerhoff, J. L., Smith, H. R., Oleshansky, M. A., et al. (1995). Cognition, anxiety and performance on a career-related oral examination. *Journal of Counseling Psychology, 42,* 47–54.

Gollwitzer, P. M., & Bargh, J. A. (Eds.). (1996). *The psychology of action: Linking cognition and motivation to behavior.* New York: Guilford Press.

Gollwitzer, P. M., & Brandstatter, V. (1997). Implementation intentions and effective goal pursuit. *Journal of Personality and Social Psychology, 73,* 186–199.

Gove, P. B. (Ed.). (1976). *Webster's third new international dictionary of the English language, unabridged.* Springfield, MA: Merriam.

Graham, S. (1997). Using attribution theory to understand social and academic motivation in African American youth. *Educational Psychologist, 32*(1), 21–34.

Graham, S., MacArthur, C., & Schwartz, S. (1995). Effects of goal setting and procedural facilitation on the revising behavior and writing performance of students with writing and learning problems. *Journal of Educational Psychology, 87,* 230–240.

Gresham, F. M., Quinn, M. M., & Restori, A. (1999). Methodological issues in functional analysis: Generalizability to other disability groups. *Behavioral Disorders, 24,* 180–182.

Griffin, B., & Hesketh, B. (2001, April). *Some questions about the relationship between conscientiousness and performance.* Poster session presented at the Society of Industrial and Organizational Psychology, San Diego, CA.

Gustafson, J. P. (1992). *Self-delight in a harsh world: The main stories of individual, marital and family psychotherapy.* New York: Norton.

Hamachek, D. E. (1978). Psychodynamics of normal and neurotic perfectionism. *Psychology, 15,* 27–33.

Hattie, J., Biggs, J., & Purdie, N. (1996). Effects of learning skills interventions on student learning: A meta-analysis. *Review of Educational Research, 66,* 99–136.

Haycock, L. A., McCarthy, P., & Skay, C. L. (1998). Procrastination in college students: The role of self-efficacy and anxiety. *Journal of Counseling and Development, 76,* 317–324.

Hershberger, W. A. (1988). Psychology as a conative science. *American Psychologist, 43,* 823–824.

Hess, B., Sherman, M. F., & Goodman, M. (2000). Eveningness predicts academic procrastination: The mediating role of neuroticism. *Journal of Social Behavior and Personality, 15,* 61–74.

Hewitt, P. L., & Flett, G. L. (1991). Perfectionism in the self and social contexts: Conceptualization, assessment, and association with psychopathology. *Journal of Personality and Social Psychology, 60*, 456–470.

Hewitt, P. L., & Flett, G. L. (2002). Perfectionism and stress in psychopathology. In G. L. Flett & P. L. Hewitt (Eds.), *Perfectionism: Theory, research, and treatment* (pp. 255–284). Washington, DC: American Psychological Association.

Hewitt, P. L., Flett, G. L., & Ediger, E. (1996). Perfectionism and depression: Longitudinal assessment of a specific vulnerability hypothesis. *Journal of Abnormal Psychology, 105*, 276–280.

Hewitt, P. L., Flett, G. L., Sherry, S. B., Habke, M., Parkin, M., Lam, R. W., et al. (2003). The interpersonal expression of perfection: Perfectionistic self-presentation and psychological distress. *Journal of Personality and Social Psychology, 84*, 1303–1325.

Higgins, E. T. (1987). Self-discrepancy: A theory relating self and affect. *Psychological Review, 94*, 319–340.

Hill, M. B., Hill, D. A., Chabot, A. E., & Barrall, J. F. (1978). A survey of college faculty and student procrastination. *College Student Personnel Journal, 12*, 256–262.

Hirsch, C. R., & Hayward, P. (1998). The perfect patient: Cognitive–behavioural therapy for perfectionism. *Behavioural and Cognitive Psychotherapy, 26*, 359–364.

Hollender, M. H. (1965). Perfectionism. *Comprehensive Psychiatry, 6*, 94–103.

Hollon, S. D., & Kendall, P. C. (1980). Cognitive self-statements in depression: Development of an Automatic Thoughts Questionnaire. *Cognitive Therapy and Research, 4*, 383–395.

Jackson, T., Weiss, K. E., & Lundquist, J. J. (2000). Does procrastination mediate the relationship between optimism and subsequent stress? *Journal of Social Behavior and Personality, 15*, 203–212.

Jiao, Q. G., & Onwuegbuzie, A. J. (1998). Perfectionism and library anxiety among graduate students. *Journal of Academic Librarianship, 24*, 365–371.

John, O. (1990). The "Big Five" factor taxonomy: Dimensions of personality in the natural language and in questionnaires. In A. Pervin (Ed.), *Handbook of personality* (pp. 66–100). New York: Guilford Press.

Johnson, B. T., Mullen, B., & Salas, E. (1995). Comparison of three major meta-analytic approaches. *Journal of Applied Psychology, 80*, 94–106.

Johnson, J. L., & Bloom, A. M. (1995). An analysis of the contribution of the five factors of personality to variance in academic procrastination. *Personality and Individual Differences, 18*, 127–133.

Kabat-Zinn, J. (1994). *Mindfulness meditation for everyday life.* London: Piatkus.

Kanfer, F. H. (1975). Self-management methods. In F. H. Kanfer & A. P. Goldstein (Eds.), *Helping people change* (pp. 309–355). New York: Pergamon Press.

Kavale, K. A., Forness, S. R., & Walker, H. M. (1999). Interventions for oppositional defiant disorder and conduct disorder in the schools. In H. C. Quay &

A. E. Hogan (Eds.), *Handbook of disruptive behavior disorders* (pp. 441–454). New York: Kluwer Academic/Plenum.

King, L. A., McKee-Walker, L., Broyles, S. J. (1996). Creativity and the five-factor model. *Journal of Research in Personality, 30,* 189–203.

Kleijn, W. C., van der Ploeg, H. M., & Topman, R. M. (1994). Cognition, study habits, test anxiety and academic performance. *Psychological Reports, 75,* 1219–1226.

Klinger, E. (1977). *Meaning and void: Inner experience and the incentives in people's lives.* Minneapolis: University of Minnesota Press.

Klinger, E. (1987). Current concerns and disengagement from incentives. In F. Halisch & J. Kuhl (Eds.), *Motivation, intention, and volition* (pp. 337–347). New York: Springer-Verlag.

Knaus, W. J. (1998). *Do it now!* New York: Wiley.

Kohut, H. (1971). *The analysis of the self.* New York: International Universities Press.

Kuehlwein, K. T., & Rosen, H. (Eds.). (1993). *Cognitive therapies in action: Evolving innovative practice.* San Francisco: Jossey-Bass.

Kuhl J. (2000). A functional-design approach to motivational and self-regulation: The dynamics of personality systems interactions. In M. Boekaerts, P. R. Pintrich, & M. Zeidner (Eds.), *Handbook of self-regulation* (pp. 111–169). San Diego, CA: Academic.

Kuhl, J., & Goschke, T. (1994). State orientation and the activation and retrieval of intentions in memory. In J. Kuhl & J. Beckmann (Eds.), *Volition and personality: Action versus state orientation* (pp. 127–153). Toronto, Ontario, Canada: Hogrefe & Huber.

Lay, C. H. (1986). At last, my research article on procrastination. *Journal of Research in Personality, 20,* 474–495.

Lay, C. H. (1987). A modal profile analysis of procrastinators: A search for types. *Personality and Individual Differences, 8,* 705–714.

Lay, C. H. (1988). The relation of procrastination and optimism to judgements of time to complete an essay and anticipation of setbacks. *Journal of Social Behavior and Personality, 3,* 201–214.

Lay, C. H. (1990). Working to schedule on personal projects: An assessment of person-project characteristics and trait procrastination. *Journal of Social Behavior and Personality, 5,* 91–103.

Lay, C. H. (1992). Trait procrastination and the perception of person-task characteristics. *Journal of Social Behavior and Personality, 7,* 483–494.

Lay, C. H. (1994). Trait procrastination and affective experiences: Describing past study behavior and its relation to agitation and dejection. *Motivation and Emotion, 18,* 269–284.

Lay, C. H. (1995). Trait procrastination, agitation, dejection, and self-discrepancy. In J. R. Ferrari, J. L. Johnson, & W. G. McCown (Eds.), *Procrastination and task avoidance* (pp. 97–112). New York: Plenum.

Lay, C. H. (1997). Explaining lower-order traits through higher-order factors: The case of trait procrastination, conscientiousness and the specificity dilemma. *European Journal of Personality, 11,* 267–278.

Lay, C. H., & Brokenshire, R. (1997). Conscientiousness, procrastination, and person-task characteristics in job searching by unemployed adults. *Current Psychology, 16*(1), 83–96.

Lay, C. H., & Burns, P. (1991). Intentions and behavior in studying for an examination: The role of trait procrastination and its interaction with optimism. *Journal of Social Behavior and Personality, 6,* 605–617.

Lay, C. H., Edwards, J. M., Parker, J. D. A., & Endler, N. S. (1989). An assessment of appraisal, anxiety, coping, and procrastination during an examination period. *European Journal of Personality, 3,* 195–208.

Lay, C. H., Knish, S., & Zanatta, R. (1992). Self-handicappers and procrastinators: A comparison of their practice behavior prior to an evaluation. *Journal of Research in Personality, 26,* 242–257.

Lay, C. H., Kovacs, A., & Danto, D. (1998). The relation of trait procrastination to the big-five factor conscientiousness: An assessment with primary-junior school children based on self-reports. *Personality and Individual Differences, 25,* 187–193.

Lay, C. H., & Schouwenburg, H. C. (1993). Trait procrastination, time management, and academic behavior. *Journal of Social Behavior and Personality, 8,* 647–662.

Lay, C. H., & Silverman, S. (1996). Trait procrastination, anxiety, and dilatory behavior. *Personality and Individual Differences, 21,* 61–67.

Lazarus, A. A. (1971). *Behavior therapy and beyond.* New York: McGraw-Hill.

Lazarus, A. A. (1989). *The practice of multimodal therapy; systematic, comprehensive and effective psychotherapy.* Baltimore: John Hopkins University Press.

Leahy, R. L. (2001). *Overcoming resistance in cognitive therapy.* New York: Guilford Press.

Lens, W., & Depreeuw, E. (1998). *Studiemotivatie en faalangst nader bekeken: Tussen kunnen en moeten staat willen* [Study motivation and test anxiety explored: Between can and must comes will]. Leuven, Belgium: Universitaire Pers.

Little, B. R. (1983). Personal projects: A rationale and method for investigation. *Environment and Behaviour, 15,* 273–309.

Little, B. R. (1987). Personal projects analysis: A new methodology for counselling psychology. *Natcom, 13,* 591–614.

Little, B. R. (1989). Personal projects analysis: Trivial pursuits, magnificent obsessions, and the search for coherence. In D. Buss & N. Cantor (Eds.), *Personality psychology: Recent trends and emerging directions* (pp. 15–31). New York: Springer-Verlag.

Little, B. R. (1999). Personality and motivation: Personal action and the conative evolution. In L. A. Pervin & O. P. John (Eds.), *Handbook of personality: Theory and research* (2nd ed.). New York: Guilford Press.

Locke, E. A., & Latham, G. P. (1990). *A theory of goal setting and task performance*. Englewood Cliffs, NJ: Prentice Hall.

Locke, E. A., Shaw, G. P., Saari, L. M., & Latham, G. P. (1981). Goal setting and task performance: 1969–1980. *Psychological Bulletin, 90*, 125–152.

Logue, W. (1988). Research on self-control: An integrating framework. *Behavioral and Brain Sciences, 11*, 665–679.

Macran, S., Stiles, W. B., & Smith, J. A. (1999). How does personal therapy affect therapists' practice? *Journal of Counseling Psychology, 46*, 419–431.

Mahy, A. (1995). *Validation of the AMP using semi-structured diagnostic interviews to diagnose types of high school underachievers*. Unpublished master's thesis, York University, Toronto, Ontario, Canada.

Mandel, H. P. (1997). *Conduct disorder and underachievement: Risk factors, assessment, treatment, and prevention*. New York: Wiley.

Mandel, H. P., Friedland, J., & Marcus, S. I. (1996). *The Achievement Motivation Profile (AMP) manual: Administration, scoring, and interpretation*. Los Angeles, CA: Western Psychological Services.

Mandel, H. P., Friedland, J., & Marcus, S. I. (1996). *The Achievement Motivation Profile (AMP) computerized interpretive report*. Los Angeles, CA: Western Psychological Services.

Mandel, H. P., & Marcus, S. I. (1988). *The psychology of underachievement: Differential diagnosis and differential treatment*. New York: Wiley.

Mandel, H. P., & Marcus, S. I., with Dean, L. (1995). *Could do better: Why children underachieve and what to do about it*. New York: Wiley.

Mandel, H. P., Roth, R. M., & Berenbaum, H. L. (1968). Relationship between personality change and achievement change as a function of psychodiagnosis. *Journal of Counseling Psychology, 15*, 500–505.

Mandel, H. P., & Uebner, J. (1971). "If you never chance for fear of losing . . ." *Personnel and Guidance Journal, 50*, 192–197.

Markus, H., & Nurius, P. (1986). Possible selves. *American Psychologist, 41*, 954–969.

Martin, T. R., Flett, G. L., Hewitt, P. L., Krames, L., & Szanto, G. (1996). Personality correlates of depression and health symptoms: A test of a self-regulation model. *Journal of Research in Personality, 31*, 264–277.

Mathur, S. R., Quinn, M. M., & Rutherford, R. B., Jr. (1996). *Teacher-mediated behavior management strategies for children with emotional/behavioral disorders*. Reston, VA: Council for Exceptional Children.

McAdam, D. P. (1993). *The stories we live by: Personal myths and the making of the self*. New York: Guilford Press.

McCall, R. B., Evahn, C., & Kratzer, L. (1992). *High school underachievers: What do they achieve as adults?* Newbury Park, CA: Sage.

McClelland, D. C. (1965). Toward a theory of motive acquisition. *American Psychologist, 20*, 321–333.

McClelland, D. C. (1979). *Increasing achievement motivation*. Boston: McBer and Company.

McCown, W. (1986). Behavior of chronic college student procrastinators: An experimental study. *Social Science and Behavioral Documents, 17*, 133.

McCown, W., Johnson, J., & Petzel, T. (1989). Procrastination, a principal components analysis. *Personality and Individual Differences, 10*, 197–202.

McCown, W., Johnson, J., & Shure, M. B. (Eds.). (1993). *The impulsive client: Theory, research, and treatment*. Washington, DC: American Psychological Association.

McCown, W., Petzel, T., & Rupert, P. (1987). An experimental study of some hypothesized behaviors and personality variables of college student procrastinators. *Personality and Individual Differences, 8*, 781–786.

McCown, W., & Roberts, R. (1994). Personal and chronic procrastination by university students during an academic examination period. *Personality and Individual Differences, 12*, 413–415.

McCrae, R. R., & Costa, P. T. (1999). A five-factor theory of personality. In L. A. Pervin & O. P. John (Eds.), *Handbook of personality: Theory and research* (2nd ed., pp. 139–153). New York: Guilford Press.

McGregor, I. (2003). Defensive zeal: Compensatory conviction about attitudes, values, goals, groups, and self-definition in the face of personal uncertainty. In S. J. Spencer, S. Fein, M. P. Zanna, & J. M. Olson (Eds.), *Motivated social perception: The Ontario symposium* (pp. 73–92). Mahwah, NJ: Erlbaum.

McGregor, I., & Little, B. R. (1998). Personal projects, happiness, and meaning: On doing well and being yourself. *Journal of Personality and Social Psychology, 74*, 492–512.

McKay, J. (1985). *The relationships among sex, age, ability, and achievement patterns in differentially diagnosed high school students*. Unpublished master's thesis, York University, Toronto, Ontario, Canada.

McKean, K. J. (1994). Using multiple risk factors to assess the behavioral, cognitive, and affective effects of learned helplessness. *Journal of Personality, 128*, 177–183.

McLeod, J. (1997). *Narrative and psychotherapy*. London: Sage.

McMillan, J. H., Simonetta, L. G., & Singh, J. (1994). Student opinion survey—Development of measures of student motivation. *Educational and Psychological Measurement, 54*, 496–505.

McMullin, R. E. (2000). *The new handbook of cognitive therapy techniques*. New York: Norton.

McMurran, M. (1994). *The psychology of addiction*. London: Taylor & Francis.

Meichenbaum, D. (1977). *Cognitive–behavior modification: An integrative approach*. New York: Plenum.

Milgram, N. A. (1991). Procrastination. In R. Dulbecco (Ed.), *Encyclopedia of human biology* (Vol. 6, pp. 149–155). New York: Academic Press.

Milgram, N. A., Batori, G., & Mowrer, D. (1993). Correlates of academic procrastination. *Journal of School Psychology, 31,* 487–500.

Milgram, N. A., Gehrman, T., & Keinan, G. (1992). Procrastination and emotional upset: A typological model. *Personality and Individual Differences, 13,* 1307–1313.

Milgram, N. A., Marshevsky, S., & Sadeh, C. (1995). Correlates of academic procrastination: Discomfort, task aversiveness, and task capability. *Journal of Psychology, 129,* 145–155.

Milgram, N. A., Mey-Tal, G., & Levison, Y. (1998). Procrastination, generalized or specific, in college students and their parents. *Personality and Individual Differences, 25,* 297–316.

Milgram, N. A., & Naaman, N. (1996). Typology in procrastination. *Personality and Individual Differences, 20,* 679–683.

Milgram, N. A., Sroloff, B., & Rosenbaum, M. (1988). The procrastination of everyday life. *Journal of Research in Personality, 22,* 197–212.

Milgram, N. A., & Tenne, R. (2000). Personality correlates of decisional and task avoidant procrastination. *European Journal of Personality, 14,* 141–156.

Milgram, N., & Toubiana, Y. (1999). Academic anxiety, academic procrastination, and parental involvement in students and their parents. *British Journal of Educational Psychology, 69,* 345–361.

Milgram, N. A., Weizman, D., & Raviv, A. (1991). Situational and personal determinants of academic procrastination. *Journal of General Psychology, 119,* 123–133.

Miller, W. R. (1983). Motivational interviewing with problem drinkers. *Behavioral Psychotherapy, 1,* 147–172.

Miller, W. R., & Rollnick, S. (2002). *Motivational interviewing: Preparing people to change addictive behavior* (2nd ed.). New York: Guilford Press.

Millon, T. (1994). Personality disorders: Conceptual distinctions and classification issues. In P. T. Costa & T. A. Widiger (Eds.), *Personality disorders and the five-factor model of personality* (pp. 279–301). Washington, DC: American Psychological Association.

Mirande, M. (1999). Naar een educatief intranet [Toward an educational network]. *Onderzoek van Onderwijs, 28,* 41–42.

Mischel, W. (1981). Metacognition and the rules of delay. In J. H. Flavell & L. Ross (Eds.), *Social cognitive development: Frontiers and possible futures* (pp. 240–271). Cambridge, England: Cambridge University Press.

Mischel, W., Cantor, N., & Feldman, S. (1996). Principles of self-regulation: The nature of willpower and self-control. In E. T. Higgins & A. W. Kruglanski (Eds.), *Social psychology: Handbook of basic principles* (pp. 329–359). New York: Guilford Press.

Mischel, W., & Shoda, Y. (1998). Reconciling processing dynamics and personality dispositions. *Annual Review of Psychology, 49,* 229–258.

Missildine, H. (1963). *Your inner child of the past.* New York: Simon & Schuster.

Mitchell, R. (2003). *A cross-sectional examination of self-perceptions related to academic achievement and underachievement across adolescence*. Unpublished doctoral dissertation, York University, Toronto, Ontario, Canada.

Mullen, B. (1989). *Advanced BASIC meta-analysis*. Hillsdale, NJ: Erlbaum.

Muraven, M., Tice, D. M., & Baumeister, R. F. (1998). Self-control as limited resource: Regulatory depletion patterns. *Journal of Personality and Social Psychology, 74*, 774–789.

Musznyski, S. Y., & Akamatsu, T. J. (1991). Delay in completion of doctoral dissertations in clinical psychology. *Professional Psychology: Research and Practice, 22*, 119–123.

Myers, I. B., & McCaulley, M. (1985). *Manual: A guide to the development and use of the Myers–Briggs Type Indicator*. Palo Alto, CA: Consulting Psychologist Press.

Nielsen, A. D., Hewitt, P. L., Han, H., Habke, A. M., Cockell, S. J., Stager, G., et al. (1997, June). *Perfectionistic self-presentation and attitudes toward seeking professional help*. Paper presented at the annual meeting of the Canadian Psychological Association, Toronto, Ontario, Canada.

Noy, S. (1969). Comparison of three psychotherapies in promoting growth in behavior disorders. *Dissertation Abstracts International, 29*, 3919B.

Omodei, M. M., & Wearing, A. J. (1990). Need satisfaction and involvement in personal projects: Toward an integrative model of subjective well-being. *Journal of Personality and Social Psychology, 59*, 762–769.

Onwuegbuzie, A. J. (2000). Academic procrastination and perfectionistic tendencies among graduate students. *Journal of Social Behavior and Personality, 15*, 103–110.

Onwuegbuzie, A. J., & Collins, K. M. T. (2001). Writing apprehension and academic procrastination among graduate students. *Psychological Reports, 92*, 560–562.

Onwuegbuzie, A. J., & Jiao, Q. C. (2000). I'll go to the library later: The relationship between academic procrastination and library anxiety. *College and Research Libraries, 4*, 45–52.

Oosterhuis, J. A. (1995). *Probes: Procedure ter bevordering van effectief en efficient studeergedrag* [Procedure for encouraging effective and efficient study behavior]. Unpublished dissertation, University of Amsterdam, the Netherlands.

Ottens, A. J. (1982). A guaranteed scheduling technique to manage students' procrastination. *College Student Journal, 16*, 371–376.

Owens, A. M., & Newbegin, I. (1997). Procrastination in high school achievement. *Journal of Social Behavior and Personality, 12*, 869–887.

Pacht, A. R. (1984). Reflections on perfection. *American Psychologist, 39*, 386–390.

Parry, A., & Doan, R. E. (1994). *Story re-visions: Narrative therapy in the postmodern world*. New York: Guilford Press.

Paunonen, S. V., & Ashton, M. C. (2001). Big Five predictors of academic achievement. *Journal of Research in Personality, 35*, 78–90.

Perry, R. P. (1991). Perceived control in college students: Implications for instruction in higher education. In J. Smart (Ed.), *Higher education: Handbook of theory and research* (Vol. 7, pp. 1–56). New York: Agathon.

Pervin, L. A. (1989). *Goal concepts in personality and social psychology*. Hillsdale, NJ: Erlbaum.

Pervin, L. A., & John, O. P. (Eds.). (1999). *Handbook of personality: Theory and research* (2nd ed.). New York: Guilford Press.

Polkinghorne, D. E. (1988). *Narrative knowing and the human sciences*. Albany: State University of New York Press.

Prochaska, J. O., & DiClemente, C. C. (1984). *The transtheoretical approach: Crossing traditional boundaries of therapy*. Homewood, IL: Dow Jones/Irwin.

Prochaska, J. O., DiClemente, C. C., & Norcross, J. C. (1992). In search of how people change: Applications to addictive behaviors. *American Psychologist, 47,* 1102–1114.

Procter, P. (Ed.). (1995). *Cambridge international dictionary of English*. Cambridge, England: Cambridge University Press.

Prohaska, W., Morrill, P., Atiles, I., & Perez, A. (2000). Academic procrastination by nontraditional students. *Journal of Social Behavior and Personality, 15,* 125–134.

Provost, J. A. (1988). *Procrastination: Using psychological type concepts to help students*. Gainesville, FL: Center for Application of Psychological Type.

Pychyl, T. A. (1995). *Personal projects, subjective well-being and the lives of doctoral students*. Unpublished doctoral dissertation, Carleton University, Ottawa, Ontario, Canada.

Pychyl, T. A., Coplan, R. J., & Reid, P. A. M. (2002). Parenting and procrastination: Gender differences in the relations between procrastination, parenting style and self-worth in early adolescence. *Personality and Individual Differences, 33,* 271–285.

Pychyl, T. A., Lee, J. M., Thibodeau, R., & Blunt, A. (2000). Five days of emotion: An experience sampling study of undergraduate student procrastination. *Journal of Social Behavior and Personality, 15,* 239–254.

Pychyl, T. A., & Little, B. R. (1998). Dimensional specificity in the prediction of subjective well-being: Personal projects in pursuit of the PhD. *Social Indicators Research, 45,* 423–473.

Pychyl, T. A., Morin, R. W., & Salmon, B. R. (2000). Procrastination and planning fallacy: An examination of the study habits of university students. *Journal of Social Behavior and Personality, 15,* 135–150.

Quattrone, G. A. (1985). On the congruity between internal states and action. *Psychological Bulletin, 98,* 3–40.

Robinson, T. E., & Berridge, K. C. (2003). Addiction. *Annual Review of Psychology, 54,* 25–53.

Rosenthal, R. (1991). *Meta-analytic procedures for social research*. Newbury Park, CA: Sage.

Roth, R. M. (1970). *Underachieving students and guidance*. Boston: Houghton Mifflin.

Roth, R. M., Mauksch, H. O., & Peiser, K. (1967). The non-achievement syndrome, group therapy, and achievement change. *Personnel and Guidance Journal, 46,* 393–398.

Rothblum, E. D. (1990). Fear of failure: The psychodynamic, need achievement, fear of success, and procrastination models. In H. Leitenberg (Ed.), *Handbook of social and evaluation anxiety* (pp. 497–537). New York: Plenum.

Rothblum, E. D., Solomon, L. J., & Murakami, J. (1986). Affective, cognitive, and behavioral differences between high and low procrastinators. *Journal of Counseling Psychology, 33,* 387–394.

Saddler, C. D., & Sacks, L. A. (1993). Multidimensional perfectionism and academic procrastination: Relationships with depression in university students. *Psychological Reports, 73,* 863–871.

Salkovskis, P. (Ed.). (1996). *Frontiers of cognitive therapy*. New York: Guilford Press.

Sanderson, C., & Clarkin, J. F. (1994). Use of the NEO–PI personality dimensions in differential treatment planning. In P. T. Costa & T. A. Widiger (Eds.), *Personality disorders and the five-factor model of personality* (pp. 219–235). Washington, DC: American Psychological Association.

Sapadin, L. (1997). *It's about time! The six styles of procrastination and how to overcome them*. New York: Penguin.

Sarmány Schuller, I. (1999). Procrastination, need for cognition, and sensation seeking. *Studia Psychologica, 41,* 73–85.

Schafer, R. (1992). *Retelling a life: Narration and dialogue in psychoanalysis*. New York: Basic Books.

Scher, S. J., & Ferrari, J. R. (2000). The recall of completed and non-completed tasks through daily logs to measure procrastination. *Journal of Social Behavior and Personality, 15,* 255–265.

Schouwenburg, H. C. (1992). Procrastinators and fear of failure: An exploration of reasons for procrastination. *European Journal of Personality, 6,* 225–236.

Schouwenburg, H. C. (1993). Procrastination and failure-fearing students in terms of personality-describing adjectives. *Nederlands Tijdschrift voor de Psychologie en Haar Grensgebieden, 48,* 43–44.

Schouwenburg, H. C. (1994). *Uitstelgedrag bij studenten* [Academic procrastination]. Unpublished dissertation, University of Groningen, the Netherlands.

Schouwenburg, H. C. (1995). Academic procrastination: Theoretical notions, measurement, and research. In J. R. Ferrari, J. L. Johnson, & W. G. McCown (Eds)., *Procrastination and task avoidance: Theory, research, and treatment* (pp. 71–96). New York: Plenum.

Schouwenburg, H. C. (1996). *Personality and academic competence*. Unpublished report, University of Groningen, the Netherlands.

Schouwenburg, H. C. (1997). *Results of questionnaire among participants of skills courses taught by the Academic Assistance Center of the University of Groningen from Janu-*

ary 1995 to August 1996. Unpublished report, University of Groningen, the Netherlands.

Schouwenburg, H. C. (2002, July). *Procrastination, persistence, work discipline, and impulsivity: A nomological network of self-control*. Poster session presented at the 11th European Conference on Personality, Jena, Germany.

Schouwenburg, H. C., & Groenewoud, J. T. (1997). *Studieplanning: Een werkboek voor studenten* [Study planning: A workbook for students]. Groningen, the Netherlands: Wolters-Noordhoff.

Schouwenburg, H. C., & Lay, C. H. (1995). Trait procrastination and the big-five factors of personality. *Personality and Individual Differences, 18,* 481–490.

Schwartz, R. M., & Garamoni, G. L. (1986). A structural model of positive and negative states of mind: Asymmetry in the internal dialogue. In P. C. Kendall (Ed.), *Advances in cognitive–behavioral research and therapy* (Vol. 4, pp. 1–62). New York: Academic Press.

Senécal, C., Koestner, R., & Vallerand, R. J. (1995). Self-regulation and academic procrastination. *Journal of Social Psychology, 135,* 607–619.

Senécal, C., Lavoie, K., & Koestner, R. (1997). Trait and situational factors in procrastination. *Journal of Social Behavior and Personality, 12,* 889–903.

Sherry, S. B., Hewitt, P. L., Flett, G. L., & Harvey, M. (2003). Perfectionism dimensions, perfectionistic attitudes, dependent attitudes, and depression in psychiatric patients and university students. *Journal of Counseling Psychology, 50,* 373–386.

Silver, M., & Sabini, J. (1981). Procrastinating. *Journal of the Theory of Social Behaviour, 11,* 207–221.

Sinclair, J., et al. (Ed.) (1987). *Collins Cobuild English language dictionary*. London: Collins.

Smith, J. A. (1996). Beyond the divide between cognition and discourse: Using interpretative phenomenological analysis in health psychology. *Psychology and Health, 11,* 261–271.

Smith, T. W. (1989). Assessment in R.E.T. In M. E. Bernard & R. DiGiuseppe (Eds.), *Inside rational–emotive therapy: A critical appraisal of the theory and therapy of Albert Ellis* (pp. 135–153). San Diego, CA: Academic Press.

Solomon, L. J., & Rothblum, E. D. (1984). Academic procrastination: Frequency and cognitive–behavioral correlates. *Journal of Counseling Psychology, 31,* 503–509.

Specter, M. H., & Ferrari, J. R. (2000). Time orientations of procrastinators: Focusing on the past, present, or future? *Journal of Social Behavior and Personality, 15,* 197–202.

Spence, D. P. (1982). *Narrative truth and historical truth: Meaning and interpretation in psychoanalysis*. New York: Norton.

Stainton, M., Lay, C. H., & Flett, G. L. (2000). Trait procrastinators and behavior/trait specific cognitions. *Journal of Social Behavior and Personality, 15,* 297–312.

Stark, J. W., Shaw, K. M., & Lowther, M. A. (1989). *Student goals for college and courses: A missing link in assessing and improving academic achievement* (ASHE-ERIC Higher Education Report No. 6). Washington, DC: George Washington University.

Steel, P. (2003). *The nature of procrastination.* Unpublished manuscript, University of Calgary, Alberta, Canada.

Steel, P., Brothen, T., & Wambach, C. (2001). Procrastination and personality, performance, and mood. *Personality and Individual Differences, 30,* 95–106.

Stein, N. L., & Policastro, M. (1984). The concept of a story: A comparison between children's and teachers' viewpoints. In H. Mandl, N. L. Stein, & T. Trabasso (Eds.), *Learning and comprehension of text* (pp. 113–155). Hillsdale, NJ: Erlbaum.

Stöber, J. (1998). The Frost Multidimensional Perfectionism Scale revisited: More perfect with four (instead of six) dimensions. *Personality and Individual Differences, 24,* 481–491.

Stöber, J., & Joormann, J. (2001). Worry, procrastination, and perfectionism: Differentiating amount of worry, pathological worry, anxiety, and depression. *Cognitive Therapy and Research, 25,* 49–60.

Thoresen, C. E., & Mahoney, M. J. (1974). *Behavioral self-control.* New York: Holt, Rinehart & Winston.

Tice, D. M., & Baumeister, R. F. (1997). Longitudinal study of procrastination, performance, stress, and health: The costs and benefits of dawdling. *Psychological Science, 8,* 454–458.

Topman, R. M., & Jansen, T. (1984). "I really can't do it, anyway": The treatment of test anxiety. In H. M. van der Ploeg, R. Schwarzer, & C. D. Spielberger (Eds.), *Advances in test anxiety research* (Vol. 3, pp. 243–251). Lisse, the Netherlands: Swets & Zeitlinger.

Topman, R. M., & Kleijn, W. C. (1996). Vrees voor spreken in groepen: Ervaringen met de Vragenlijst Spreken in Groepen [Fear of speaking in groups: Experiences with the Speaking in Groups Questionnaire]. *Gedragstherapie, 29,* 79–91.

Topman, R. M., Kleijn, W. C., & van der Ploeg, H. M. (1990). "Eigenlijk weet je dat wel, maar ja. . .": Zelfselectie: De diagnostische en de gedragskant ["In fact you know, but . . . ": Self-selection: Diagnostic and behavioral aspects]. *Underzoek van Onderwijs, 19,* 23–24.

Topman, R. M., Kleijn, W. C., & van der Ploeg, H. M. (1997). Cognitive balans van negatieve en positieve gedachten en examenvrees [Cognitive balance of negative and positive thought and test anxiety]. *Gedragstherapie, 30,* 85–102.

Topman, R. M., Kleijn, W. C., van der Ploeg, H. M., & Masset, E. A. E. A. (1992). Test anxiety, cognitions, study habits and academic performance: A prospective study. In K. A. Hagvet & T. Backer Johnsen (Eds.), *Advances in test anxiety research* (Vol. 7, pp. 221–240). Lisse, the Netherlands: Swets & Zeitlinger.

Topman, R. M., & Stoutjesdijk, E. T. (1995). "Nu je dit weet, wat doe je er mee": Ontwikkeling van een korte studievragenlijst en de effecten van feedback op de aanpak van studieproblemen ["Now that you know, what are you going to do": Development of a short questionnaire and the effects of feedback on solving study problems]. In H. C. Schouwenburg & J. T. Groenewoud (Eds.), *Studievaardigheid en leerstijlen* (pp. 133–149). Groningen, the Netherlands: Wolters-Noordhof.

Topman, R. M., & Stoutjesdijk, E. T. (1998). *Persoonlijke verwachtingen en de aanpak van studieproblemen door eerstejaars studenten* [Personal expectations of first-year students and their approach to study problems]. Unpublished report, University of Leiden, the Netherlands.

Tuckman, B. W. (1991). The development and concurrent validity of the Procrastination Scale. *Educational and Psychological Measurement, 51*, 473–480.

Tuckman, B. W. (1996). The relative effectiveness of incentive motivation and prescribed learning strategy in improving college students' course performance. *Journal of Experimental Education, 64*(3), 197–210.

Tuckman, B. W. (1998). Using tests as an incentive to motivate procrastinators to study. *Journal of Experimental Education, 66*, 141–147.

Tuckman, B. W. (2002a). *Academic procrastinators: Their rationalizations and Web-based performance.* Paper presented at the national conference of the American Psychological Association, Chicago.

Tuckman, B. W. (2002b). Evaluating ADAPT: A hybrid instructional model combining Web-based and classroom components. *Computers & Education, 39*, 216–269.

Tuckman, B. W. (2003). The effect of learning and motivation strategies training on college students' achievement. *Journal of College Student Development, 44*, 430–437.

Tuckman, B. W., Abry, D. A., & Smith, D. R. (2002). *Learning and motivation strategies: Your guide to success.* Upper Saddle River, NJ: Prentice Hall.

Tuckman, B. W., & Sexton, J. L. (1990). The relation between self-beliefs and self-regulated performance. *Journal of Social Behavior and Personality, 5*, 465–472.

Tuckman, B. W., & Sexton, T. L. (1992). Self-believers are self-motivated; self-doubters are not. *Personality and Individual Differences, 13*, 425–428.

Vallacher, R. R., & Wegner, D. M. (1987). What do people think they're doing? Action identification and human behavior. *Psychological Review, 94*, 3–15.

Vanden Auweele, Y., Depreeuw, E., Rzewnicki, R., & Ballon, F. (1999). Optimal functioning versus dysfunctioning of athletes: A comprehensive model for the practice of sport psychology. *European Yearbook of Sport Psychology, 3*, 1–37.

Walker, C. E. (1975). *Learn to relax: Thirteen ways to reduce tension.* Englewood Cliffs, NJ: Prentice Hall.

Walker, L. J. S. (1988). Procrastination: Fantasies and fears. *Manitoba Journal of Counseling, 25*(11), 23–25.

Walker, L. J. S., & Stewart, D. (2000). Overcoming the powerlessness of procrastination. *Guidance and Counselling, 16*(1), 39–42.

Warshaw, P. R., & Davis, F. D. (1985). Disentangling behavioral intention and behavioral expectation. *Journal of Experimental Social Psychology, 21*, 213–228.

Watson, D. C. (2001). Procrastination and the five-factor model: A facet level analysis. *Personality and Individual Differences, 30,* 149–158.

Weiner, B. (1986). *An attributional theory of motivation and emotion.* New York: Springer-Verlag.

Weiner, B. (1995). *Judgments of responsibility: A foundation for a theory of social conduct.* New York: Guilford Press.

Welsley, J. C. (1994). Effects of ability, high school achievement, and procrastinatory behavior on college performance. *Educational and Psychological Measurement, 54,* 404–408.

West, R. (1991). Psychological theories of addiction. In I. B. Glass (Ed.), *The international handbook of addiction behaviour* (pp. 20–24). London: Tavistock/Routledge.

White, M. (1995). *Re-authoring lives: Interviews and essays.* Adelaide, South Australia: Dulwich Centre Publications.

White, M., & Epston, D. (1990). *Narrative means to therapeutic ends.* New York: Norton.

Wolfradt, U., & Pretz, J. E. (2001). Individual differences in creativity: Personality, story writing, and hobbies. *European Journal of Personality, 15,* 297–310.

Zimmerman, B. J. (1998). Academic studying and the development of personal skill: A self-regulatory perspective. *Educational Psychologist, 33*(2/3), 73–86.

Zimmerman, B. J., & Bandura, A. (1994). Impact of self-regulatory influences on writing course attainment. *American Educational Research Journal, 31,* 845–862.

Zimmerman, B. J., Bandura, A., & Martinez-Pons, M. (1992). Self-motivation for academic attainment: The role of self-efficacy beliefs and personal goal setting. *American Educational Research Journal, 29,* 663–676.

AUTHOR INDEX

SUBJECT INDEX

and narrative intervention, 176, 179
and PPA interventions, 164
of procrastinators, 21, 22, 77
reduction of, 17, 188
in resistance, 192
and student procrastination, 13–14, 76
Applied behavioral analysis, 108, 110–113
example of, in procrastination, 111
Approach goals, 164
AP procrastinator. *See* Academic problem procrastinator or underachiever
APSI (Academic Procrastination State Inventory), 4, 7, 13, 20, 67, 69–70, 103, 154, 206, 207
Assessment
for AP procrastinators, 121
effect, 206–207
ATP. *See* Academic trait procrastination/procrastinator
Attitudes Toward Seeking Professional Help Scale, 191
Automatic process, procrastination as, 172
Automatic thoughts, 17, 121, 185, 187, 193
Automatic Thoughts Questionnaire, 185–186
Autonomy, procrastination as proof of, 52
Aversiveness of task, 23, 24
Avoidance, 7, 76
as easy strategy, 173, 174
Avoidance goals, 164
Awareness, narrative techniques for, 173
Awareness discussion, in counseling model, 80

Balance, in procrastinating students' lives, 49–50
Behavioral control, and interventions, 17
Behavioral flexibility, 37
Behavioral intervention programs, 91–92, 103, 198
in self-management courses, 71–72
Strategies for Achievement, 91, 93–99
Task Management Groups, 91, 99–103
See also Cognitive–behavioral approach in therapy
Behavioral problem, procrastination as (mainly), 199–200, 203
Beliefs, debilitating or self-defeating, 140, 148. *See also* Irrational cognitions
Belief system, 61
Big Five model of personality, 5–6
and level of analysis, 150

and procrastination, 5–6, 8, 20
and conscientiousness, 14–15
meta-analysis on, 30–40
research related to, 32
Breadth of interest measure, 52

Carleton University, treatment program at, 153
Catastrophizing, and REBT, 62
Change
and group counseling program, 57–58
operations toward, 46
orientations toward, 46, 55
stages of, 110
Choices, confronting of, 125–129
Cognitions
and interventions, 17
and trait procrastination, 16
See also Beliefs, debilitating or self-defeating; Irrational cognitions
Cognitive–behavioral approach in therapy, 119, 198
and AP procrastination, 121 (*see also* Confrontive CBT approach)
in group treatment (University of Louvain), 105, 118
aim of, 108
participating group characteristics for, 115–116
problems in, 116–117
program evaluation in, 113–115, 116, 118
program procedure in, 113, 114
relapse prevention in, 117–118
and student contact with Psychotherapeutic Student Center, 107–108
target group for, 106
theoretical background of, 108–113
in self-management courses, 60, 61–67, 73 (*see also* Rational–emotive behavioral therapy)
Cognitive perspective, procrastination and perfectionism from, 185–187
Cognitive problem, procrastination as (mainly), 200–201, 203
Cognitive scripts, parental style in, 157
Cognitive strategies, 77, 85, 89
Commitment
Digital Coaching as increasing, 145
vs. intention, 47, 128
in personal project analysis, 158

and trait procrastination, 7, 15–16
    See also Procrastination
Dilatory study behavior, 12
Discounting, 8
    and long- vs. short-term goals, 65
    and self-control theory, 205
    and self-management course, 64
    and trait procrastination, 16
Discovery, counseling-model session for, 81–82
Disorganization, neurotic, 51
Doing It Now program, 153–154

Effect assessment, 206–207
Efficacy, as factor, 152–153, 160, 162. *See also* Self-efficacy
Emotional Stability, and procrastination, 5–6
Energy level, 51–52
Environment, restructuring of, 92, 97–98, 101, 202
Excuses
    and ATP, 24–26
    confronting of, 17
Expectancy, in "ideal" intervention program, 204
Expectancy value theory of motivation, 201, 205
Expectations, vs. intentions, 47
Experiential confrontations, 122
External attributions, 25
Extraversion–introversion, and procrastination, 5, 31, 32–33, 34, 37
    and taxonomy of procrastination, 14, 15

Factual confrontations, 122
Fantasy, and procrastination, 33, 36
Fear of failure
    and perfectionism, 184
    and procrastination, 15, 21, 22, 23, 149
        in perfectionistic procrastinators, 182, 188
        in personal projects analysis, 157
Fears, counseling-model session on, 85–86
Fear of success, in personal project analysis, 157
Feedback
    on different trait measures, 199
    in Digital Coaching, 144, 147
Feelings, and interventions, 17
Five Factor model, 186. *See also* Big Five model of personality

Flexibility, behavioral, 37
Flow experience, from narrative intervention, 179
Frost Multidimensional Perfectionism Scale (FMPS), 183, 184
Frustration tolerance, and REBT, 62–63
Functional analysis, 92

Gender differences, 26, 120
Goals
    approach, 164
    avoidance, 164
    guidelines for meeting of, 158
    and "ideal" intervention characteristics, 204
    long-term vs. short-term, 65
Goal setting, 17, 52–53, 87
    in Digital Coaching, 141, 145
    and division into subgoals, 10, 101, 141, 198
    as procrastinators' weakness, 9
Groningen, University of
    self-management course at, 59–73
    Task Management Groups at, 99–100, 102
Group influence, 198. *See also at* Peer
Guilt
    in personal project analysis, 157
    and procrastination (meta-analysis), 36
    of procrastinators, 21, 22, 77
    reducing of, 17

Habit pattern, procrastination as, 77
"Hello–goodbye" effect, 207
Human worth rating, 63

"Ideal" intervention program, 203–207
Identity consolidation, 46–47
Illinois Institute of Technology (IIT), procrastination and underachievement research at, 119–120
Imagery, rational–emotive, 63
Impulsiveness, 8, 32, 202
Individual differences, in procrastination, 29
Information communication technology (ICT), 133
    Digital Coaching, 139–148
    Strategies for achievement, 93
    Study Support Web site, 134–139
Inspiration, as necessary condition for working, 63

240   SUBJECT INDEX

Institute on Achievement and Motivation (IAM) at York University, Toronto, 120

Intellect or Openness to Experience (factor), and procrastination, 5–6. *See also* Openness to experience

Intelligence, 21

Intentions
  and behavior, 4, 108, 198
  vs. commitment, 47, 128
  vs. expectations, 47
  goal vs. implementation, 48, 55
  for procrastinators, 47, 55
  timely pursuit and enactment of, 43, 45, 46, 50, 56–57

Interest, breadth of, 52

International Personality Item Pool, 186

Interpretation of situation, feelings and behavior from, 111

Interpretive phenomenological analysis, 169, 171, 180

Intervention(s)
  difference in approach of, 16–17
  features of, 17
  as promoting cognitive control, 16
  and self-control theory, 10
  See also Counseling of student procrastinators

Intervention methods
  and Big Five model of personality traits, 6
  See also Behavioral intervention programs; Cognitive–behavioral approach in therapy; Information communication technology; Narrative approach; Personal project analysis; Rational–emotive behavioral therapy; Self-management courses

Intervention program details
  confrontive CBT, 122–129
  counseling using personal projects, 153–159
  digital coaching, 142–145
  group counseling, York University, 48–57
  group training, University of Louvain, 109–113, 114
  narrative approach, 169–170
  powerlessness group counseling, 81–87
  self-management training, Universities of Groningen/Utrecht, 61–67, 68
  strategies for achievement, 93–98

task management group, 100–102

Intervention program, "ideal," 203–207
  components, 204
  effect assessment, 206–207
  identification of procrastinators, 205–206

Intervention programs
  general themes across, 198
  some uncommon themes within, 199

Intrusive thoughts, 187

Irrational cognitions (beliefs, thinking)
  and perfectionistic procrastinator, 182, 187
  from powerlessness, 76
  and procrastination, 76
  and REBT/RET, 61, 62–63, 64, 112–113

Irrational negative self-talk, 157

Isolation, Digital Coaching as overcoming, 145

Journal of Social Behavior and Personality, special issue of, xi

Journals on procrastination (group participants), 82, 86

Lay Procrastination Scale, 5, 6, 7, 12, 13, 15, 16, 32, 44, 81, 89, 186, 207
  Dutch adaptation of, 136, 137, 138, 142, 146
  frequency distribution of scores, 12

Learning experiences, 176–178

Learning and Motivation Strategies: Your Guide to Success (Tuckman), 95

Learning performance activities, 96–97

Leiden University, ICT approach at, 133
  Digital Coaching project, 141–142, 147 (*see also* Digital Coaching)
  Study Support Web site, 134 (*see also* Study Support Web site)

Louvain, group training at University of, 113
  intervention program content, 114

Meaning
  creation of (narrative approach), 168, 180
  as factor, 152–153, 160

Measurement scales, 5
  Academic Competence scale, 70
  Academic Procrastination State Inventory (APSI), 4, 7, 13, 20, 67, 69–70, 103, 154, 206, 207

group training in, 105–118
PsycINFO database of American Psychological Association, 30
Punisher, as procrastinator style, 80
Punishment
    in cognitive–behavioral program, 112
    in self-management courses, 65

Quantitative research, in self-management courses, 69–70, 72
Questionnaire, in group counseling program, 45–46, 49, 50–51

Rational–emotive behavioral therapy (REBT), 6–7, 198, 200
    in counseling session for powerlessness, 85
    for perfectionism, 187
    and self-management courses, 61–64, 68, 70, 71–72, 73
Rational–emotive therapy (RET), 112–113
Rebelliousness, and procrastination, 14, 52
REBT. See Rational–emotive behavioral therapy
Reciprocal determinism, 95
Regulation, embodied, 178
Relapse
    after group program, 58
    after personal project analysis, 161
    and procrastination as addiction, 201
Relapse prevention, in cognitive–behavioral program (University of Louvain), 117–118
Relaxation and visualization techniques, in self-management course, 66, 71–72
Research on procrastination, 30
    and academic settings, 3
    and cognitive approach, 201
    in cognitive–behavioral program, 112
    and confrontive CBT approach, 119–120
    with AP procrastinators, 130–131
    and effect assessment, 206–20
    and meta-analysis on procrastination and Big Five model, 30–40
    and meta-analysis supporting intervention targets, 204
Resistance, 199
    of AP procrastinator, 125
    and competing alternatives, 48
    of perfectionistic students, 192
RET (rational–emotive therapy), 112–113

Reward
    in self-management courses, 65
    perceived, 8, 9
    subjective value of, 9
Rituals, as preparation, for work, 178

Satisfaction With Life Scale (SWLS), 154, 159
Scales, measurement. See Measurement scales
Scheduling, 17
    by procrastinating students, 50
    and significance of procrastination, xi
    with un-schedule, 156–157
    See also Time management
Scripts, parental style in, 157
Self, sense of, 174–176
Self-acceptance
    and rational–emotive techniques, 187–188
    unconditional, 63, 73
Self-concept
    and group counseling program, 57
    and trait procrastination, 46
Self-confidence, 21, 22
Self-consciousness, and procrastination, 36, 76
Self-control, 8
    and personal power vs. powerlessness, 76, 77
    in students, 11
Self-controlling procedures, in cognitive–behavioral program, 112
Self-control theory, 8–9, 10, 201, 205
Self-critic, 176
Self-discrepancy, Higgins's theory of, 66
Self-efficacy, xii, 17, 22, 198, 203
    and Digital Coaching, 148
    and explanation of behavior, 65
    and "ideal" intervention characteristics, 204
    and personal power, 77
    and powerlessness, 76
    and self-management courses, 65, 70, 72
    and trait procrastination, 16
    See also Efficacy, as factor
Self-efficacy approach, 89
Self-efficacy expectations (expectancies), 139–140, 201
Self-esteem
    and group counseling program, 53, 57
    and narrative interventions, 179
    and procrastination, 149

Worksheet, procrastination, 82, 83
Writing intervention. *See* Narrative approach

York University, group counseling at, 44

Zen meditation, concentration exercise from, 65

ABOUT THE EDITORS

Henri C. Schouwenburg, PhD, is a psychological counselor, trainer for students, and researcher in educational psychology at the University of Groningen, the Netherlands. He received his PhD from the University of Groningen and wrote his dissertation on academic procrastination. He is the cofounder of the Academic Assistance and Counseling Center at the University of Groningen and has been affiliated with that center since 1980. His research on study problems and learning styles served as a basis for developing supportive training programs for university students. He is the author of Dutch books on approaches to learning and study problems and cofounder of the Dutch National Study Skills Association; he is a nationwide active promoter of professional skills for the psychological counseling of students. He is Web master of the Internet sites of the Dutch Association of Psychological Student Counselors and of the Dutch National Study Skills Association. In cooperation with Dr. Clarry H. Lay, he founded the biennial international conferences on counseling the procrastinator in academic settings. He is presently living in Belgium.

Clarry H. Lay, PhD, recently retired as professor of psychology at York University, Toronto, Ontario, Canada, although he continues to teach, do research, and counsel student procrastinators. His research areas have included person perception, procrastination, and assessment of the Big Five personality factors with younger children, as well as acculturation, ethnic identity, and related matters. Along with Dr. Henri Schouwenburg, he founded the biennial international conferences on counseling the procrastinator in academic settings. On the basis of his own disposition, he maintains an unhealthy interest in procrastination.

Timothy A. Pychyl, PhD, is associate professor in the Department of Psychology and Centre for Initiatives in Education at Carleton University, Ottawa, Ontario, Canada. The author of numerous publications and conference presentations on procrastination, he finds that his research complements his teaching very well, as both are focused on student learning and academic success. His scholarship of teaching and learning has been recognized with a number of awards, including a national 3M Teaching Fellowship from the Society for Teaching and Learning in Higher Education. He is the founder of facultydevelopment.ca, a Web-based resource for faculty development in higher education. With degrees in science, linguistics, and education, as well as a PhD in psychology, his academic interests and research have varied widely.

Joseph R. Ferrari, PhD, is professor and director of the community psychology doctoral program in the Department of Psychology at DePaul University in Chicago. He also is editor-in-chief of the *Journal of Prevention & Intervention in the Community* since 1994. The author of 100 scholarly journal articles, 7 books, and 230 conference presentations, he is internationally known in the field of social personality as the leading researcher on the study of chronic procrastination. He is a social community psychologist whose service and research interests include adult community service and volunteerism, undergraduate education in community psychology, sense of community, mutual support, addictions and recovery, and caregiver stress and satisfaction.